EU DATA PROTECTION AND THE GDPR

ASPEN SELECT SERIES

EU DATA PROTECTION AND THE GDPR

Daniel J. Solove
John Marshall Harlan Research Professor of Law
George Washington University Law School

Paul M. Schwartz
Jefferson E. Peyser Professor of Law
U.C. Berkeley Law School
Faculty Director, Berkeley Center for Law & Technology

 Wolters Kluwer

Published by Wolters Kluwer in New York.

Wolters Kluwer Legal & Regulatory U.S. serves customers worldwide with CCH, Aspen Publishers, and Kluwer Law International products. (www.WKLegaledu.com)

Cover image: artjazz/Adobe Stock

To contact Customer Service, e-mail customer.service@wolterskluwer.com, call 1-800-234-1660, fax 1-800-901-9075, or mail correspondence to:

Wolters Kluwer
Attn: Order Department
PO Box 990
Frederick, MD 21705

Printed in the United States of America.

1 2 3 4 5 6 7 8 9 0

ISBN 978-1-5438-3263-1

Library of Congress Cataloging-in-Publication Data application is in process.

SUSTAINABLE FORESTRY INITIATIVE

Certified Chain of Custody
Promoting Sustainable Forestry

www.sfiprogram.org

About Wolters Kluwer Legal & Regulatory U.S.

Wolters Kluwer Legal & Regulatory U.S. delivers expert content and solutions in the areas of law, corporate compliance, health compliance, reimbursement, and legal education. Its practical solutions help customers successfully navigate the demands of a changing environment to drive their daily activities, enhance decision quality and inspire confident outcomes.

Serving customers worldwide, its legal and regulatory portfolio includes products under the Aspen Publishers, CCH Incorporated, Kluwer Law International, ftwilliam.com and MediRegs names. They are regarded as exceptional and trusted resources for general legal and practice-specific knowledge, compliance and risk management, dynamic workflow solutions, and expert commentary.

To my Pamela and Griffin—DJS

To Steffie, Clara, and Leo—PMS

SUMMARY OF CONTENTS

CONTENTS

PREFACE

Due to the significance of international flows of personal data, there are high stakes today for the United States and the European Union (EU) when it comes to information privacy law. The annual digital services trade between the U.S. and EU is worth approximately $260 billion, and cross-border data flows represent a fast-growing component of trade for these two entities. Yet, differences in transatlantic regulations potentially imperil critical international data flows involving personal information.

This volume, *EU Data Protection and the GDPR*, examines the EU approach to data privacy. It considers the development of the European approach beginning with developments such as the OECD Guidelines and the European Convention on Human Rights. These documents provided the background for the rise of EU data protection through Articles 7 and 8 of the Charter of Fundamental Rights, and then the Data Protection Directive. The Directive, which was created in 1995, established a basic legislative framework for the processing of personal information in the EU.

The EU then replaced the Directive with the General Data Protection Regulation (GDPR), which took effect on May 25, 2018. The GDPR is the strictest and most influential privacy law in the world. This volume's second chapter provides an edited version of the GDPR with its most important sections. In contrast to the Directive, which required EU Member States to pass enacting legislation, the GDPR has direct effect in Member States.

EU Data Protection and the GDPR also looks at the issue of international transfers of data. Personal information increasingly flows across the borders of different nations around the world, and transferring data from the EU to the U.S. has been a complex and controversial matter.

With the profound worldwide influence of the GDPR, it is an exciting time to be studying EU data protection law.

A Note on the Casebook Website. We strive to keep the book up to date between editions, and we maintain a web page for the book with downloadable updates and other useful information. We invite you to visit the website:

https://informationprivacylaw.com

The website contains links to useful news sites, blogs, and online resources pertaining to information privacy law issues. We also provide a list of recommended books that can be read in conjunction with this book.

A Note on Privacy Law Fundamentals. Students may find our short volume, *Privacy Law Fundamentals,* to be a useful companion to the casebook. *Privacy Law Fundamentals* is designed to be a distilled overview of information privacy law for both practitioners and students. More information about this book can be found at http://informationprivacylaw.com.

A Note on the Editing. We have deleted many citations and footnotes from the cases to facilitate readability. The footnotes that have been retained in the cases have been renumbered.

Daniel J. Solove
Paul M. Schwartz

November 2020

ACKNOWLEDGMENTS

Daniel J. Solove: I would like to thank Carl Coleman, Scott Forbes, Susan Freiwald, Tomás Gómez-Arostegui, Stephen Gottlieb, Marcia Hofmann, Chris Hoofnagle, John Jacobi, Orin Kerr, Raymond Ku, Peter Raven-Hansen, Joel Reidenberg, Neil Richards, Michael Risinger, Lior Strahilevitz, Peter Swire, William Thompson, and Peter Winn for helpful comments and suggestions. Charlie Sullivan and Jake Barnes provided indispensable advice about how to bring this project to fruition. Special thanks to Richard Mixter at Aspen Publishers for his encouragement and faith in this project. Thanks as well to the other folks at Aspen who have contributed greatly to the editing and development of this book: John Devins, Christine Hannan, Carmen Reid, Jessica Barmack, John Burdeaux, and Sandra Doherty. I would like to thank my research assistants Jasmine Arooni, Peter Choy, Monica Contreras, Carly Grey, Maeve Miller, James Murphy, Poornima Ravishankar, Sheerin Shahinpoor, Mingli Shi, Vladimir Semendyai, John Spaccarotella, Tiffany Stedman, Shannon Sylvester, Lourdes Turrecha, Eli Weiss, and Kate Yannitte. I would also like to thank Dean Dayna Matthew for providing the resources I needed. And thanks to my wife Pamela Solove and son Griffin Solove, who kept me in good cheer throughout this project.

Paul M. Schwartz: For their suggestions, encouragement, and insights into information privacy law, I would like to thank Ken Bamberger, Fred Cate, Malcolm Crompton, Christopher Gulotta, Andrew Guzman, Chris Hoofnagle, Ted Janger, Ronald D. Lee, Lance Liebman, Steven McDonald, Viktor Mayer-Schönberger, Deirdre Mulligan, Karl-Nikolaus Peifer, Ira Rubinstein, Pam Samuelson, Lior Strahilevitz, Peter Swire, William M. Treanor, and Peter Winn. I benefited as well through the years from the help of my talented research assistants: Cesar Alvarez, Benedikt Burger, Kai-Dieter Classen, Leah Duranti, David Fang, Natalie Heim, Alpa Patel, Karl Saddlemire, Brian St. John, Laura Sullivan, Kevin Yang, and Sebastian Zimmeck. Many thanks to my co-author, Daniel Solove. Many thanks as well to my mother, Nancy Schwartz, and to Laura Schwartz and Ed Holden; David Schwartz; and Daniel Schwartz.

A profound debt is owed to Spiros Simitis. My interest in the subject of information privacy began in 1985 with his suggestion that I visit his office of the Hessian Data Protection Commissioner in Wiesbaden and sit in on meetings there. Through his scholarship, example, and friendship, Professor Simitis has provided essential guidance during the decades since that initial trip to Wiesbaden.

In April 2020, privacy law lost a giant: my dear friend Joel Reidenberg. Professor Reidenberg's insights helped shaped our field, and his loss is deeply felt. Our community has benefited from his contributions, his warmth, and his friendship.

My portion of the book is dedicated to Steffie, Clara, and Leo, with my gratitude and love.

We are grateful to the following sources for their permission to reprint excerpts of their scholarship:

American Law Institute. *Restatement (Third) of Foreign Relations Law*. Copyright © 1987. Reproduced with permission. All rights reserved.

Joel Reidenberg, *E-Commerce and Trans-Atlantic Privacy*. Houston Law Review, Vol. 38 (2001). University of Houston Law Center. Copyright © 2001.

Paul M. Schwartz & Karl-Nikolaus Peifer, *Transatlantic Data Privacy Law*. Georgetown Law Journal, Vol. 106 (2017). Georgetown University Law Center. Copyright © 2017.

James Q. Whitman, *The Two Western Cultures of Privacy: Dignity Versus Liberty,* 113 Yale L.J. 1151 (2004). Reprinted with permission.

EU DATA PROTECTION AND THE GDPR

CHAPTER 1

EU DATA PROTECTION AND THE GDPR

CHAPTER OUTLINE

The study of information privacy provides an opportunity to understand privacy law in different countries. This chapter explores the European Union General Data Protection Regulation and important European privacy case law. It focuses on European Union legal developments that will have an impact in the United States as well as on texts that offer a comparative perspective on the U.S. privacy regime.

United States and foreign privacy regimes differ in some respects. Consider the standard description of privacy legislation in Europe as "omnibus" and privacy law in the United States as "sectoral." In Europe, one statute typically regulates the processing of personal information in public and private sectors alike. In the absence of more specific legislation, the general information privacy law in Europe sets the initial terms for the processing, storage, and transfer of personal information. The omnibus law is often accompanied, moreover, by more specific privacy laws. These typically regulate certain areas of data use such as telecommunications, health care, and social welfare programs. In the United States, in contrast, there are only sectoral laws. These statutes focus on specific sectors of the economy or certain technologies.[1]

Outside of Europe, other countries around the world are moving toward adopting comprehensive privacy legislation based on the European model. According to Graham Greenleaf, there are now 120 data privacy laws in the world.[2] In his assessment, the trend since the start of the 21st Century has been for enactment of laws in OECD countries in the Asia-Pacific region with activity in Latin America, Africa, the Middle East, and Central Asia as well. He notes, "Since 2010 the average number of new laws per year has increased to 5.5, double the 2.7 average over the whole 44 years" from enactment of the first national data protection law in Sweden in 1973.[3] Moreover, Greenleaf notes that a large portion of the laws of these countries reflect European standards. In his assessment, "[S]omething reasonably described as 'European standard' data privacy laws are becoming the norm in most parts of the world with data privacy laws."[4]

In Europe, privacy law is shaped by the Council of Europe and the European Union (EU) and entities within these institutions. It was Article 8 of the Council of Europe's Convention on Human Rights of 1950, which firmly established privacy protection as a critical human rights claim in postwar Europe. The Council of Europe, located in Strasbourg, France, is Europe's leading human rights organization. Forty-seven Member States belong to it; 28 of these belong to the EU as well.

The privacy provisions in Article 8 have been given effect both by the decisions of the European Court of Human Rights, which is located in Strasbourg,

---

[1] Joel R. Reidenberg, *Setting Standards for Fair Information Practice in the U.S. Private Sector*, 80 Iowa L. Rev. 497, 500 (1995).

[2] Graham Greenleaf, *Countries with Data Privacy Laws — by Year 1973-2016*, 146 Privacy Laws & Business Int'l Rep. 18 (2017).

[3] Id. For a comprehensive list of the world's data protection statutes, see Graham Greenleaf, Global Tables of Data Privacy Laws and Bills (5th ed. 2017, updated March 2017), 145 Privacy Laws & Business Int'l Rep. 14-26 (2017).

[4] GRAHAM GREENLEAF, ASIAN DATA PRIVACY LAWS 57 (2014). Moreover, as Greenleaf states, "One of the most-implemented 'European' principles outside Europe is 'Data export restrictions based on destination,' which could also be named the 'adequacy requirement' for data exports." Id.

France, and by the Convention on Data Protection established by the Council of Europe in 1980. The counter-party in litigation under Article 8 is the respective Member State whose law or other activity is challenged as violative of privacy. An interpretation of Article 8 by the European Court of Human Rights can lead it to remand the case back to the judiciary in the Member State for a further proceeding in light of its ruling on the applicable law.

Beyond the European Convention of Human Rights, the EU has a Charter of Fundamental Rights, which contains key privacy protections. The Convention and Charter function as the two pillars of fundamental rights in Europe. The former is an international treaty; the latter is a key constitutional document of the EU.

In its Article 8, the Convention grants everyone a "right to respect for his private and family life, his home and his correspondence." The EU's Charter of Fundamental Rights has more detailed protection for privacy. Its Article 7 protects private life and family life. In its Article 8, however, the Charter more specifically articulates "a right to the protection of personal data concerning him or her." In addition, the EU's Lisbon Treaty of 2007 explicitly recognized a right to data protection and also made the Charter of Fundamental Rights a legally enforceable document within the EU. The highest court in the EU is the European Court of Justice. It is located in Luxembourg City, Luxembourg.

One of the most important areas of European privacy law for almost a decade has been the Data Protection Directive of the European Union. Enacted in 1995, the Data Protection Directive establishes a basic legislative framework for the processing of personal information in the European Union. The EU Data Protection Directive has exercised a profound effect on the development of privacy law, not only in Europe but around the world. The EU has now replaced the Directive with the General Data Protection Regulation, which takes effect on May 25, 2018.

In the view of Gregory Schaffer, there has been a "ratcheting up" effect in the relationship between the United States and Europe in the area of privacy policy.[5] As a consequence of laws in Europe that safeguard privacy, Schaffer predicted in 2000 that it was more likely that similar laws will be adopted in the United States or at least that U.S. firms will improve their privacy protection. While there is no omnibus bill in the United States, there has been considerable regulatory activity. In addition, Kenneth Bamberger and Deirdre Mulligan attribute the rise of Chief Privacy Officers in U.S. corporations at least in part to their role "smoothing interactions with European regulators under the Safe Harbor Agreement."[6]

It is worth noting that the phrase "data protection" is frequently used to describe privacy protection in the European context. This term reflects the modern concept of privacy protection that emerged in the 1970s as computer systems were increasingly used to process information on citizens. At the same time, a concept of "privacy," sometimes referred to as that of private life or the private domain, continues to play an important role in the European conception of information privacy.

---

[5] Gregory Shaffer, *Globalization and Social Protection: The Impact of EU and International Rules in the Ratcheting Up of U.S. Privacy Standards*, 25 Yale J. Int'l L. 1 (2000).

[6] Kenneth Bamberger & Deirdre Mulligan, *Privacy on the Books and on the Ground*, 63 Stan. L. Rev. 247, 262 (2014).

Beyond Europe, important international and regional agreements have helped shape the structure of national privacy law and influenced the development of privacy as a legal claim in particular countries. The Privacy Guidelines of the Organization for Economic Cooperation and Development (OECD), adopted in 1980, represent a consensus position of countries from North America, Europe, and East Asia as to the basic structure of privacy law. This non-binding framework was supplemented in 2013 by additional OECD privacy guidelines.

Other privacy laws follow from Article 12 of the Universal Declaration of Human Rights, adopted by the United Nations in 1948, which states that "[n]o one shall be subjected to arbitrary interference with his privacy, family, home or correspondence, nor to attacks upon his honor and reputation. Everyone has the right to the protection of the law against such interference or attacks."

A. THE OECD PRIVACY GUIDELINES

1. THE 1980 ORIGINAL GUIDELINES

On September 23, 1980, the Organization for Economic Cooperation and Development (OECD), a group of leading industrial countries concerned with global economic and democratic development, issued guidelines for privacy protection in the transfer of personal information across national borders. The United States is a member of the OECD, which has 34 member countries. Its 1980 document is the Guidelines on the Protection of Privacy and Transborder Flows of Personal Data (the Guidelines), which establish eight key principles for the protection of personal information. It creates a non-binding framework that is intended to influence policymaking about privacy throughout the world.

Scope. The Guidelines "apply to personal data, whether in the public or private sectors, which, because of the manner in which they are processed, or because of their nature or the context in which they are used, pose a danger to privacy and individual liberties." "Personal data" is defined as "any information relating to an identified or identifiable individual (data subject)." § 1(b). The Guidelines provide a floor of protection; member countries can adopt more stringent protections. It is important to note, however, that the Guidelines are not binding on the member nations of the OECD. Rather, they offer suggestions to lead to a more uniform treatment throughout different countries of personal data processing and to a free international flow of information. Their goal is to promote and protect, by recommending the implementation of uniform principles across member states, "the fundamental values of privacy, individual liberties and the global free flow of information."[7]

Principles. The OECD Privacy Guidelines establish eight principles regarding the processing of personal data:

---

[7] OECD, *Recommendation of the Council concerning Guidelines governing the Protection of Privacy and Transborder Flows of Personal Data (2013)*, C(80)58/FINAL, as amended on 11 July 2013 by C(2013)79, at 11.

1. *Collection Limitation Principle.* There should be limits to the collection of personal data and any such data should be obtained by lawful and fair means and, where appropriate, with the knowledge or consent of the data subject.

2. *Data Quality Principle.* Personal data should be relevant to the purposes for which they are to be used, and, to the extent necessary for those purposes, should be accurate, complete and kept up-to-date.

3. *Purpose Specification Principle.* The purposes for which personal data are collected should be specified not later than at the time of data collection and the subsequent use limited to the fulfillment of those purposes or such others as are not incompatible with those purposes and as are specified on each occasion of change of purpose.

4. *Use Limitation Principle.* Personal data should not be disclosed, made available or otherwise used for purposes other than those specified in accordance with [the Purpose Specification Principle] except: a) with the consent of the data subject; or b) by the authority of law.

5. *Security Safeguards Principle.* Personal data should be protected by reasonable security safeguards against such risks as loss or unauthorised access, destruction, use, modification or disclosure of data.

6. *Openness Principle.* There should be a general policy of openness about developments, practices and policies with respect to personal data. Means should be readily available of establishing the existence and nature of personal data, and the main purposes of their use, as well as the identity and usual residence of the data controller.

7. *Individual Participation Principle.* An individual should have the right: (a) to obtain from a data controller, or otherwise, confirmation of whether or not the data controller has data relating to him; (b) to have communicated to him, data relating to him (i) within a reasonable time; (ii) at a charge, if any, that is not excessive; (iii) in a reasonable manner; and (iv) in a form that is readily intelligible to him; (c) to be given reasons if a request made under subparagraphs (a) and (b) is denied, and to be able to challenge such denial; and (d) to challenge data relating to him and, if the challenge is successful to have the data erased, rectified, completed or amended.

8. *Accountability Principle.* A data controller should be accountable for complying with measures which give effect to the principles stated above. . . .

Self-Regulation and International Data Flow. The OECD Guidelines stress the importance of self-regulation and the free flow of data on a global basis. They call in § 19(b) for Member countries to "in particular endeavor to . . . encourage and support self-regulation, whether in the form of codes of conduct or otherwise." Sections 15-18 establish the "basic principles" of "free flow" of personal data and of transborder data flow. For example, § 16 of the Guidelines states: "Member countries should take all reasonable and appropriate steps to ensure that transborder flows of personal data, including transit through a member country are uninterrupted and secure." Section 18 permits restriction on these flows, but seeks to limit the conditions under which these limits can be exercised. This section provides: "A Member country should refrain from restricting transborder flows of personal data between itself and another Member country except where the latter does not yet substantially observe these Guidelines or where the re-export of such data would circumvent its domestic privacy legislation."

The Worldwide Influence of the OECD Privacy Guidelines. As noted, the OECD Privacy Guidelines are non-binding on members of the OECD. Nonetheless, they have had a significant impact on the development of national law in North America, Europe, and East Asia.[8] For example, in the United States, the subscriber privacy provisions in the Cable Act of 1984 include many of the principles of the OECD Privacy Guidelines. In Australia, the Privacy Act of 1988 establishes 11 privacy principles based on the OECD Privacy Guidelines. New Zealand's 1993 Privacy Act, which regulates both the public and private sectors, adopts 12 principles based on the OECD Privacy Guidelines. South Korea's Act on the Protection of Personal Information Managed by Public Agencies of 1994 follows a number of the OECD Privacy Guidelines.

The Working Party on Information Security and Privacy (WPISP). WPISP is an important forum at the OECD for the development of policy options. It brings together both government and representatives of "[b]usiness, civil society, other international organizations and non-members." The WPISP has published white papers and guidances on policy and practices, including a paper on "Making privacy notices simple" and a "privacy policy statement generator."[9] It also played a key role in the formulation of the 2013 update to the 1980 Guidelines. It developed the Terms of Reference that served as a roadmap for the review process and delivered important preparatory work to the Expert Group that was formed to review the 1980 Guidelines.

2. THE 2013 OECD PRIVACY GUIDELINES

The OECD released a set of new guidelines in 2013 that update the 1980 Guidelines but do not replace them. A volunteer Expert Group led the revision process; it was chaired by Jennifer Stoddart, Privacy Commissioner of Canada. Omer Tene, an international privacy expert, served as rapporteur for the project.

New Concepts in the 2013 Guidelines. The new guidelines emphasize the need for multifaceted national privacy strategy, privacy management programs, and data security breach notification. The 2013 guidelines provide additional details about accountability in organizations, an idea already present in the 1980 Guidelines, and simplify and consolidate the OECD approach to transborder data flows.

Multifaceted National Privacy Strategies. National strategies should "reflect a coordinated approach across governmental bodies." Article 19(a). This approach should include establishment of "privacy enforcement authorities with the governance, resources and technical expertise necessary to exercise their powers effectively and to make decisions on an objective, impartial and consistent basis." Article 19(c).

---

[8] For an analysis of privacy laws around the world, see EPIC & Privacy International, Privacy and Human Rights (2006).

[9] OECD, *What Is the Working Party on Information Security and Privacy (WPISP)?*, at http://www.oecd.org/document/46/0,3746,en_2649_34255_36862382_1_1_1_1,00.html.

Privacy Management Programs. A "data controller" is required to establish a privacy management program with a number of elements including the ability to give "effect to these Guidelines for all personal data under its control." Article 15(a). The Guidelines define a data controller as "a party who, according to national law, is competent to decide about the contents and use of personal data regardless of whether or not such data are collected, stored, processed or disseminated by that party or by an agent on its behalf." Article 1(a).

Data Security Breach Notification. Notification is to be given both to an authority and to the affected individual affected by the security breach. Article 15(c). Notice must be given to an authority only when a "significant security breach affecting personal data" occurs. Article 15(c). Notification to data subjects is required only where the breach "is likely to adversely affect" these persons. The *Supplementary Explanatory Memorandum to the Revised OECD Guidelines* explains that it seeks a "risk-based approach to notification." It seeks to curb excessive notifications, which can create an undue burden on data controllers and enforcement authorities as well as encourage affected individuals to ignore breach notices.

Expanding Accountability. The original OECD Guidelines already contained a principle of "accountability." The 2013 Guidelines provide more details about the steps that an accountable organization should take. These include establishment of a privacy management program, as discussed above, and being able to demonstrate that the management program is appropriate. Article 15(b).

Transborder Data Flows. Regarding international data flows, a data controller is "accountable for personal data under its control without regard to the location of the data." Article 16. As the Supplementary Explanatory Memorandum points out, this paragraph "restates the basic principle of accountability . . . in the context of transborder data flows." Article 17 establishes a principle of free flow of international data. It states:

> A Member country should refrain from restricting transborder data flows . . . where (a) the other country substantially observes these Guidelines or (b) sufficient safeguards exist, including effective enforcement mechanisms and appropriate measures put in place by the data controller, to ensure a continuing level of protection consistent with these Guidelines.

Finally, Article 18 requires any restriction to transborder flows to be "proportionate to the risks presented, taking into account the sensitivity of the data, and the purpose and context of the processing."

NOTES & QUESTIONS

1. *The OECD Privacy Guidelines, Old and New, and the Fair Information Practices.* How do the 1980 OECD Privacy Guidelines compare with the 2013 Guidelines? What do the new areas of emphasis demonstrate about trends in information privacy law? Do the two OECD Guidelines compare favorably

with the articulation of Fair Information Practices in the Department of Housing, Education, and Welfare (HEW) Report of 1973. Is either framework more comprehensive? More detailed? Which framework would be easier to comply with? To enforce?

B. PRIVACY PROTECTION IN EUROPE

1. DIVERGENCE OR CONVERGENCE?

JAMES Q. WHITMAN, *THE TWO WESTERN CULTURES OF PRIVACY: DIGNITY VERSUS LIBERTY*

113 Yale L.J. 1151 (2004)

Continental law is avidly protective of many kinds of "privacy" in many realms of life, whether the issue is consumer data, credit reporting, workplace privacy, discovery in civil litigation, the dissemination of nude images on the Internet, or shielding criminal offenders from public exposure. To people accustomed to the continental way of doing things, American law seems to tolerate relentless and brutal violations of privacy in all these areas of law. I have seen Europeans grow visibly angry, for example, when they learn about routine American practices like credit reporting. How, they ask, can merchants be permitted access to the entire credit history of customers who have never defaulted on their debts? Is it not obvious that this is a violation of privacy and personhood, which must be prohibited by law?

[Differences about privacy in the United States and Europe] are clashes in attitude that go well beyond the occasional social misunderstanding. In fact, they have provoked some tense and costly transatlantic legal and trade battles over the last decade and a half. Thus, the European Union and the United States slid into a major trade conflict over the protection of consumer data in the 1990s, only problematically resolved by a 2000 "safe harbor" agreement. Europeans still constantly complain that Americans do not accept the importance of protecting consumer privacy. Those tensions have only grown in the aftermath of September 11. . . .

For sensitive Europeans, indeed, a tour through American law may be an experience something like a visit to the latrines of Ephesus. Correspondingly, it has become common for Europeans to maintain that they respect a "fundamental right to privacy" that is either weak or wholly absent in the "cultural context" of the United States. Here, Europeans point with pride to Article 8 of the European Convention on Human Rights, which protects "the right to respect for private and family life," and to the European Union's new Charter of Fundamental Rights, which demonstratively features articles on both "Respect for Private and Family Life" and "Protection of Personal Data." By the standards of those great documents, American privacy law seems, from the European point of view, simply to have "failed.". . .

What we must acknowledge, instead, is that there are, on the two sides of the Atlantic, two different cultures of privacy, which are home to different intuitive sensibilities, and which have produced two significantly different laws of privacy. . . .

So why do these sensibilities differ? Why is it that French people won't talk about their salaries, but will take off their bikini tops? Why is it that Americans comply with court discovery orders that open essentially all of their documents for inspection, but refuse to carry identity cards? Why is it that Europeans tolerate state meddling in their choice of baby names? Why is it that Americans submit to extensive credit reporting without rebelling? . . .

At its conceptual core, the American right to privacy still takes much the form that it took in the eighteenth century: It is the right to freedom from intrusions by the state, especially in one's own home. The prime danger, from the American point of view, is that "the sanctity of [our] home[s]," in the words of a leading nineteenth-century Supreme Court opinion on privacy, will be breached by government actors. American anxieties thus focus comparatively little on the media. Instead, they tend to be anxieties about maintaining a kind of private sovereignty within our own walls.

Such is the contrast that lies at the base of our divergent sensibilities about what counts as a "privacy" violation. On the one hand, we have an Old World in which it seems fundamentally important not to lose public face; on the other, a New World in which it seems fundamentally important to preserve the home as a citadel of individual sovereignty. . . . When Americans seem to continental Europeans to violate norms of privacy, it is because they seem to display an embarrassing lack of concern for public dignity — whether the issue is the public indignity inflicted upon Monica Lewinsky by the media, or the self-inflicted indignity of an American who boasts about his salary. Conversely, when continental Europeans seem to Americans to violate norms of privacy, it is because they seem to show a supine lack of resistance to invasions of the realm of private sovereignty whose main citadel is the home — whether the issue is wiretapping or baby names. . . .

Where do the peculiar continental anxieties about "privacy" come from? To understand the continental law of privacy, we must start by recognizing how deeply "dignity" and "honor" matter in continental law more broadly. Privacy is not the only area in which continental law aims to protect people from shame and humiliation, from loss of public dignity. The law of privacy, in these continental countries, is only one member of a much wider class of legal protections for interpersonal respect. The importance of the value of respect in continental law is most familiar to Americans from one body of law in particular: the continental law of hate speech, which protects minorities against disrespectful epithets. But the continental attachment to norms of respect goes well beyond hate speech. Minorities are not the only ones protected against disrespectful epithets on the Continent. Everybody is protected against disrespect, through the continental law of "insult," a very old body of law that protects the individual right to "personal honor." Nor does it end there. Continental law protects the right of workers to respectful treatment by their bosses and coworkers, through what is called the law of "mobbing" or "moral harassment." This is law that protects employees against being addressed disrespectfully, shunned, or even assigned humiliating tasks like xeroxing. Continental law also protects the right of women to respectful treatment through its version of the law of sexual harassment. It even tries to protect the right of prison inmates to respectful treatment . . . to a degree almost unimaginable for Americans. . . .

If I may use a cosmological metaphor: American privacy law is a body caught in the gravitational orbit of liberty values, while European law is caught in the orbit of dignity. . . . Continental Europeans are consistently more drawn to problems touching on public dignity, while Americans are consistently more drawn to problems touching on the depredations of the state. . . .

Why does continental law work so hard to guarantee norms of "respect," "dignity," and "personal honor" in so many walks of life? This is a question to which I believe we must give a different answer from the one Europeans themselves commonly give. Europeans generally give a dramatic explanation for why dignity figures so prominently in their law: They assert that contemporary continental dignity is the product of a reaction against fascism, and especially against Nazism. Having experienced the horrific indignities of the 1930s and 1940s, continental societies, Europeans say, have mended their ways. Europe has dignity today because Europe was traumatized seventy years ago. . . .

In fact, the history of the continental law of dignity begins long before the postwar period. It begins in the eighteenth, and even the seventeenth, centuries. The continental societies that we see today are the descendants of the sharply hierarchical societies that existed two or two-and-a-half centuries ago — of the aristocratic and monarchical societies of which the France of Louis XIV was the model. In point of fact, continental law has enforced norms of respect and dignity for a very long time. In earlier centuries, though, only persons of high social status could expect their right to respect to be protected in court. Indeed, well into the twentieth century, only high-status persons could expect to be treated respectfully in the daily life of Germany or France, and only high-status persons could expect their "personal honor" to be protected in continental courts. . . .

What we see in continental law today is the result of a centuries-long, slow-maturing revolt against that style of status privilege. Over time, it has come to seem unacceptable that only certain persons should enjoy legal protections for their "dignity." Indeed, the rise of norms of respect for everybody — even minorities, even prison inmates — represents a great social transformation on the Continent. Everybody is now supposed to be treated in ways that only highly placed and wealthy people were treated a couple of centuries ago. . . .

The uncomfortable paradox . . . is that much of this leveling up took place during the fascist period, for fascist politics involved precisely the promise that all members of the nation-state would be equal in "honor" — that all racial Germans, for example, would be "masters." For that very reason, some of the fundamental institutions of the continental law of dignity experienced significant development under the star of fascism. In fact, the fascist period, seen in proper sociological perspective, was one stage in a continuous history of the extension of honor throughout all echelons of continental society.

This long-term secular leveling-up tendency has shaped continental law in a very fundamental way. Contemporary continental hate speech protections, for example, can be traced back to dueling law: In the nineteenth century, continental courts protected the right to respect only of the dueling classes. Today they protect everybody's right to respect; indeed, the rules of dueling have had a striking influence in the Continent, sometimes being imported bodily into the law. . . . As for Americans: They have their own concepts of personhood, their own traditions, and their own values. And the consequence is that there will always be practices that intuitively seem to represent obvious violations to Americans. Most especially, state action will raise American hackles much more often than European ones.

This is indeed almost too obvious to need describing for American readers. Suspicion of the state has always stood at the foundation of American privacy thinking, and American scholarly writing. . . .

What matters in America, over the long run, is liberty against the state within the privacy of one's home. This does not mean that the American approach to "privacy" is narrowly limited to Fourth Amendment search and seizure problems, of course. Lawyers do ingenious things, and the conception of privacy as liberty within the sanctity of the home can be extended in important ways. This has been notably true, of course, in the famous series of "constitutional privacy" decisions that began with *Griswold v. Connecticut*. . . .

Nevertheless, the fundamental limit on American thinking always remains: American "privacy" law, however ingenious its elaborations, always tends to imagine the home as the primary defense, and the state as the primary enemy. This gives American privacy law a distinctive coloration. Where American law perceives a threat to privacy, it is typically precisely because the state has become involved in the transaction. . . .

In truth, there is little reason to suppose that Americans will be persuaded to think of their world of values in a European way any time soon; American law simply does not endorse the general norm of personal dignity found in Europe. Nor is there any greater hope that Europeans will embrace the American ideal; the law of Europe does not recognize many of the antistatist concerns that Americans seem to take for granted. Of course we are all free to plead for a different kind of law — in Europe or in the United States. But pleading for privacy as such is not the way to do it. There is no such thing as privacy as such. The battle, if it is to be fought, will have to be fought over more fundamental values than that.

PAUL M. SCHWARTZ & KARL-NIKOLAUS PEIFER,
TRANSATLANTIC DATA PRIVACY LAW
106 Georgetown L.J. 115 (2017)

Rights talk forms an essential part of the European project, and one that has become more central over time. As Fabbrini notes, there has been a "growth of a fundamental rights culture in Europe in the last few decades."[10] Data protection law is at the front ranks of this effort. The EU began as an economic trading zone, but has always been about more than rationalizing a trade in coal and steel or safeguarding the free movement of goods. Constructed in the aftermath of the destruction of World War II, the European Community rests on a desire for a new model of political cooperation with the goal of bringing lasting peace to Europe.

---

[10] Federico Fabbrini, *Fundamental Rights in Europe* 13 (2014).

Meeting this goal led to creation of a supranational authority, and one with "the power to bind its constituent member states."[11] Yet, the rise of these largely Brussels-based institutions has not been without challenges.

Of the considerable hurdles faced by the EU project, one of the most significant has been the "democratic deficit" of its institutions. The ordinary European citizen feels bound to her national government, but is likely to have a more distant relationship to the EU as a sovereign entity. Too often, the EU is considered a distant, inaccessible institution. There are complaints about its transparency, complexity, the dominance of its executive institutions, the inability of its citizens to replace important decision makers, and the lack of power for more democratic EU institutions.

One response has been to increase the power of the European Parliament. Starting in 1979, EU reforms have made it a directly elected body and assigned it more traditional kinds of legislative power. Nonetheless, as Paul Craig and Grainne de Búrca warn, "The problems of secrecy, impenetrability, accountability, and representativeness are not addressed simply by giving added powers to the European Parliament."[12] Another response to the democratic deficit in the EU has been made at the constitutional level.

The hope has been to create a sense of European citizenship through development and enforcement of European constitutional rights. Jürgen Habermas, the German philosopher, has emerged as one of the clearest voices for constitutionality as the key to Europe's future. In his analysis, the European Union is made up of citizens of the member states ("We the People") as well as the nations of Europe.[13] Each individual therefore participates in the EU in a double fashion: both as a European citizen and through a role in her home nation.

In turn, the EU must provide its citizens with constitutional guarantees of justice and freedom. Human dignity is the bedrock on which these guarantees rest. As the Charter of Fundamental Rights states in its Article 1: "Human dignity is inviolable. It must be respected and protected." Above all, Habermas stresses the need for construction of a "common public sphere" in which citizens of Europe will engage in democratic deliberation. Rather than as Croatians, Czechs, Frenchmen, or Italians, Europeans are to discuss issues that require transnational solutions in a new shared, deliberative space.

This new communicative area, Habermas' "common public sphere" for EU citizens, is far from established. But the EU is further along in development of a shared political identity based on common fundamental rights. The rights talk around data protection should be understood within this context. Here is the forward-looking focus of EU data protection; it seeks to create a constitutional basis for a pan-European identity. To be sure, there are other foundational elements for the EU's interest in privacy and data protection. The first element concerns integration of member states around a common market. As Abraham Newman argues, one goal of EU regulators has been to draw on their powers to further market integration.[14] Similarly, both the Directive and GDPR reflect, in part, such

---

[11] Paul Craig & Grainne de Búrca, *EU Law: Texts, Cases, and Materials* 5 (4th ed. 2008).

[12] *Id.* at 133.

[13] Jürgen Habermas, *Zur Verfassung Europas* 66 (2011).

[14] Abraham Newman, *Protectors of Privacy* 75 (2008).

a market purpose.[15] Early caselaw of the European Court of Justice interpreting the Directive also emphasize this "market integration objective."[16]

The second element is the continent's terrible experience of fascism, totalitarianism, and authoritarianism. The experience with the data gathering of different kinds of secret police in Western and Eastern Europe alike has profoundly heightened sensitivities towards data protection throughout the EU. The rise of dignity and personality interests in European law after World War II played important part in the later development of information privacy rights.

To view EU data protection law, however, as resting only on the internal market and the lessons of the past, however crucial, would be to ignore its equally important role in a rights-oriented European project. As one German law professor has stated, Europe is no longer conversing in different languages when it comes to data protection law, but now speaks "European." The European language of data protection is now formed through the decisions of the European Court of Human Rights, the European Court of Justice, the GDPR, and a shared institutional structure, which includes the European Data Protection Board, the European Data Protection Supervisor, and national data protection authorities. Data protection is a critical part of the EU's development of European human rights law. In this regard, Fabbrini points to a 2014 decision of the European Court of Justice invalidating the EU's Data Retention Directive as the ruling that "crowns a decade of progressive jurisprudential developments in the field of human rights."[17]

III. The United States: Protecting the Privacy Consumer

U.S. privacy law situates the consumer within a marketplace for data trade. In it, the FTC has a central role through its policing data exchanges against the most deceptive kinds of practices. There is considerable distance here from the EU's rights discourse about data subjects. There are equally important differences between the U.S. and EU regarding the comparative constitutional aspects of information privacy law and data protection law, and the incorporation of doctrines of contract and consent.

NOTES & QUESTIONS

1. *U.S. vs. EU Privacy Regulation of the Private Sector.* Is Whitman correct that the United States has little concern about privacy with regard to private actors? As you read this chapter, consider whether there are areas where U.S. information privacy regulation might exceed those of the Europeans.

2. *The Rise of the European Union.* Writing over a decade after Whitman, and taking a different approach to the question of U.S. and European privacy,

---

[15] Orla Lynskey, *The Foundations of EU Data Protection Law* 8 (2015).

[16] *Id.* at 51-54.

[17] Federico Fabbrini, *Human Rights in the Digital Age: The European Court of Justice Ruling in the Data Retention Case and Its Lessons for Privacy and Surveillance in the United States,* 28 Harv. Hum. Rts. J. 65, 81 (2015). The 2014 case that Fabbrini points to as a turning point has been expanded by a subsequent 2016 data retention decision of the same court, Tele2 Sverige AB v. Post-och telestyreisen, ECLI:EU:C:2016:970 (Dec. 21, 2016) (Data Retention).

Schwartz and Peifer situate privacy in a development that they call the "EU project." In their view, data protection rests on three elements. These are, first, the integration of EU member states around a common market. Second, there is "the continent's terrible experience of fascism, totalitarianism, and authoritarianism." Finally, data protection law has a central role in the development of a rights-oriented EU. How does this interpretation follow or differ from Whitman's concept of "two cultures" of privacy?

3. *Regional Variation in Privacy Norms.* How well does Whitman's analysis apply to regional diversities for privacy culture within the United States or Europe? Are individuals in New York City more likely to share the views of those in Paris or London, or those in a small town in South Carolina?

4. *The U.S. Privacy Consumer.* Rather than the "rights talk" in the EU, Schwartz and Peifer describe the U.S. as protecting a "privacy consumer." In their view, "the U.S. anchors its information privacy law in the marketplace." In their summary regarding the U.S., "[T]he rhetoric of bilateral self-interest holds sway." They state: "Personal information is another commodity in the market, and human flourishing is furthered to the extent that the individual can maximize her preferences regarding data trades. The focus of information privacy in the U.S. is policing fairness in exchanges of personal data." Does this summary seem to be a correct or complete assessment of U.S. privacy law?

5. *Divergence or Convergence?* Whitman describes a divergence between European and U.S. views toward privacy. In 1992, Colin Bennett, a Canadian political scientist, proposed that convergence was taking place between U.S. and European information privacy law. He argued:

> The process of policy making in the data protection area is clearly one where broad transnational forces for convergence have transcended variations in national characteristics. The background to the legislation is the rapid technological process that is commonly recognized to be restructuring individual, social, economic, and political relationships. . . .
>
> The technology, however, should not be regarded as an independent force that "causes" anything. The crucial variable is the common set of attitudes that developed about the technology. . . .
>
> In this context, the salience of national factors as independent variables has been reduced. The partisan orientation of governments has been insignificant. . . . Fair information practice exposes the commonalities among the closely interlinked historical, cultural, and political developments of these societies.[18]

Subsequently, Bennett modified his views regarding convergence. In *The Governance of Privacy*, Bennett and Charles Raab identify a "decentering of privacy." In their view, "The governance of privacy is exercised through a variety of institutional forms — public and private, domestic and transnational, with the result that in certain contexts the government regulators are not necessarily the most important actors, and the laws they enact not necessarily the most important instruments." There is now a "fragmentation" with privacy

---

[18] Colin J. Bennett, *Regulating Privacy: Data Protection and Public Policy in Europe and the United States* 150-53 (1992).

regulation involving "a plurality of actors and a range of methods of operation and coordination." As a consequence, Bennett and Raab point to a lack of any single race to the bottom or top among different countries in different policy areas: "There are many races, many tops and many bottoms as a host of actors, public and private, use or resist the expanding repertoire of privacy instruments to encourage or obstruct the more responsible use of personal information within modern organizations."[19]

Compare Whitman's concluding paragraph to Bennett and Raab's argument that the many different policy areas and policy instruments throughout the world make any single comparison impossible. Is there an unbridgeable rift between the privacy laws in different countries based on different cultural values? Or is increasing globalization forcing countries to resolve these rifts?

6. ***Culture and Privacy Norms.*** As you go through the materials in this chapter, consider whether privacy claims vary in different parts of the world, and more generally, which factors contribute to the structuring of privacy norms. For example, is the concept of privacy determined by cultural traditions, trade requirements, legal developments, or technological influences?

2. EUROPEAN CONVENTION ON HUMAN RIGHTS, ARTICLE 8

The European Convention on Human Rights (ECHR), an international convention covering a wide range of civil and political rights, was adopted in 1950, shortly after the Universal Declaration of Human Rights of the United Nations. It was drafted under the auspices of the Council of Europe, an international organization composed today of over 40 European states, which was formed in 1949 as a result of a strong political willingness to unify European countries, to consolidate and stabilize its democracies after World War II, to prevent any future violations of human rights such as those that had taken place during the Nazi regime, and to establish a bulwark against Communism. The European Convention was intended to bring violations of human rights to the attention of the international community. As commentators have observed:

> In practice, this function of the ECHR, which imagines large-scale violations of human rights, has largely remained dormant. The ECHR has instead been used primarily to raise questions of isolated weaknesses in legal systems that basically conform to its requirements and which are representative of the "common heritage of political traditions, ideals, freedom and the rule of law" to which the Preamble to the ECHR refers.[20]

Protocol No. 11 to the Convention (1994) altered the path to the European Court of Human Rights.[21] Under the previous system, there had been a complicated system of referral to the Court involving the European Commission on Human

---

[19] Colin J. Bennett & Charles D. Raab, *The Governance of Privacy: Policy Instruments in Global Perspective* 294 (2006).

[20] S.H. Bailey, D.J. Harris & B.L. Jones, *Civil Liberties — Cases and Materials* 749-50 (3d ed. 1991).

[21] Protocol No. 11 to the Convention for the Protection of Human Rights and Fundamental Freedoms, restructuring the control machinery established thereby (ETS No. 155) (11 May 1994).

Rights. Once Protocol No. 11 entered into force in November 1998, however, the Court was able to receive applications directly "from any person, non-governmental organization or group of individuals claiming to be a victim of a violation . . . of the rights set forth in the Convention and the protocols thereto." In addition, member countries are able to refer to the Court violations of the Convention and its protocols by another member country. Finally, the Committee of Ministers is permitted to request advisory opinions from the European Court of Human Rights.

The Court's judgment is binding upon the member state against which the application was brought. It is normally declaratory. If the Court finds that a breach of the Convention has occurred, it brings into operation the defendant state's obligation in international law to make reparation. However, the Court may always award "just satisfaction" to the injured if the internal law of the defendant state allows only partial reparation.

The whole procedure can take up to five years between the registration of the application and the Court's final ruling. Although this is a slow procedure, "the primary purpose of state and individual applications is not to offer an international remedy for individual victims of violations of the Convention but to bring to light violations of an inter-state guarantee."[22]

The role of the European Court is of particular importance for several reasons. First, the volume of cases brought to the Court has increased over the years and has raised more complex jurisprudential issues than those that came before the court in earlier years. Second, the Court is the longest standing international human rights court; it is considered the model against which other regional courts can be measured. Finally, the jurisprudence of the court has influenced the normative development of other parts of the international human rights system. The Convention itself has a fundamental role in the European legal system as it has gradually acquired the status of a "constitutional instrument of European public order in the field of human rights."[23]

The critical privacy provision in the European Convention on Human Rights is Article 8. The language in Article 8 of the ECHR is similar to Article 12 of the Universal Declaration of Human Rights.

ECHR ARTICLE 8

Article 8 — Right to Respect for Private and Family Life

1. Everyone has the right to respect for his private and family life, his home and his correspondence.

2. There shall be no interference by a public authority with the exercise of this right except such as is in accordance with the law and is necessary in a democratic society in the interests of national security, public safety or the economic well-

---

[22] S.H. Bailey, D.J. Harris & B.L. Jones, *Civil Liberties: Cases and Materials* 761 (3d ed. 1991).

[23] J. Polakiewicz & V. Jacob-Foltzer, *The European Human Rights Convention in Domestic Law,* 12 Hum. Rts. L.J. 65, 125 (1991).

being of the country, for the prevention of disorder or crime, for the protection of health or morals, or for the protection of the rights and freedoms of others.

NOTES & QUESTIONS

1. *"In Accordance with Law."* As John Wadham describes it, a central requirement of Article 8 is "the rule of law":

> No matter how desirable the end to be achieved, no interference with a right protected under the Convention is permissible unless the citizen knows the basis for the interference because it is set out in an ascertainable law. In the absence of such detailed authorisation by the law, any interference, however justified, will violate the Convention. . . . No such interference can be permitted by executive rules alone.
>
> To be "prescribed by law" or "in accordance with law" means that there must be an ascertainable legal regime governing the interference in question. The Strasbourg court explained the concept in *Sunday Times v. United Kingdom* (1979) 2 EHRR 245 at paragraph 49: "Firstly, the law must be adequately accessible: the citizens must be able to have an indication that is adequate in the circumstances of the legal rules applicable to a given case. Secondly, a norm cannot be regarded as a 'law' unless it is formulated with sufficient precision to enable the citizen to regulate his conduct."
>
> The common law may be sufficiently clear for this purpose and statute law or regulation is not necessary. . . .
>
> It is not acceptable for an interference with a Convention right to occur without any legal regulation. . . .

Moreover, "any interference by a public authority with a Convention right must be directed towards an identified legitimate aim. . . . The sorts of aims which are legitimate are the interests of public safety, national security, the protection of health and morals and the economic well-being of the country or the protection of the rights and freedoms of others."[24]

2. *A Two-Stage Inquiry.* Orla Lynsky has provided an overview of the "non-exhaustive elements" that the ECHR uses in deciding whether there has been an interference with a protected interest under Article 8(1).[25] First, sometimes the mere storage of data relating to the private life of an individual may interfere with Article 8(1). Second, even for non-private information, a "systematic collection and storage of the information by a public authority" can be an activity that implicates this part of the Convention. Third, "the Court takes into consideration whether the use of information collected goes beyond that which was reasonably foreseeable by the applicant." Fourth, the Court has been more willing to find impingement of Article 8(1) "when the data concerned constitutes sensitive personal information." Finally, the Court considers whether consent was given for the processing.

---

[24] John Wadham, *Human Rights and Privacy — The Balance,* speech given at Cambridge (Mar. 2000), http://www.liberty-human-rights.org.uk/mhrp6j.html.

[25] Orly Lynskey, The Foundations of EU Data Protection Law 108-110 (2015).

If the CJEU finds an interference, with Article 8(1), it moves to the second stage of its inquiry, which concerns whether the action can be justified as in accordance with the law as well as necessary in a democratic society.

3. *"Necessary in a Democratic Society."* Wadham notes:

> Although a few rights in the Convention are absolute, most are not. The Convention approach is to decide whether a particular limitation from a right is justified in the sense of being "proportionate to the legitimate aim pursued."
>
> This means that even if a policy which interferes with a Convention right might be aimed at securing a legitimate aim of social policy, for example, the prevention of crime, this will not in itself justify the violation if the means adopted to secure the aim are excessive in the circumstances. . . .
>
> Where the Convention allows restrictions on rights it requires them to be justified by a legitimate aim and proportional to the need at hand, that is, "necessary in a democratic society." The case law interprets this to mean that there must be a "pressing social need" for the interference. . . . [T]he state's desire to protect a legitimate aim does not allow it to restrict the right of the individual disproportionately — the state cannot use a sledgehammer to crack a nut.[26]

4. ***The Council of Europe's Convention 108 on Privacy.*** Another important document for European privacy is the Council of Europe's Convention for the Protection of Individuals with Regard to Automatic Processing of Personal Data, ETS No. 108 (1981) (Convention 108). The convention is a "non-self-executing treaty." Its standards do not directly impose binding norms on signatory nations. It requires signatory nations to establish domestic data protection legislation that gives effect to the Convention's principles. These principles provide a common core of safeguards for the processing of personal data. Convention 108 permits domestic standards to exceed its basic safeguards.

Throughout the 1980s, the Convention was the most important European-wide agreement for privacy. Fifty-one nations have acceded to it. The members of the Council of Europe that have recently adopted the Convention include Armenia (2008), Monaco (2009), Azerbaijan (2010), and the Ukraine (2011). Non-member nations that have adopted the Convention include Uruguay (2013), Senegal (2016), and Tunisia (2017).

VON HANNOVER V. GERMANY [NO. 1]

59320/00 [2004] ECHR 294 (June 24, 2004)

1. The case originated in an application against the Federal Republic of Germany lodged with the Court under Article 34 of the Convention for the Protection of Human Rights and Fundamental Freedoms ("the Convention") by a national of Monaco, Caroline von Hannover ("the applicant"), on 6 June 2000.

---

[26] John Wadham, *Human Rights and Privacy — The Balance,* speech given at Cambridge (Mar. 2000), http://www.liberty-human-rights.org.uk/mhrp6j.html.

2. The applicant alleged that the German court decisions in her case had infringed her right to respect for her private and family life as guaranteed by Article 8 of the Convention. . . .

THE FACTS

8. The applicant, who is the eldest daughter of Prince Rainier III of Monaco, was born in 1957. Her official residence is in Monaco but she lives in the Paris area most of the time. . . .

9. Since the early 1990s the applicant has been trying — often through the courts — in a number of European countries to prevent the publication of photos about her private life in the tabloid press.

10. The photos that were the subject of the proceedings described below were published by the publishing company Burda in the German magazines *Bunte* and *Freizeit Revue* and by the publishing company Heinrich Bauer in the German magazine *Neue Post*.

11. [Five photos in *Freizeit Revue* magazine] show her with the actor Vincent Lindon at the far end of a restaurant courtyard in Saint-Rémy-de-Provence. [Photos in the magazine *Bunte* show her riding on horseback, with her children Peter and Andrea, in a canoe with her daughter, in a restaurant, on a bicycle, shopping in a market, skiing, leaving her house, and playing tennis. Photos in *Neue Post* magazine show her at a beach club in a swimsuit and wrapped up in a bathing towel. In this sequence, she tripped over an obstacle and fell down. The photos, which were described as "quite blurred," were accompanied by an article entitled, "Prince Ernst August played fisticuffs and Princess Caroline fell flat on her face."]
. . .

[The regional court denied her application under German law, reasoning that she did not have a right to protection against photos taken in public places. The case was appealed to the German Federal Court of Justice, and then to the German Federal Constitutional Court.] . . .

25. In a landmark judgment of 15 December 1999, delivered after a hearing, the Constitutional Court allowed the applicant's appeal in part on the ground that the three photos that had appeared in the 32nd and 34th editions of *Bunte* magazine, dated 5 August 1993 and 19 August 1993, featuring the applicant with her children had infringed her right to the protection of her personality rights guaranteed by sections 2(1) and 1(1) of the Basic Law, reinforced by her right to family protection under section 6 of the Basic Law. It referred the case to the Federal Court of Justice on that point. However, the Constitutional Court dismissed the applicant's appeal regarding the other photos.

The relevant extract of the judgment reads as follows:

> The fact that the press fulfils the function of forming public opinion does not exclude entertainment from the functional guarantee under the Basic Law. The formation of opinions and entertainment are not opposites. Entertainment also plays a role in the formation of opinions. It can sometimes even stimulate or influence the formation of opinions more than purely factual information. Moreover, there is a growing tendency in the media to do away with the distinction between information and entertainment both as regards press coverage generally and individual contributions, and to disseminate information in the form

of entertainment or mix it with entertainment ("infotainment"). Consequently, many readers obtain information they consider to be important or interesting from entertaining coverage. . . .

Nor can mere entertainment be denied any role in the formation of opinions. That would amount to unilaterally presuming that entertainment merely satisfies a desire for amusement, relaxation, escapism or diversion. Entertainment can also convey images of reality and propose subjects for debate that spark a process of discussion and assimilation relating to philosophies of life, values and behaviour models. In that respect it fulfils important social functions. . . . When measured against the aim of protecting press freedom, entertainment in the press is neither negligible nor entirely worthless and therefore falls within the scope of application of fundamental rights. . . .

The same is true of information about people. Personalization is an important journalistic means of attracting attention. Very often it is this which first arouses interest in a problem and stimulates a desire for factual information. Similarly, interest in a particular event or situation is usually stimulated by personalised accounts. Additionally, celebrities embody certain moral values and lifestyles. Many people base their choice of lifestyle on their example. They become points of crystallisation for adoption or rejection and act as examples or counter-examples. This is what explains the public interest in the various ups and downs occurring in their lives. . . .

The public has a legitimate interest in being allowed to judge whether the personal behaviour of the individuals in question, who are often regarded as idols or role models, convincingly tallies with their behaviour on their official engagements. . . .

The decision of the Federal Court of Justice cannot be criticised under constitutional law regarding the photos of the appellant at a market, doing her market shopping accompanied by her bodyguard or dining with a male companion at a well-attended restaurant. The first two cases concerned an open location frequented by the general public. The third case admittedly concerned a well circumscribed location, spatially speaking, but one in which the appellant was exposed to the other people present.

It is for this reason, moreover, that the Federal Court of Justice deemed it legitimate to ban photos showing the applicant in a restaurant garden, which were the subject of the decision being appealed but are not the subject of the constitutional appeal.

The presence of the applicant and her companion there presented all the features of seclusion. The fact that the photographs in question were evidently taken from a distance shows that the applicant could legitimately have assumed that she was not exposed to public view.

Nor can the decision being appealed be criticised regarding the photos of the applicant alone on horseback or riding a bicycle. In the Federal Court of Justice's view, the appellant had not been in a secluded place, but in a public one. That finding cannot attract criticism under constitutional law. The applicant herself describes the photos in question as belonging to the intimacy of her private sphere merely because they manifest her desire to be alone. In accordance with the criteria set out above, the mere desire of the person concerned is not relevant in any way.

The three photos of the applicant with her children require a fresh examination, however, in the light of the constitutional rules set out above. We cannot rule out the possibility that the review that needs to be carried out in the light of the relevant criteria will lead to a different result for one or other or all the photos.

The decision must therefore be set aside in that respect and remitted to the Federal Court of Justice for a fresh decision. . . .

39. The relevant provisions of the Basic Law are worded as follows:

Section 1(1) — "The dignity of human beings is inviolable. All public authorities have a duty to respect and protect it."

Section 2(1) — "Everyone shall have the right to the free development of their personality provided that they do not interfere with the rights of others or violate the constitutional order or moral law (*Sittengesetz*)."

Section 5(1) — "(1) Everyone shall have the right freely to express and disseminate his or her opinions in speech, writing and pictures and freely to obtain information from generally accessible sources. Freedom of the press and freedom of reporting on the radio and in films shall be guaranteed. There shall be no censorship. (2) These rights shall be subject to the limitations laid down by the provisions of the general laws and by statutory provisions aimed at protecting young people and to the obligation to respect personal honour (*Recht der persönlichen Ehre*)."

Section 6(1) and (2) — "(1) Marriage and the family enjoy the special protection of the State. (2) The care and upbringing of children is the natural right of parents and a duty primarily incumbent on them. The State community shall oversee the performance of that duty."

40. Section 22(1) of the Copyright (Arts Domain) Act provides that images can only be disseminated with the express approval of the person concerned.

41. Section 23(1) no. 1 of that Act provides for exceptions to that rule, particularly where the images portray an aspect of contemporary society (*Bildnisse aus dem Bereich der Zeitgeschichte*) on condition that publication does not interfere with a legitimate interest (*berechtigtes Interesse*) of the person concerned (section 23(2)). . . .

THE LAW

43. The applicant submitted that the German court decisions had infringed her right to respect for her private and family life guaranteed by Article 8 of the Convention. . . .

44. The applicant stated that she had spent more than ten years in unsuccessful litigation in the German courts trying to establish her right to the protection of her private life. She alleged that as soon as she left her house she was constantly hounded by paparazzi who followed her every daily movement, be it crossing the road, fetching her children from school, doing her shopping, out walking, practising sport or going on holiday. In her submission, the protection afforded to the private life of a public figure like herself was minimal under German law because the concept of a "secluded place" as defined by the Federal Court of Justice and the Federal Constitutional Court was much too narrow in that respect. Furthermore, in order to benefit from that protection the onus was on her to establish every time that she had been in a secluded place. She was thus deprived

of any privacy and could not move about freely without being a target for the paparazzi. She affirmed that in France her prior agreement was necessary for the publication of any photos not showing her at an official event. Such photos were regularly taken in France and then sold and published in Germany. The protection of private life from which she benefited in France was therefore systematically circumvented by virtue of the decisions of the German courts. On the subject of the freedom of the press the applicant stated that she was aware of the essential role played by the press in a democratic society in terms of informing and forming public opinion, but in her case it was just the entertainment press seeking to satisfy its readers' voyeuristic tendencies and make huge profits from generally anodyne photos showing her going about her daily business. Lastly, the applicant stressed that it was materially impossible to establish in respect of every photo whether or not she had been in a secluded place. As the judicial proceedings were generally held several months after publication of the photos, she was obliged to keep a permanent record of her every movement in order to protect herself from paparazzi who might photograph her. With regard to many of the photos that were the subject of this application it was impossible to determine the exact time and place at which they had been taken.

45. The Government submitted that German law, while taking account of the fundamental role of the freedom of the press in a democratic society, contained sufficient safeguards to prevent any abuse and ensure the effective protection of the private life of even public figures. In their submission, the German courts had in the instant case struck a fair balance between the applicant's rights to respect for her private life guaranteed by Article 8 and the freedom of the press guaranteed by Article 10, having regard to the margin of appreciation available to the State in this area. The courts had found in the first instance that the photos had not been taken in a secluded place and had, in the second instance, examined the limits on the protection of private life, particularly in the light of the freedom of the press and even where the publication of photos by the entertainment press were concerned. The protection of the private life of a figure of contemporary society "*par excellence*" did not require the publication of photos without his or her authorisation to be limited to showing the person in question engaged in their official duties. The public had a legitimate interest in knowing how the person behaved generally in public. The Government submitted that this definition of the freedom of the press by the Federal Constitutional Court was compatible with Article 10 and the European Court's relevant case-law. Furthermore, the concept of a secluded place was only one factor, albeit an important one, of which the domestic courts took account when balancing the protection of private life against the freedom of the press. Accordingly, while private life was less well protected where a public figure was photographed in a public place other factors could also be taken into consideration, such as the nature of the photos, for example, which should not shock the public. Lastly, the Government reiterated that the decision of the Federal Court of Justice — which had held that the publication of photos of the applicant with the actor Vincent Lindon in a restaurant courtyard in Saint-Rémy-de-Provence were unlawful — showed that the applicant's private life was protected even outside her home. . . .

B. The Court's Assessment

50. The Court reiterates that the concept of private life extends to aspects relating to personal identity, such as a person's name or a person's picture.

Furthermore, private life, in the Court's view, includes a person's physical and psychological integrity; the guarantee afforded by Article 8 of the Convention is primarily intended to ensure the development, without outside interference, of the personality of each individual in his relations with other human beings. . . .

52. As regards photos, with a view to defining the scope of the protection afforded by Article 8 against arbitrary interference by public authorities, the Commission had regard to whether the photographs related to private or public matters and whether the material thus obtained was envisaged for a limited use or was likely to be made available to the general public.

53. In the present case there is no doubt that the publication by various German magazines of photos of the applicant in her daily life either on her own or with other people falls within the scope of her private life.

54. The Court notes that, in its landmark judgment of 15 December 1999, the Federal Constitutional Court interpreted sections 22 and 23 of the Copyright (Arts Domain) Act (see paragraphs 40-41 above) by balancing the requirements of the freedom of the press against those of the protection of private life, that is, the public interest in being informed against the legitimate interests of the applicant. In doing so the Federal Constitutional Court took account of two criteria under German law, one functional and the other spatial. It considered that the applicant, as a figure of contemporary society *"par excellence"*, enjoyed the protection of her private life even outside her home but only if she was in a secluded place out of the public eye "to which the person concerned retires with the objectively recognisable aim of being alone and where, confident of being alone, behaves in a manner in which he or she would not behave in public". In the light of those criteria the Federal Constitutional Court held that the Federal Court of Justice's judgment of 19 December 1995 regarding publication of the photos in question was compatible with the Basic Law. The court attached decisive weight to the freedom of the press, even the entertainment press, and to the public interest in knowing how the applicant behaved outside her representative functions. . . .

56. In the present case the applicant did not complain of an action by the State, but rather of the lack of adequate State protection of her private life and her image.

57. The Court reiterates that although the object of Article 8 is essentially that of protecting the individual against arbitrary interference by the public authorities, it does not merely compel the State to abstain from such interference: in addition to this primarily negative undertaking, there may be positive obligations inherent in an effective respect for private or family life. These obligations may involve the adoption of measures designed to secure respect for private life even in the sphere of the relations of individuals between themselves. . . .

58. That protection of private life has to be balanced against the freedom of expression guaranteed by Article 10 of the Convention. In that context the Court reiterates that the freedom of expression constitutes one of the essential foundations of a democratic society. Subject to paragraph 2 of Article 10, it is applicable not only to "information" or "ideas" that are favourably received or regarded as inoffensive or as a matter of indifference, but also to those that offend,

shock or disturb. Such are the demands of that pluralism, tolerance and broadmindedness without which there is no "democratic society."

In that connection the press plays an essential role in a democratic society. Although it must not overstep certain bounds, in particular in respect of the reputation and rights of others, its duty is nevertheless to impart — in a manner consistent with its obligations and responsibilities — information and ideas on all matters of public interest. . . .

59. Although freedom of expression also extends to the publication of photos, this is an area in which the protection of the rights and reputation of others takes on particular importance. The present case does not concern the dissemination of "ideas", but of images containing very personal or even intimate "information" about an individual. Furthermore, photos appearing in the tabloid press are often taken in a climate of continual harassment which induces in the person concerned a very strong sense of intrusion into their private life or even of persecution. . . .

61. The Court points out at the outset that in the present case the photos of the applicant in the various German magazines show her in scenes from her daily life, thus engaged in activities of a purely private nature such as practising sport, out walking, leaving a restaurant or on holiday. . . .

63. The Court considers that a fundamental distinction needs to be made between reporting facts — even controversial ones — capable of contributing to a debate in a democratic society relating to politicians in the exercise of their functions, for example, and reporting details of the private life of an individual who, moreover, as in this case, does not exercise official functions. While in the former case the press exercises its vital role of "watchdog" in a democracy by contributing to "impart[ing] information and ideas on matters of public interest, it does not do so in the latter case.

64. Similarly, although the public has a right to be informed, which is an essential right in a democratic society that, in certain special circumstances, can even extend to aspects of the private life of public figures, particularly where politicians are concerned, this is not the case here. The situation here does not come within the sphere of any political or public debate because the published photos and accompanying commentaries relate exclusively to details of the applicant's private life.

65. As in other similar cases it has examined, the Court considers that the publication of the photos and articles in question, of which the sole purpose was to satisfy the curiosity of a particular readership regarding the details of the applicant's private life, cannot be deemed to contribute to any debate of general interest to society despite the applicant being known to the public. . . .

68. The Court finds another point to be of importance: even though, strictly speaking, the present application concerns only the publication of these photos and articles by various German magazines, the context in which these photos were taken — without the applicant's knowledge or consent — and the harassment endured by many public figures in their daily lives cannot be fully disregarded.

In the present case this point is illustrated in particularly striking fashion by the photos taken of the applicant at the Monte Carlo Beach Club tripping over an obstacle and falling down. . . .

69. The Court reiterates the fundamental importance of protecting private life from the point of view of the developments of every human being's personality.

That protection . . . extends beyond the private family circle and also includes a social dimension. . . . [A]nyone, even if they are known to the general public, must be able to enjoy a "legitimate expectation" of protection of and respect for their private life.

74. The Court therefore considers that the criteria on which the domestic courts based their decisions were not sufficient to protect the applicant's private life effectively. As a figure of contemporary society *"par excellence"* she cannot — in the name of freedom of the press and the public interest — rely on protection of her private life unless she is in a secluded place out of the public eye and, moreover, succeeds in proving it (which can be difficult). Where that is not the case, she has to accept that she might be photographed at almost any time, systematically, and that the photos are then very widely disseminated even if, as was the case here, the photos and accompanying articles relate exclusively to details of her private life.

75. In the Court's view, the criterion of spatial isolation, although apposite in theory, is in reality too vague and difficult for the person concerned to determine in advance. In the present case merely classifying the applicant as a figure of contemporary society *"par excellence"* does not suffice to justify such an intrusion into her private life.

76. As the Court has stated above, it considers that the decisive factor in balancing the protection of private life against freedom of expression should lie in the contribution that the published photos and articles make to a debate of general interest. It is clear in the instant case that they made no such contribution since the applicant exercises no official function and the photos and articles related exclusively to details of her private life.

77. Furthermore, the Court considers that the public does not have a legitimate interest in knowing where the applicant is and how she behaves generally in her private life even if she appears in places that cannot always be described as secluded and despite the fact that she is well known to the public.

Even if such a public interest exists, as does a commercial interest of the magazines in publishing these photos and these articles, in the instant case those interests must, in the Court's view, yield to the applicant's right to the effective protection of her private life.

78. Lastly, in the Court's opinion the criteria established by the domestic courts were not sufficient to ensure the effective protection of the applicant's private life and she should, in the circumstances of the case, have had a "legitimate expectation" of protection of her private life.

79. Having regard to all the foregoing factors, and despite the margin of appreciation afforded to the State in this area, the Court considers that the German courts did not strike a fair balance between the competing interests.

80. There has therefore been a breach of Article 8 of the Convention. . . .

85. The Court considers the question of the application of Article 41 [providing for "just satisfaction to the injured party," i.e., damages] is not ready for decision. Accordingly, it shall be reserved and the subsequent procedure fixed having regard to any agreement which might be reached between the Government and the applicant.

NOTES & QUESTIONS

1. **Von Hannover*'s* Impact on German Law.** *Von Hannover I* represents what one law professor has termed the European Court of Human Rights' (ECHR) "censure" of the German Constitutional Court, the highest German court, and its case law regarding the press and privacy.[27] For Andreas Heldrich, the European Court of Human Rights in its decision "overruled nearly point for point" the German Court's arguments in its decisions. Heldrich points in particular to the German court's need to change, after *Von Hannover I,* its existing jurisprudence, which had required "absolute persons of contemporary history" (*absolute Personen der Zeitgeschichte*) to accept being photographed anywhere outside of their homes as long as they did not retreat into a private place to be alone. In Heldrich's prediction, *Von Hannover I* means that in the future, "we will be able to enjoy colorful pictures from the private life of our celebrities only with their permission. Nonetheless, we need not worry. There will be enough of them left over."

   In contrast, Stefan Engels and Uwe Jürgens describe a path by which German courts might integrate *Von Hannover I* with existing case law. For them, the core of the decision of the European Court of Human Rights turns on whether there has been "constant annoyances that the affected party feels as a weighty invasion of her private life and even as a persecution."[28] Yet, not every such confrontation with the press will qualify under this proposed test. Engels and Jürgens argue that "prominent persons of public life" who jog by a river in Hamburg or leave a famous nightclub in Munich cannot claim that they have retreated to the private sphere. In their view, the law must accept that there is also a "reverse side" to fame, namely, public attention. The plaintiff must demonstrate that an image has been taken in the context of a "weighty persecution" by the press of her, and the court must evaluate the image in the context of the journalist's report that accompanies it. Do Engels and Jürgens or Heldrich make the more convincing case about the extent of the impact of *Von Hannover I* with existing German protection of the press?

2. **Von Hannover II *and* Von Hannover III.** Subsequent to *Von Hannover I,* the European Court of Human Rights issued opinions in two more cases brought by Princess Caroline, who lost both appeals.

   In *Von Hannover II,* Princess Caroline argued that a decision of the German Federal Constitutional Court from 2008 violated her Article 8 rights. Case of Von Hannover v. Germany (no. 2), no. 40660/08 and 60641/08, ECHR 228 (Feb. 7, 2012). She objected to the publication of photographs of her on vacation that were published in German magazines. The underlying case involved the German Federal Constitutional Court's review of a decision of the

---

[27] Andreas Heldrich, Persönlichkeitsschutz und Pressefreiheit nach der Europäischen Menschenrechtskonvention, NJW 2634 (2004).

[28] Stefan Engels & Uwe Jürgens, Auswirkungen der EGMR-Rechtsprechung zum Privatsphärenschutz-Möglichkeiten und Grenzen der Umsetzung des "Caroline"-Urteils im deutschen Recht, NJW 2517, 2521 (2007).

Federal Court of Justice (*Bundesgerichtshof*).[29] The Federal Court of Justice found that some of the photographs of Princess Caroline contributed to a debate of general interests and some did not. The photographs that contributed to the public debate were protected by freedom of the press, and Princess Caroline appealed this part of the decision to the Constitutional Court. The core issue for the Constitutional Court was "the question of the extent to which articles may be illustrated using photographs showing the private life of celebrities." For it, the key was whether a photograph, even one that showed a celebrity on vacation, "dealt with relevant factual topics that affect a democratic society."

The Constitutional Court found against Caroline, and agreed with the Federal Court of Justice, in holding that some of the contested photographs met this standard. Photographs were published, for example, of Princess Caroline on vacation with her husband in St. Moritz, a Swiss winter sport resort. The photograph accompanied an article about the illness of her father, Prince Rainier, that discussed how his children, including Caroline, were taking turns caring for him. The Constitutional Court stated that "the illness of the reigning Prince of Monaco constitutes an event of general public interest and . . . the press should also be allowed, in connection with such an event, to report on the way his children including [Caroline] were managing to reconcile their duties towards solidarity within the family with their legitimate interest in safeguarding the needs of their own private lives including the desire to go on holiday." Regarding the relevant European precedent, the Constitutional Court argued, "The European Court of Human Rights in its [*Von Hannover* opinion] did not categorically exclude the possibility that a report which contributes to the treatment of important factual issues that are of interest to the general public may also be illustrated using pictures taken from the everyday life of persons who are part of public or political life."

In *Von Hannover II*, the European Court of Human Rights decided that the German national courts did not violate the requirements of Article 8. It found that the national courts "explicitly took account of the [European Court of Human Right's] relevant case law." Indeed, the German Federal Constitutional Court had "undertaken a detailed analysis of the [European Court's] case-law in response to the applicants' complaints. . . ." The Court of Human Rights stated that it accepted "that the photos in question, considered in the light of the accompanying articles, did contribute, at least to some degree, to a debate of general interest." It added that the press had the task of imparting information and ideas on all matters of public interest, and the public had a right to receive the resulting information and ideas.

Von Hannover III concerned a further complaint by Princess Caroline against the German press. After losing her case in German courts, Princess Caroline again appealed and again lost before the European Court of Human Rights. *Affaire Von Hannover c. Allemagne* (No. 3) no. 8772/10, ECHR 835

---

[29] Order of the First Senate of 26 February 2008, German Federal Constitutional Court (1 BcR 1602, 1606, 1626/07 (official English translation), at http://www.bverfg.de/entscheidungen/rs20080226_1bvr160207en.html.

(Sept. 19, 2013).[30] The photographs in question accompanied, among other articles in the popular press, one regarding a trend in which Hollywood stars and royalty rented out their vacation homes. The European Court of Human Rights found that it could accept the decision of the German courts that the photographs contributed to a debate of general interest.

3. *Axel Springer.* In *Von Hannover II* and *Von Hannover III*, the European Court of Justice found that the German courts had adequately balanced privacy and the freedom of the press. In *Case of Axel Springer v. Germany*, No. 39954, ECHR 227 (Feb. 7, 2012), it reached a different conclusion.

In *Springer*, German courts had placed restrictions on the publication in the *Bild Zeitung*, a daily newspaper, of articles about the arrest of "TV star X" for possession of cocaine at the Oktoberfest in Munich. Ironically, TV star X was famous for playing "a police superintendent, whose mission was law enforcement and crime prevention." Regarding X's role as a TV cop, the European Court of Human Rights stated: "The fact was such as to increase the public's interest in being informed of X's arrest for a criminal offence." It also noted that X "was arrested in public, in a tent at the beer festival in Munich." The Court of Human Rights found that the German courts failed to give adequate weight to the public interest in the publication. It added that, "The fact that the first article contained certain expressions which, to all intents and purposes, were designed to attract the public's attention cannot in itself raise an issue under the Court's case-law . . . ." The expressions in question included the article's headline: "TV star X caught in possession of cocaine. A bretzel (*Brezn*), a beer mug [containing a litre of beer — *Maß*] and a line of coke (*Koks*)."[31]

4. *Privacy in Public.* How would the *Von Hannover* cases and the *Axel Springer* case be decided under the American privacy torts? Is the ECHR's protection of privacy in public too strong? For Nicholas Nohlen, "German courts had long given too much weight to the freedom of the press (even protecting 'news' that was merely entertaining), to the disadvantage of the individual's right to protection of private life."[32] In contrast, Nohlen states that the ECHR emphasized that "the decisive factor for balancing the right to private life and freedom of the press lies in the contribution of the delivered information to a debate of general interest." In other words, the focus should now be placed on the value of the information that the press delivers.

How is a court to assess the whether information is connected to a "debate of general interest" (the ECHR's test)? Nohlen concedes:

> The ECHR's criterion in *Von Hannover* remains unclear. The Court held that the decisive criterion in balancing the right to private life against freedom of the press is whether the published photos contribute to a debate of general interest.

[30] Only a French official version of the decision and an unofficial German translation of the decision are available.

[31] For two 2014 cases of the Court of Human Rights applying the *Von Hannover* criteria, see Case of Lillo-Stenberg and Saether v. Norway, No. 13258/09 (Apr. 16, 2014); Case of Ruusunen v. Finland, No. 73579/10, ECHR (Apr. 14, 2014).

[32] Nicholas Hohlen, Case Note: Von Hannover v. Germany, 100 Am. J. Int'l L. 196, 198 (2006).

It did not then establish a criterion, however, for determining what is to be considered as contributing to such a debate.

Nohlen then proposes a series of examples of the kinds of press reports that would possibly contribute to such a debate of general interest: "published articles with photos showing a well-known musician, who was said to be a family man, secretly cheating on his wife, or of a young soccer star, who always appeared to be shy and reserved, involved in a street fight." As he notes, moreover, nothing in *Von Hannover I* limits the test of a "debate of general interest" to merely political topics.

Consider as well the reasoning of the German Constitutional Court, which noted that the "applicant herself describes the photos in question as belonging to the intimacy of her private sphere merely because they manifest her desire to be alone. . . . [T]he mere desire of the person concerned is not relevant in any way." Does the ECHR have a satisfactory answer to this objection—namely, that there must be more objective criteria to define what is private than merely an individual's desires? Does the ruling of the ECHR threaten to make privacy too subjective a matter by not relying as heavily upon the fact that at least some of the photographs of Princess Caroline were taken while she was in public places?

5. *Article 8 vs. Article 10.* Whereas Article 8 of the Convention protects privacy, Article 10 protects freedom of speech and press:

> 1. Everyone has the right to freedom of expression. This right shall include freedom to hold opinions and to receive and impart information and ideas without interference by public authority and regardless of frontiers. This article shall not prevent States from requiring the licensing of broadcasting, television or cinema enterprises.
> 2. The exercise of these freedoms, since it carries with it duties and responsibilities, may be subject to such formalities, conditions, restrictions or penalties as are prescribed by law and are necessary in a democratic society, in the interests of national security, territorial integrity or public safety, for the prevention of disorder or crime, for the protection of health or morals, for the protection of the reputation or rights of others, for preventing the disclosure of information received in confidence, or for maintaining the authority and impartiality of the judiciary.

How are Article 8 and Article 10 to be reconciled? In *Von Hannover,* how does the ECHR's balance between Articles 8 and 10 compare to the U.S. Supreme Court's analysis of privacy laws that conflict with the First Amendment right to freedom of speech and press? How does the ECHR differ from the German Constitutional Court on the scope of freedom of press?

Does *Von Hannover* strike the right balance between privacy and free speech? Consider Barbara McDonald:

> [E]ven in the case of public figures, the court's decision [in *Von Hannover*] indicates a greater respect for the notion that some aspects of their lives should remain private and free of intrusion even when they are in public. The applicable tests — whether the information came within their "legitimate expectation" of privacy so as to invoke a need to be balanced with the right to

freedom of expression, and if so, whether it contributes to a debate of general interest — is a fairly high bar for the media to overcome.[33]

IN THE CASE OF MOSLEY V. THE UNITED KINGDOM
48009/08 [2011] ECHR 774 (10 May 2011)

---

8. The applicant was born in 1940 and lives in Monaco.

9. On 30 March 2008, the *News of the World*, a Sunday newspaper owned by News Group Newspapers Limited, published on its front page an article headed "F1 boss has sick Nazi orgy with 5 hookers." The article opened with the sentence, "Formula 1 motor racing chief Max Mosley is today exposed as a secret sadomasochistic sex pervert." Several pages inside the newspaper were also devoted to the story, which included still photographs taken from video footage secretly recorded by one of the participants in the sexual activities, who was paid in advance to do so. An edited extract of the video as well as still images were also published on the newspaper's website and reproduced elsewhere on the internet. The print version of the newspaper invited readers to view the video, providing the website address of the newspaper. . . .

13. On 6 April 2008 a second series of articles on the applicant's sexual activities was published in the *News of the World*. . . .

22. On 24 July 2008 judgment was handed down in the privacy proceedings. . . .

25. Eady J concluded that the newspaper articles and images constituted a breach of the applicant's right to privacy. He found that there were no Nazi connotations in the applicant's sexual activities and that there was therefore no public interest or justification in the publication of the article about his personal life and the accompanying images.

26. On the question of damages, Eady J declined to award exemplary damages and limited the damages available to a compensatory award. He considered it questionable whether deterrence should have a distinct, as opposed to a merely incidental, role to play in the award of compensatory damages, noting that it was a notion more naturally associated with punishment. He further observed that if damages were paid to an individual for the purpose of deterring the defendant it would naturally be seen as an undeserved windfall. He added that if damages for deterrence were to have any prospect of success it would be necessary to take into account the means of the relevant defendant. Any award against the *News of the World* would have to be so large that it would fail the test of proportionality when seen as fulfilling a compensatory function and would risk having a "chilling effect" on freedom of expression.

27. Eady J recognized that the sum awarded would not constitute adequate redress, noting:

"231. . . . . it has to be accepted that an infringement of privacy cannot ever be effectively compensated by a monetary award. Judges cannot achieve what is, in the nature of things, impossible. That unpalatable fact cannot be mitigated by

---

[33] Barbara McDonald, *Privacy, Princesses, and Paparazzi*, 50 N.Y. L. Sch. L. Rev. 205, 223 (2005).

simply adding a few noughts to the number first thought of. Accordingly, it seems to me that the only realistic course is to select a figure which marks the fact that an unlawful intrusion has taken place while affording some degree of *solatium* to the injured party. . . .''[34]

28. The applicant was awarded GBP 60,000 in damages and recovered approximately GBP 420,000 in costs.[35] The judge noted that the applicant was hardly exaggerating when he said that his life was ruined. A final injunction was granted against the newspaper. . . .

65. The applicant complained that the United Kingdom had violated its positive obligations under Article 8 of the Convention . . . by failing to impose a legal duty on the *News of the World* to notify him in advance in order to allow him the opportunity to seek an interim injunction and thus prevent publication of material which violated his right to respect for his private life. The Government contested that argument.

a. General principles

i. Article 8

106. It is clear that the words "the right to respect for . . . private . . . life" which appear in Article 8 require not only that the State refrain from interfering with private life but also entail certain positive obligations on the State to ensure effective enjoyment of this right by those within its jurisdiction. Such an obligation may require the adoption of positive measures designed to secure effective respect for private life even in the sphere of the relations of individuals between themselves (see *Von Hannover v. Germany*).

107. The Court emphasises the importance of a prudent approach to the State's positive obligations to protect private life in general and of the need to recognise the diversity of possible methods to secure its respect. The choice of measures designed to secure compliance with that obligation in the sphere of the relations of individuals between themselves in principle falls within the Contracting States' margin of appreciation. However, this discretion goes hand in hand with European supervision.

108. The Court recalls that a number of factors must be taken into account when determining the breadth of the margin of appreciation to be accorded to the State in a case in which Article 8 of the Convention is engaged. First, the Court reiterates that the notion of "respect" in Article 8 is not clear-cut, especially as far as the positive obligations inherent in that concept are concerned: bearing in mind the diversity of the practices followed and the situations obtaining in the Contracting States, the notion's requirements will vary considerably from case to case. Thus Contracting Parties enjoy a wide margin of appreciation in determining the steps to be taken to ensure compliance with the Convention. . . .

---

[34] Editors' Note: In English law, *solatium* is a term used for general damages. It is given as compensation for suffering, loss, or injured feelings.

[35] Editors' Note: GBP 60,000 is approximately $100,000, and GBP 420,000 is approximately $700,000.

109. Second, the nature of the activities involved affects the scope of the margin of appreciation. The Court has previously noted that a serious interference with private life can arise where the state of domestic law conflicts with an important aspect of personal identity. Thus, in cases concerning Article 8, where a particularly important facet of an individual's existence or identity is at stake, the margin allowed to the State is correspondingly narrowed.

110. Third, the existence or absence of a consensus across the Member States of the Council of Europe, either as to the relative importance of the interest at stake or as to the best means of protecting it, is also relevant to the extent of the margin of appreciation: where no consensus exists, the margin of appreciation afforded to States is generally a wide one.

111. Finally, in cases where measures which an applicant claims are required pursuant to positive obligations under Article 8 would have an impact on freedom of expression, regard must be had to the fair balance that has to be struck between the competing rights and interests arising under Article 8 and Article 10.

ii. Article 10

112. The Court emphasises the pre-eminent role of the press in informing the public and imparting information and ideas on matters of public interest in a State governed by the rule of law. Not only does the press have the task of imparting such information and ideas but the public also has a right to receive them. Were it otherwise, the press would be unable to play its vital role of "public watchdog." . . .

114. The Court also reiterates that there is a distinction to be drawn between reporting facts — even if controversial — capable of contributing to a debate of general public interest in a democratic society, and making tawdry allegations about an individual's private. In respect of the former, the pre-eminent role of the press in a democracy and its duty to act as a "public watchdog" are important considerations in favour of a narrow construction of any limitations on freedom of expression. However, different considerations apply to press reports concentrating on sensational and, at times, lurid news, intended to titillate and entertain, which are aimed at satisfying the curiosity of a particular readership regarding aspects of a person's strictly private life (*Von Hannover*). Such reporting does not attract the robust protection of Article 10 afforded to the press. . . . While confirming the Article 10 right of members of the public to have access to a wide range of publications covering a variety of fields, the Court stresses that in assessing in the context of a particular publication whether there is a public interest which justifies an interference with the right to respect for private life, the focus must be on whether the publication is in the interest of the public and not whether the public might be interested in reading it.

115. It is commonly acknowledged that the audiovisual media have often a much more immediate and powerful effect than the print media. Accordingly, although freedom of expression also extends to the publication of photographs, the Court recalls that this is an area in which the protection of the rights of others takes on particular importance, especially where the images contain very personal and intimate "information" about an individual or where they are taken on private

premises and clandestinely through the use of secret recording devices (see *Von Hannover*). . . .

117. Finally, the Court has emphasized that while Article 10 does not prohibit the imposition of prior restraints on publication, the dangers inherent in prior restraints are such that they call for the most careful scrutiny on the part of the Court. This is especially so as far as the press is concerned, for news is a perishable commodity and to delay its publication, even for a short period, may well deprive it of all its value and interest. The Court would, however, observe that prior restraints may be more readily justified in cases which demonstrate no pressing need for immediate publication and in which there is no obvious contribution to a debate of general public interest.

118. . . . The question for consideration in the present case is whether the specific measure called for by the applicant, namely a legally binding pre-notification rule, is required in order to discharge that obligation.

119. The Court observes at the outset that this is not a case where there are no measures in place to ensure protection of Article 8 rights. A system of self-regulation of the press has been established in the United Kingdom, with guidance provided in the Editors' Code and Codebook and oversight of journalists' and editors' conduct by the [Press Complaints Commission (PCC)]. While the PCC itself has no power to award damages, an individual may commence civil proceedings in respect of any alleged violation of the right to respect for private life which, if successful, can lead to a damages award in his favour. . . . The Court is of the view that such awards can reasonably be expected to have a salutary effect on journalistic practices. Further, if an individual is aware of a pending publication relating to his private life, he is entitled to seek an interim injunction preventing publication of the material. . . . Further protection for individuals is provided by the Data Protection Act 1998, which sets out the right to have unlawfully collected or inaccurate data destroyed or rectified.

120. The Court further observes that, in its examination to date of the measures in place at domestic level to protect Article 8 rights in the context of freedom of expression, it has implicitly accepted that *ex post facto* damages provide an adequate remedy for violations of Article 8 rights arising from the publication by a newspaper of private information. . . .

121. . . . While the specific facts of the applicant's case provide a backdrop to the Court's consideration of this question, the implications of any pre-notification requirement are necessarily far wider. However meritorious the applicant's own case may be, the Court must bear in mind the general nature of the duty called for. In particular, its implications for freedom of expression are not limited to the sensationalist reporting at issue in this case but extend to political reporting and serious investigative journalism. The Court recalls that the introduction of restrictions on the latter type of journalism requires careful scrutiny.

i. The margin of appreciation

122. The Court recalls, first, that the applicant's claim relates to the positive obligation under Article 8 and that the State in principle enjoys a wide margin of appreciation. It is therefore relevant that the respondent State has chosen to put in

place a system for balancing the competing rights and interests which excludes a pre-notification requirement. . . .

123. Second, the Court notes that the applicant's case concerned the publication of intimate details of his sexual activities, which would normally result in a narrowing of the margin of appreciation. However, the highly personal nature of the information disclosed in the applicant's case can have no significant bearing on the margin of appreciation afforded to the State in this area given that any pre-notification requirement would have an impact beyond the circumstances of the applicant's own case.

124. Third, the Court highlights the diversity of practice among member States as to how to balance the competing interests of respect for private life and freedom of expression. Indeed the applicant has not cited a single jurisdiction in which a pre-notification requirement as such is imposed. In so far as any common consensus can be identified, it therefore appears that such consensus is against a pre-notification requirement rather than in favor of it. . . . The Court therefore concludes that the respondent State's margin of appreciation in the present case is a wide one.

ii. The clarity and effectiveness of a pre-notification requirement

126. . . . [T]he Court is persuaded that concerns regarding the effectiveness of a pre-notification duty in practice are not unjustified. Two considerations arise. First, it is generally accepted that any pre-notification obligation would require some form of "public interest" exception. Thus a newspaper could opt not to notify a subject if it believed that it could subsequently defend its decision on the basis of the public interest. The Court considers that in order to prevent a serious chilling effect on freedom of expression, a reasonable belief that there was a "public interest" at stake would have to be sufficient to justify non-notification, even if it were subsequently held that no such "public interest" arose. . . .

128. Second, and more importantly, any pre-notification requirement would only be as strong as the sanctions imposed for failing to observe it. A regulatory or civil fine, unless set at a punitively high level, would be unlikely to deter newspapers from publishing private material without pre-notification. . . .

129. Although punitive fines or criminal sanctions could be effective in encouraging compliance with any pre-notification requirement, the Court considers that these would run the risk of being incompatible with the requirements of Article 10 of the Convention. It reiterates in this regard the need to take particular care when examining restraints which might operate as a form of censorship prior to publication. . . .

iii. Conclusion

130. As noted above, the conduct of the newspaper in the applicant's case is open to severe criticism. Aside from publication of the articles detailing the applicant's sexual activities, the *News of the World* published photographs and video footage, obtained through clandestine recording, which undoubtedly had a far greater impact than the articles themselves. Despite the applicant's efforts in a number of jurisdictions, these images are still available on the Internet. The Court

can see no possible additional contribution made by the audiovisual material, which appears to have been included in the *News of the World*'s coverage merely to titillate the public and increase the embarrassment of the applicant. . . .

132. However, the Court has consistently emphasized the need to look beyond the facts of the present case and to consider the broader impact of a pre-notification requirement. The limited scope under Article 10 for restrictions on the freedom of the press to publish material which contributes to debate on matters of general public interest must be borne in mind. Thus, having regard to the chilling effect to which a pre-notification requirement risks giving rise, to the significant doubts as to the effectiveness of any pre-notification requirement and to the wide margin of appreciation in this area, the Court is of the view that Article 8 does not require a legally binding pre-notification requirement. Accordingly, the Court concludes that there has been no violation of Article 8 of the Convention by the absence of such a requirement in domestic law.

FOR THESE REASONS, THE COURT UNANIMOUSLY
1. *Declares* the application admissible;
2. *Holds* that there has been no violation of Article 8 of the Convention.

NOTES & QUESTIONS

1. **Mosley:** *The European Court and "the Margin of Appreciation."* The European Court of Human Rights found that Article 8 did not require that the press engage in pre-notification of subjects before publishing articles about their private life. One of the most interesting aspects of the decision is the European Court's assessment of the extent to which it should grant deference to the way in which the legal system in the United Kingdom handled the case. The term for this principle is "the margin of appreciation" to be accorded the State. The European Court applied a multi-factor test for assessing the "breadth of the margin of appreciation to be accorded to the State in a case in which Article of the Convention is engaged." Is there any particular factor that proved especially important in this case?
2. **Mosley:** *The Decision of the U.K. High Court of Justice.* As the European Court of Human Rights noted in its opinion, the U.K. court found for Mosley. Much of its decision turned on an assessment of the contested events involving Mosley that the *News of the World* wrote about in multiple articles and that was captured in a video that it posted on its website. Specifically, the court felt obligated to consider whether the event involved "Nazi-themed or concentration camp role-play," or merely "sado-masochistic ('S and M') and some sexual activities."[36] Why did this distinction matter?

For the U.K. court, "if it really were the case, as the newspaper alleged, that the Claimant had for entertainment and sexual gratification been 'mocking the humiliating ways the Jews were treated,' or 'parodying Holocaust horrors,' there could be a public interest in that being revealed at least to those in

---

[36] Max Mosley and News Group Newspapers Limited, Case No: HQ08X01303, [2008] EWHC 1777 (QB) (24 July 2008).

[Formula 1 auto racing, or FIA] to whom he is accountable." The privacy interest in Article 8 would not protect Mosley's participation in such activities from press revelation. The court noted of Mosley:

> He had to deal with many people of all races and religions and has spoken out against racism in the sport. If he really were behaving in the way I have just described, that would, for many people, call seriously into question his suitability for his FIA role. It would be information which people arguably should have the opportunity to know and evaluate. It is probably right to acknowledge that private fantasies should not in themselves be subjected to legal scrutiny by the courts, but when they are acted out that is not necessarily so.

In its judgment, however, the U.K. court decided that "[b]eatings, humiliation and the infliction of pain are inherent to S and M activities. So too is the enactment of domination, restraints, punishment and prison scenarios. Behavior of this kind, in itself, is in this context therefore merely neutral. It does not entail Nazism." It declared, "The fact a particular relationship happens to be adulterous, or that someone's tastes are unconventional or 'perverted,' does not give the media *carte blanche*."

Did the U.K. court locate a convincing distinction for line drawing as to where the public interest begins and ends?

3. ***Mosley v. Google: Germany and France.*** In 2014, Mosley won a decision against Google in the Regional Court of Hamburg. *Injunctive Relief Claim (Unterlassungsanspruch)*, LG Hamburg 24 Zivilkammer, Jan. 24, 2014. The German court decided that Google had an obligation to prevent the re-posting of images beyond "notice-and-take" down limited to specific URL's. Once it was informed of a violation of Mosley's personality right caused by publication of specific images, the search engine company was required to prevent future similar violations by making the offending images inaccessible at its site. The Hamburg court stated that Google had a legal duty to use filtering software to stop its search engine's future distribution of these images

In 2013, Mosley won a similar judgment in France. Mosley v. S.A.R.L. Google, Tribunal de Grande Instance de Paris, Nov. 6, 2013. The French court identified an obligation of Google to automate a procedure for blocking nine images that courts had found to represent a significant violation of Mosley privacy. With approval, the court referred to an expert opinion by Viktor Mayer-Schönberg, an Oxford University professor. Mayer-Schönberg had evaluated the cost and complexity of the development or use of filtering software that would automatically recognize these images and block of them from any Google "web images" result. He concluded that the task would cost little and be attainable by a "programmer of moderate expertise."

For more on the obligations of operators of search engines under European privacy law, see below for the European Court of Justice's *Google* decision (2014) and the Notes following it.

4. ***The English Breach of Confidence Tort.*** In England, courts have frequently considered and consistently rejected recognizing the Warren and Brandeis privacy torts. Instead, the tort of breach of confidence is the primary common law protection of privacy. The tort traces back to *Prince Albert v. Strange*,

(1848) 41 Eng. Rep. 1171 (Ch.), the case that Warren and Brandeis relied heavily upon in arguing that a basis for the privacy torts existed in the common law. Later on, in *Coco v. Clark*, [1969], R.P.C. 41 (U.K.), three elements for the tort were established: (1) the information must have "the necessary quality of confidence about it"; (2) the information "must have been imparted in circumstances importing an obligation of confidence"; and (3) there must be an "unauthorised use of that information to the detriment of the party communicating it."

The English breach of confidence tort is quite broad. Unlike the American version of the tort, which applies to doctors, bankers, and other professionals, the English tort also applies to friends and family. *See Stephens v. Avery*, (1988) 1 Ch. 449 (U.K.) (breach of confidence tort applies to friends); *Argyll v. Argyll*, (1967) 1 Ch. 302 (U.K.) (breach of confidence applies to spouses). The tort even applies to lovers, such as in the case of *Barrymore v. News Group Newspapers, Ltd.*, [1997] F.S.R. 600 (Ch.) (U.K.), where the court declared: "when people kiss and later one of them tells, that second person is almost certainly breaking a confidential arrangement." In *A v. B*, [2003] Q.B. 195, 207 (U.K.), the court explained the full scope of the tort:

> A duty of confidence will arise whenever the party subject to the duty is in a situation where he either knows or ought to know that the other person can reasonably expect his privacy to be protected. The range of situations in which protection can be provided is therefore extensive. Obviously, the necessary relationship can be expressly created. More often its existence will have to be inferred from the facts. Whether a duty of confidence does exist which courts can protect, if it is right to do so, will depend on all the circumstances of the relationship between the parties at the time of the threatened or actual breach of the alleged duty of confidence.

Parties who induce breaches of confidence or receive information based on another's a breach of confidence can also be liable. Similar third-party liability exists with the American breach of confidentiality tort. Some commentators have noted that the English tort has become too broad. Consider Joshua Rozenberg:

> The need for a formal relationship between two parties has become attenuated almost to the point of non-existence. Where information has the necessary quality of confidence about it, the courts are more than willing to infer an obligation of confidence from the surrounding facts. . . . That means they will hold that someone who has received confidential information is bound by a duty of confidence. Put bluntly, if the judges think something ought to remain private then they will find a way of making it so.[37]

Although the English breach of confidence tort is quite broad, it does not cover some of the actions that the privacy torts protect against. For example, in *Kay v. Robertson*, [1991] F.S.R. 62 (C.A.) (U.K.), a famous actor suffered a severe head injury. In the hospital where he was recovering, notices were placed in several locations near his room and on the room's door that only permitted individuals would be allowed to visit him. A journalist and photographer snuck

---

[37] Joshua Rozenberg, *Privacy and the Press* 15 (2004).

in, interviewed the actor, and took photographs of him and his room. He was eventually discovered by hospital security staff and ejected. The actor was not in a good condition to be interviewed and had no recollection of the events. The actor sought to stop the publication of an article about the interview and containing the photos. The court considered whether to recognize a common law protection of privacy but concluded that doing so would be a matter for Parliament:

> It is well-known that in English law there is no right to privacy, and accordingly there is no right of action for breach of a person's privacy. The facts of the present case are a graphic illustration of the desirability of Parliament considering whether and in what circumstances statutory provision can be made to protect the privacy of individuals. . . .

What Warren and Brandeis privacy tort(s) could apply in this case? Would the actor have a successful case under the tort(s)? The English breach of confidence tort was not among the causes of action considered in the case. Would it have provided protection? If so, under what theory would it have applied?

Neil Richards and Daniel Solove contrast the American privacy torts with the English breach of confidence tort and note several important differences. Many of the privacy torts contain a "highly offensive" requirement; the breach of confidence tort does not. The public disclosure tort requires "publicity" (widespread disclosure); the breach of confidence tort does not. The public disclosure tort also does not apply when the disclosure is newsworthy; the English tort contains no such restriction.

> In contrast to Warren and Brandeis's individualistic conception of privacy, the English law of confidentiality focuses on relationships rather than individuals. Far from a right to be let alone, confidentiality focuses on the norms of trust within relationships. Indeed, most of our personal information is known by other people, such as doctors, spouses, children, and friends, as well as institutions, such as ISPs, banks, merchants, insurance companies, phone companies, and other businesses. We need to share our secrets with select others, and when we tell others a secret, we still consider it to be a secret. We confide in others, we trust them with information that can make us vulnerable, and we expect them not to betray us. These norms are missing from the Warren and Brandeis conception of privacy.
>
> The key conceptual difference between the breach of confidence tort and public disclosure of private facts tort is the nature of what is protected. The public disclosure tort focuses on the nature of the information being made public. By contrast, the focus of the tort of breach of confidentiality is on the nature of the relationship.[38]

Under the Human Rights Act (HRA) of 1998, the United Kingdom now follows the European Convention on Human Rights. This means that courts must balance Article 8 with Article 10. The result has been a broader protection of privacy as well as of free speech. The HRA prompted English courts to once

---

[38] Neil M. Richards & Daniel J. Solove, *Privacy's Other Path: Recovering the Law of Confidentiality*, 96 Geo. L.J. 123, 174 (2007).

again consider whether to recognize the Warren and Brandeis privacy torts. Instead of doing so, the courts have thus far concluded that the breach of confidence tort can be stretched to include a wider range of privacy violations. As for incorporating Article 10, England does not have a First Amendment, so Article 10 purportedly increases protection for speech. Courts consider freedom of speech and the press as a factor in assessing whether a party ought to be liable under the breach of confidence tort.

5. ***Photos of J.K. Rowling's Son in Public.*** In *Murray v. Big Pictures Ltd.,* [2008] EWCA Civ 446, the England and Wales Court of Appeal concluded that David Murray (the son of J.K. Rowling, author of the Harry Potter book series) was entitled to privacy protection from being photographed in public. When David was less than two years old, a photographer secretly snapped a photograph of him with a zoom lens when he was out in public in Edinburgh with his parents. The photo captured nothing "embarrassing or untoward." The photo appeared in a magazine in 2005. David's parents sued on his behalf. The judge below dismissed "the claim based on breach of confidence or invasion of privacy . . . [because] on my understanding of the law including *Von Hannover* there remains an area of innocuous conduct in a public place which does not raise a reasonable expectation of privacy." The judge reasoned:

> It seems to me that a distinction can be drawn between a child (or an adult) engaged in family and sporting activities and something as simple as a walk down a street or a visit to the grocers to buy the milk. The first type of activity is clearly part of a person's private recreation time intended to be enjoyed in the company of family and friends. Publicity on the test deployed in *Von Hannover* is intrusive and can adversely affect the exercise of such social activities. But if the law is such as to give every adult or child a legitimate expectation of not being photographed without consent on any occasion on which they are not, so to speak, on public business then it will have created a right for most people to the protection of their image. If a simple walk down the street qualifies for protection then it is difficult to see what would not.

The appellate court, however, disagreed:

> It seems to us that, although the judges regarded the parents' concerns as overstated, the parents' wish, on behalf of their children, to protect the freedom of the children to live normal lives without the constant fear of media intrusion is (at least arguably) entirely reasonable and, other things being equal, should be protected by the law. It is true . . . that the photographs showed no more than could be seen by anyone in the street but, once published, they would be disseminated to a potentially large number of people on the basis that they were children of well-known parents, leading to the possibility of further intrusion in the future. . . .
>
> We do not share the predisposition . . . that routine acts such as a visit to a shop or a ride on a bus should not attract any reasonable expectation of privacy. All depends upon the circumstances. The position of an adult may be very different from that of a child. In this appeal we are concerned only with the question whether David, as a small child, had a reasonable expectation of privacy, not with the question whether his parents would have had such an expectation. Moreover, we are concerned with the context of this case, which

was not for example a single photograph taken of David which was for some reason subsequently published.

It seems to us that, subject to the facts of the particular case, the law should indeed protect children from intrusive media attention, at any rate to the extent of holding that a child has a reasonable expectation that he or she will not be targeted in order to obtain photographs in a public place for publication which the person who took or procured the taking of the photographs knew would be objected to on behalf of the child. That is the context in which the photographs of David were taken.

How broadly does the *Von Hannover* decision extend? Is there any way to avoid the slippery slope problem described by the judge below, that "[i]f a simple walk down the street qualifies for protection then it is difficult to see what would not"?

6. *Use of CCTV Footage by the Media.* In England, the government uses an extensive system of millions of public surveillance cameras that are monitored via closed circuit television, a system known as CCTV. The government frequently supplies the video to the media. Consider *Peck v. United Kingdom,* 44647/98 [2003] ECHR 44 (28 January 2003):

> The present applicant was in a public street but he was not there for the purposes of participating in any public event and he was not a public figure. It was late at night, he was deeply perturbed and in a state of distress. While he was walking in public wielding a knife, he was not later charged with any offence. The actual suicide attempt was neither recorded nor therefore disclosed. However, footage of the immediate aftermath was recorded and disclosed by the Council directly to the public in its CCTV News publication. In addition, the footage was disclosed to the media for further broadcasting and publication purposes. Those media included the audiovisual media: Anglia Television broadcast locally to approximately 350,000 people and the BBC broadcast nationally, and it is "commonly acknowledged that the audiovisual media have often a much more immediate and powerful effect than the print media." The Yellow Advertiser was distributed in the applicant's locality to approximately 24,000 readers. The applicant's identity was not adequately, or in some cases not at all, masked in the photographs and footage so published and broadcast. He was recognised by certain members of his family and by his friends, neighbours and colleagues.
>
> As a result, the relevant moment was viewed to an extent which far exceeded any exposure to a passer-by or to security observation . . . and to a degree surpassing that which the applicant could possibly have foreseen when he walked in Brentwood on 20 August 1995. . . .
>
> [T]he Court appreciates the strong interest of the State in detecting and preventing crime. It is not disputed that the CCTV system plays an important role in these respects and that that role is rendered more effective and successful through advertising the CCTV system and its benefits.
>
> However, the Court notes that the Council had other options available to it to allow it to achieve the same objectives. In the first place, it could have identified the applicant through enquiries with the police and thereby obtained his consent prior to disclosure. Alternatively, the Council could have masked the relevant images itself. A further alternative would have been to take the utmost care in ensuring that the media, to which the disclosure was made, masked those images. The Court notes that the Council did not explore the first

and second options and considers that the steps taken by the Council in respect of the third were inadequate. . . .

In sum, the Court does not find that, in the circumstances of this case, there were relevant or sufficient reasons which would justify the direct disclosure by the Council to the public of stills from the footage in its own CCTV News article without the Council obtaining the applicant's consent or masking his identity, or which would justify its disclosures to the media without the Council taking steps to ensure so far as possible that such masking would be effected by the media. The crime-prevention objective and context of the disclosures demanded particular scrutiny and care in these respects in the present case. . . .

Accordingly, the Court considers that the disclosures by the Council of the CCTV material in the CCTV News and to the Yellow Advertiser, Anglia Television and the BBC were not accompanied by sufficient safeguards to prevent disclosure inconsistent with the guarantees of respect for the applicant' private life contained in Article 8. As such, the disclosure constituted a disproportionate and therefore unjustified interference with his private life and a violation of Article 8 of the Convention.

Could the English breach of confidentiality tort have provided an adequate remedy for the plaintiff?

As the *von Hannover* and *Mosley* decisions demonstrate, the Convention on Human Rights protects both privacy and freedom of expression. Its protection of the latter is found in Article 10, which states: "Everyone has the right to freedom of expression. This right shall include freedom to hold opinions and to receive and impart information and ideas without interference by public authority and regardless of frontiers." Article 10 also makes clear that this right is not absolute: "The exercise of these freedoms, since it carries with it duties and responsibilities, may be subject to such formalities, conditions, restrictions or penalties as are prescribed by law and are necessary in a democratic society. . . ." In the following decision, the ECHR seeks, in its words, "to retain the essence" of both Articles 8 (privacy) and Article 10 (freedom of expression).

SATUKUNNAN MARKKINAPÖRSSI OY AND SATAMEDIA OY V. FINLAND

ECHR, No. 931/13, Grand Chamber (June 22, 2017)

I. THE CIRCUMSTANCES OF THE CASE

A. Background to the case

1. Since 1994 the first applicant company, Satakunnan Markkinapörssi Oy collected data from the Finnish tax authorities for the purpose of publishing information about natural persons' taxable income and assets in the Veropörssi newspaper. Several other publishing and media companies also publish such data which, pursuant to Finnish law, are accessible to the public

2. In 2002 Veropörssi appeared 17 times, with each issue concentrating on a certain geographical area of the country. The data published comprised the surnames and forenames of approximately 1.2 million natural persons whose

annual taxable income exceeded certain thresholds, mainly from 60,000 to 80,000 Finnish marks (approximately 10,000 to 13,500 euros (EUR)), as well as the amount, to the nearest EUR 100, of their earned and unearned income and taxable net assets. When published in the newspaper, the data were set out in the form of an alphabetical list and organised according to municipality and income bracket.

3. The first applicant company worked in cooperation with the second applicant company, Satamedia Oy, and both were owned by the same shareholders. In 2003 the first applicant company started to transfer personal data published in Veropörssi, in the form of CD-ROM discs, to the second applicant company which, together with a mobile telephone operator, started a text-messaging service (SMS service). By sending a person's name to a service number, taxation information could be obtained concerning that person, on the requesting person's mobile telephone, if information was available in the database or register created by the second applicant company. This database was created using personal data already published in the newspaper and transferred in the form of CD-ROM discs to the second applicant company. From 2006 the second applicant company also published Veropörssi.

4. In September 2000 and November 2001, the applicant companies ordered taxation data from the Finnish National Board of Taxation (verohallitus, skattestyrelsen). Following the first order, the Board requested an opinion from the Data Protection Ombudsman, on the basis of which the Board invited the applicant companies to provide further information regarding their request and indicating that the data could not be disclosed if Veropörssi continued to be published in its usual form. The applicant companies subsequently cancelled their data request and paid people to collect taxation data manually at the local tax offices.

D. The Court's assessment

1. Preliminary remarks on the scope and context of the Court's assessment

5. The Court notes at the outset that the present case is unusual to the extent that the taxation data at issue were publicly accessible in Finland. Furthermore, as emphasised by the applicant companies, they were not alone amongst media outlets in Finland in collecting, processing and publishing taxation data such as the data which appeared in Veropörssi. Their publication differed from that of those other media outlets by virtue of the manner and the extent of the data published.

6. In addition, ... only a very small number of Council of Europe member States provide for public access to taxation data, a fact which raises issues regarding the margin of appreciation which Finland enjoys when providing and regulating public access to such data and reconciling that access with the requirements of data protection rules and the right to freedom of expression of the press.

7. Given this context and the fact that at the heart of the present case lies the question whether the correct balance was struck between that right and the right to privacy as embodied in domestic data protection and access to information legislation, it is necessary, at the outset, to outline some of the general principles deriving from the Court's case-law on Article 10 and press freedom, on the one

hand, and the right to privacy under Article 8 of the Convention in the particular context of data protection on the other.

8. Bearing in mind the need to protect the values underlying the Convention and considering that the rights under Articles 10 and 8 of the Convention deserve equal respect, it is important to remember that the balance to be struck by national authorities between those two rights must seek to retain the essence of both.

(a) Article 10 and press freedom

9. The Court has consistently held that freedom of expression constitutes one of the essential foundations of a democratic society and one of the basic conditions for its progress and for each individual's self-fulfilment. Subject to paragraph 2 of Article 10, it is applicable not only to "information" or "ideas" that are favourably received or regarded as inoffensive or as a matter of indifference, but also to those that offend, shock or disturb. Such are the demands of pluralism, tolerance and broadmindedness without which there is no "democratic society". As enshrined in Article 10, freedom of expression is subject to exceptions which must, however, be construed strictly, and the need for any restrictions must be established convincingly.

10. Although the press must not overstep certain bounds, regarding in particular protection of the reputation and rights of others, its task is nevertheless to impart – in a manner consistent with its obligations and responsibilities — information and ideas on all matters of public interest . . . .

(b) Article 8, the right to privacy and data protection

11. As regards whether, in the circumstances of the present case, the right to privacy under Article 8 of the Convention is engaged given the publicly accessible nature of the taxation data processed and published by the applicant companies, the Court has constantly reiterated that the concept of "private life" is a broad term not susceptible to exhaustive definition.

12. Leaving aside the numerous cases in which the Court has held that the right to privacy in Article 8 covers the physical and psychological integrity of a person, private life has also been held to include activities of a professional or business nature.

13. The fact that information is already in the public domain will not necessarily remove the protection of Article 8 of the Convention. Thus, in Von Hannover v. Germany (no. 59320/00, §§ 74-75 and 77, ECHR 2004 VI), concerning the publication of photographs which had been taken in public places of a known person who did not have any official function, the Court found that the interest in publication of that information had to be weighed against privacy considerations, even though the person's public appearance could be assimilated to "public information".

14. It follows from well-established case-law that where there has been compilation of data on a particular individual, processing or use of personal data or publication of the material concerned in a manner or degree beyond that normally foreseeable, private life considerations arise.

15. The protection of personal data is of fundamental importance to a person's enjoyment of his or her right to respect for private and family life, as guaranteed by Article 8 of the Convention. The domestic law must afford appropriate safeguards to prevent any such use of personal data as may be inconsistent with the guarantees of this Article. Article 8 of the Convention thus provides for the right to a form of informational self-determination, allowing individuals to rely on their right to privacy as regards data which, albeit neutral, are collected, processed and disseminated collectively and in such a form or manner that their Article 8 rights may be engaged.

16. In the light of the foregoing considerations and the Court's existing case-law on Article 8 of the Convention, it appears that the data collected, processed and published by the applicant companies in Veropörssi, providing details of the taxable earned and unearned income as well as taxable net assets, clearly concerned the private life of those individuals, notwithstanding the fact that, pursuant to Finnish law, that data could be accessed, in accordance with certain rules, by the public.

5. Necessary in a democratic society

17. The core question in the instant case, as indicated previously, is whether the interference with the applicant companies' right to freedom of expression was "necessary in a democratic society" and whether, in answering this question, the domestic courts struck a fair balance between that right and the right to respect for private life.

18. [T]he Court considers it useful to reiterate the criteria for balancing these two rights in the circumstances of a case such as the present one.

(a) General principles concerning the margin of appreciation and balancing of rights

19. According to the Court's established case-law, the test of necessity in a democratic society requires the Court to determine whether the interference complained of corresponded to a pressing social need, whether it was proportionate to the legitimate aim pursued and whether the reasons given by the national authorities to justify it are relevant and sufficient. The margin of appreciation left to the national authorities in assessing whether such a need exists and what measures should be adopted to deal with it is not, however, unlimited but goes hand in hand with European supervision by the Court, whose task it is to give a final ruling on whether a restriction is reconcilable with freedom of expression as protected by Article 10. As indicated above, when exercising its supervisory function, the Court's task is not to take the place of the national courts but rather to review, in the light of the case as a whole, whether the decisions they have taken pursuant to their power of appreciation are compatible with the provisions of the Convention relied on. Where the balancing exercise has been undertaken by the national authorities in conformity with the criteria laid down in the Court's case-law, the Court would require strong reasons to substitute its view for that of the domestic courts.

20. The Court has already had occasion to lay down the relevant principles which must guide its assessment — and, more importantly, that of domestic courts — of necessity. It has thus identified a number of criteria in the context of balancing the competing rights. The relevant criteria have thus far been defined as: contribution to a debate of public interest, the degree of notoriety of the person affected, the subject of the news report, the prior conduct of the person concerned, the content, form and consequences of the publication, and, where it arises, the circumstances in which photographs were taken. Where it examines an application lodged under Article 10, the Court will also examine the way in which the information was obtained and its veracity, and the gravity of the penalty imposed on the journalists or publishers.

(b) Application of the relevant general principles to the present case

(i) Contribution of the impugned publication to a debate of public interest

21. In order to ascertain whether a publication concerning an individual's private life is not intended purely to satisfy the curiosity of a certain readership, but also relates to a subject of general importance, it is necessary to assess the publication as a whole and have regard to the context in which it appears.

22. Public interest ordinarily relates to matters which affect the public to such an extent that it may legitimately take an interest in them, which attract its attention or which concern it to a significant degree, especially in that they affect the well-being of citizens or the life of the community. This is also the case with regard to matters which are capable of giving rise to considerable controversy, which concern an important social issue, or which involve a problem that the public would have an interest in being informed about. The public interest cannot be reduced to the public's thirst for information about the private life of others, or to an audience's wish for sensationalism or even voyeurism.

23. It is unquestionable that permitting public access to official documents, including taxation data, is designed to secure the availability of information for the purpose of enabling a debate on matters of public interest. Such access, albeit subject to clear statutory rules and restrictions, has a constitutional basis in Finnish law and has been widely guaranteed for many decades.

24. . . . Taking the publication as a whole and in context and analysing it in the light of the above-mentioned case-law, the Court, like the Supreme Administrative Court, is not persuaded that publication of taxation data in the manner and to the extent done by the applicant companies contributed to such a debate or indeed that its principal purpose was to do so.

25. . . . . While the information might have enabled curious members of the public to categorise named individuals, who are not public figures, according to their economic status, this could be regarded as a manifestation of the public's thirst for information about the private life of others and, as such, a form of sensationalism, even voyeurism.

26. In the light of these considerations, the Court cannot but agree with the Supreme Administrative Court that the sole object of the impugned publication was not, as required by domestic and EU law, the disclosure to the public of information, opinions and ideas, a conclusion borne out by the layout of the

publication, its form, content and the extent of the data disclosed. Furthermore, it does not find that the impugned publication could be regarded as contributing to a debate of public interest or assimilated to the kind of speech, namely political speech, which traditionally enjoys a privileged position in its case-law, thus calling for strict Convention scrutiny and allowing little scope under Article 10 § 2 of the Convention for restrictions.

(ii) Subject of the impugned publication and how well-known were the persons concerned

27. The data published in Veropörssi comprised the surnames and names of natural persons whose annual taxable income exceeded certain thresholds (see paragraph 9 above). The data also comprised the amount, to the nearest EUR 100, of their earned and unearned income as well as details relating to their taxable net assets. When published in the newspaper, the data were set out in the form of an alphabetical list and were organised according to municipality and income bracket.

28. . . . . Unlike other Finnish publications, the information published by the applicant companies did not pertain specifically to any particular category of persons such as politicians, public officials, public figures or others who belonged to the public sphere by dint of their activities or high earnings. As the Court has previously stated, such persons inevitably and knowingly lay themselves open to close scrutiny by both journalists and the public at large.

(iv) Content, form and consequences of the publication and related considerations

29. It is noteworthy that the CJEU has made clear . . . . that the public character of data processed does not exclude such data from the scope of the Data Protection Directive and the guarantees the latter lays down for the protection of privacy.

30. Whilst the taxation data in question were publicly accessible in Finland, they could only be consulted at the local tax offices and consultation was subject to clear conditions. The copying of that information on memory sticks was prohibited. Journalists could receive taxation data in digital format, but retrieval conditions also existed and only a certain amount of data could be retrieved. Journalists had to specify that the information was requested for journalistic purposes and that it would not be published in the form of a list. Therefore, while the information relating to individuals was publicly accessible, specific rules and safeguards governed its accessibility.

31. The fact that the data in question were accessible to the public under the domestic law did not necessarily mean that they could be published to an unlimited extent. Publishing the data in a newspaper, and further disseminating that data via an SMS service, rendered it accessible in a manner and to an extent not intended by the legislator.

32. As indicated previously, the gathering of information is an essential preparatory step in journalism and an inherent, protected part of press freedom. It is noteworthy that, in the instant case, the Supreme Administrative Court did not seek to interfere with the collection by the applicant companies of raw data, an

activity which goes to the heart of press freedom, but rather with the dissemination of data in the manner and to the extent outlined above.

(v) Gravity of the sanction imposed on the journalists or publishers

33. As indicated in the Chamber judgment, the applicant companies were not prohibited from publishing taxation data or from continuing to publish Veropörssi, albeit they had to do so in a manner consistent with Finnish and EU rules on data protection and access to information. The fact that, in practice, the limitations imposed on the quantity of the information to be published may have rendered some of their business activities less profitable is not, as such, a sanction within the meaning of the case-law of the Court.

(vi) Conclusion

34. In the light of the aforementioned considerations, the Court considers that, in assessing the circumstances submitted for their appreciation, the competent domestic authorities and, in particular, the Supreme Administrative Court gave due consideration to the principles and criteria as laid down by the Court's case-law for balancing the right to respect for private life and the right to freedom of expression. In so doing, the Supreme Administrative Court attached particular weight to its finding that the publication of the taxation data in the manner and to the extent described did not contribute to a debate of public interest and that the applicants could not in substance claim that it had been done solely for a journalistic purpose within the meaning of domestic and EU law. The Court discerns no strong reasons which would require it to substitute its view for that of the domestic courts and to set aside the balancing done by them. It is satisfied that the reasons relied upon were both relevant and sufficient to show that the interference complained of was "necessary in a democratic society" and that the authorities of the respondent State acted within their margin of appreciation in striking a fair balance between the competing interests at stake.

35. The Court therefore concludes that there has been no violation of Article 10 of the Convention.

NOTES & QUESTIONS

1. ***The Holding.*** The publisher in *Satamedia Oy* gathered Finnish individuals' publicly-available tax data. It then collaborated with a service provider to send out tax information via text message following a customer's request. The ECHR found that such extensive publication of personal tax information violated Article 8. Although tax information was publicly available in Finland, the Finnish legislator had not intended to permit publication of this information "to an unlimited extent," such as via a text messaging service. The ECHR also found that the publication of this information did not enable "a debate of public interest." Hence, there was no violation of Article 10's protection of freedom of expression and press freedom.

2. *Assessing the Public Interest.* The ECHR built on its earlier decisions in *Satamedia Oy* concerning when a publication contributed to a debate of public interest. All publicly accessible information does not advance such a discussion; the ECHR spoke in negative terms of "the public's thirst for information about the private life of others," especially those who are not public figures, which it termed "a form of sensationalism, even voyeurism." *Satamedia Oy*, ¶ 22. In contrast, it defined the concept of "public interest" as "matters which affect the public to such an extent that it may legitimately take an interest in them, which attract its attention or which concern it to a significant degree, especially in that they affect the well-being of citizens or the life of the community." Id. How does this approach differ from that of U.S. courts when deciding newsworthiness? How does U.S. court typically assess the privacy impact of publicly-accessible information?

3. EUROPEAN UNION DATA PROTECTION

(a) The European Charter of Fundamental Rights, Articles 7 and 8

The European Union Data Protection Directive of 1995 established common rules for data protection among Member States of the European Union. The Directive was created in the early 1990s and formally adopted in 1995. The Directive will be replaced by the General Data Protection Regulation on May 25, 2018.

Another milestone in EU privacy law was the adoption of the European Charter of Fundamental Rights. In December 2000, the leaders of the institutions of the European Union gathered in Nice to sign this document.[39] The Charter of Fundamental Rights sets out in a single text, for the first time in the European Union's history, the whole range of civil, political, economic, and social rights of European citizens and all persons living in the European Union. It entrenches the rights found in the case law of the European Court of Justice; rights and freedoms enshrined in the European Convention on Human Rights; and other rights and principles developed through the common constitutional traditions of EU Member States and other international instruments. The Treaty of Lisbon of 2007 both specifically recognized data protection as a fundamental human right and made the Charter of Fundamental Rights a legally enforceable document within the EU. The cases from the European Court of Justice that follow will interpret both the Directive and the EU Charter of Fundamental Rights.

EU CHARTER OF FUNDAMENTAL RIGHTS, ARTICLES 7 AND 8

ARTICLE 7 — RESPECT FOR PRIVATE AND FAMILY LIFE

Everyone has the right to respect for his or her private and family life, home and communications.

---

[39] Available at http://www.europarl.eu.int/charter/default_en.htm.

ARTICLE 8 — PROTECTION OF PERSONAL DATA

1. Everyone has the right to the protection of personal data concerning him or her.

2. Such data must be processed fairly for specified purposes and on the basis of the consent of the person concerned or some other legitimate basis laid down by law. Everyone has the right of access to data which has been collected concerning him or her, and the right to have it rectified.

3. Compliance with these rules shall be subject to control by an independent authority.

(b) The Data Protection Directive

Although the General Data Protection Regulation will replace the Data Protection Directive in May 2018, it is still important to understand the Directive. First, the earlier document has played an important role in shaping the current contours of EU and world privacy. Second, important decisions of the European Court of Justice interpret and develop EU constitutional data protection through its framework. Finally, "what's past is prologue" (Shakespeare), and the development of the Directive has important lessons for the future of data protection law.

Prior to the adoption of the Directive, leading EU countries had national privacy legislation. As Abraham Newman has shown, different historically contingent factors had already smoothed the path to enactment of data protection statutes in the 1970s in France and Germany, two leaders in information privacy law.[40] For example, Newman demonstrates that French industry's potential opposition to the proposed French data protection legislation was muted by the past nationalization of many affected companies and the centralization of these industries, which minimized the impact of the statutes. As a further example, in Germany, a pro-privacy alliance benefited at a critical stage in the late 1970s from an "alignment of political actors at that time [who] neutralized key barriers to the passage of the policy."

The choice was also made in these key European nations to enact "omnibus" privacy laws. Recall that an omnibus law establishes regulatory standards for a broad area of information law. In contrast, a sectoral law regulates information use through attention only to narrower areas, such as the use of information in video rentals, or provision of cable television. After the initial choice in key European nations to enact omnibus law, the EU's "harmonizing" project in the field of data protection exercised a strong influence on other nations.[41] This term of European community law refers to formal regulatory attempts to increase the similarity of legal measures in member states. Specifically, European integration increased the sharing of data among EU Member Nations and created new demands for personal information. Due to this data sharing throughout the EU, nations with privacy statutes had incentives to advocate equivalent standards in all member nations. Without such shared levels of protection, previous efforts within individual nations

---

[40] Abraham L. Newman, *Protectors of Privacy* 60-69 (2008).
[41] Paul M. Schwartz, *Preemption and Privacy*, 118 Yale L.J. 902, 914-16 (2009).

to ensure privacy for their citizen's data would be for naught. The information could easily be transferred to other member states with weaker levels of data protection.

Thus, the Directive's purpose, somewhat paradoxically, was to facilitate the free flow of personal data within the EU by setting an equally high privacy level in all EU Member States. An increased harmonization of the privacy laws of various European nations would enable the free flow of goods and services, labor, and capital. The Directive also reinforced the preference in the EU for omnibus privacy laws. The benefit of an omnibus law is that it provides a relatively limited series of benchmarks and sets them within a single statute. In contrast, an exclusively sectoral approach would have caused far greater complexity for the EU in assessing the "equivalency" of data protection for each of the now 27 EU member states.

The Directive imposed obligations on the processors of personal data. It required technical security and the notification of individuals whose data was being collected, and outlined circumstances under which data transfer could occur. The Directive also gave individuals substantial rights to control the use of data about themselves. These rights included the right to be informed that their personal data was being transferred, the need to obtain "unambiguous" consent from the individual for the transfer of certain data, the opportunity to make corrections in the data, and the right to object to the transfer. Data regulatory authority, enforcement provisions, and sanctions were also key elements of the directive. Following passage of the Directive, the various national governments of the EU amended their own national data protection legislation to bring it into line with the Directive.

The Directive also extended privacy safeguards to personal data that was transferred outside of the European Union. Article 25 of the Directive stated that data could only be transferred to third countries that provided an "adequate level of data protection." As a result, implementation focused on both the adoption of national law within the European Union and the adoption of adequate methods for privacy protection in third party countries.[42]

Directives are a form of EU law that is binding for Member States, but only as to the result to be achieved. They allow the national authorities to choose the form and the methods of their implementation and generally fix a deadline for it. Therefore, the rules of law applicable in each Member State are the national laws implementing the directives and not the directive itself. However, the directive has a "direct effect" on individuals: it grants them rights that can be upheld by the national courts in their respective countries if their governments have not implemented the directive by the set deadline. A directive thus grants *rights* rather than creates obligations, and they are enforceable by *individuals* rather than by public authorities.

It is important to distinguish between vertical and horizontal effects. "Vertical effects" means that the rights established by a directive flow from the European

---

[42] For perspectives on the EU Directive, see Peter P. Swire & Robert E. Litan, None of Your Business: World Data Flows, Electronic Commerce, and the European *Privacy Directive* (1998); Spiros Simitis, *From the Market to the Polis: The EU Directive on the Protection of Personal Data*, 80 Iowa L. Rev. 445 (1995); Symposium, *Data Protection Law and the European Union's Directive: The Challenge for the United States*, 80 Iowa L. Rev. 431 (1995).

Union to citizens of the EU. Where a violation occurs, citizens may petition EU institution and their national government that has adopted (or "transposed") a directive into national law. But this interest does not create a right for one citizen of the EU to bring an action against another citizen. For such an impact to occur ("horizontal effects") there must be national law or an EU regulation in place. Whereas the EU "regulations" or treaty provisions are able to confer rights on private individuals and impose obligations on them, directives can only confer rights on individuals against the State; they cannot impose on them obligations in favor of the State or other individuals. Directives are only capable of "vertical" direct effect, unlike treaty provisions and regulations, which are also capable of "horizontal" direct effect.

Directives are enacted in the context of the European Community (EC)'s competences, the EC being one of the legal entities that is part of the European Union. It means that their scope is limited to the area of competence of the EC. The EU Data Directive, as a result, does not cover activities, which fall outside the scope of EC law, such as the data processing operations concerning public security, defense, State security, and the activities of the State in areas of criminal law. *See, e.g.,* EU Data Directive, Article 3(2). In such cases, the only authorities that may promulgate enforceable legislation are the Member States. The European Union, however, can voice its concerns on privacy issues regarding policing and security through its "Justice and Home Affairs" branch. Under the direction of the EU Council,[43] the Justice and Home Affairs branch can take common positions defining the approach of the EU to a particular matter or even establish conventions, although each Member State can always oppose these decisions and not implement them into national law. The EU Council is the group of delegates of the Member States, each State being represented by a government minister who is authorized to commit his government.

NOTES & QUESTIONS

1. *Defining "Personal Data," Dynamic IP Addresses, and Graffiti Registers.* The EU Data Directive's definition of "personal data" (Art. 2(a)) is one of the keys to understanding the scope and application of the Directive as it only applies to the processing of personal data. The Directive defined "personal data" as "information relating to an identified or identifiable natural person." The GDPR adopts this same definition. The determination of the scope of "personal data" constitutes a crucial issue when enforcing data protection rules, particularly in the online context.

   Paul Schwartz and Daniel Solove argue that the EU has adopted an "expansionist approach" to defining the scope of "personal data."[44] As you read the following examples involving "dynamic IP addresses" and graffiti registers,

---

[43] The EU Council is the group of delegates of the Member States, each State being represented by a government minister who is authorized to commit his government.

[44] Paul M. Schwartz & Daniel J. Solove, *The PII Problem: Privacy and a New Concept of Personally Identifiable Information,* 86 N.Y.U. L. Rev. 1814 (2011). For additional analysis of the EU definition of "personal information," see Paul M. Schwartz & Daniel J. Solove, *Reconciling Personal Information in the EU and U.S.,* 102 Cal. L. Rev. 877 (2014).

consider whether these seem to indicate such a broad definitional approach at work. Compare these notions of "personal data" with the notion of "personally identifiable information" found in U.S. privacy laws. Are they identical?

In 2007, the Article 29 Working Party, the independent advisory body made up of data protection commissioners from EU Member States, issued an opinion concerning "the concept of personal data."[45] As the opinion states, "Working on a common definition of the notion of personal data is tantamount to defining what falls inside or outside the scope of data protection rules." For the Article 29 Party, dynamic IP addresses can be considered as personal data:

> [e]specially in those cases where the processing of IP addresses is carried out with the purpose of identifying the users of the computer (for instance, by Copyright holders in order to prosecute computer users for violation of intellectual property rights), the controller anticipates that the "means likely reasonably to be used" to identify the persons will be available e.g. through the courts appealed to (otherwise the collection of the information makes no sense).
> . . .

This view has been controversial. Some experts have argued that ISPs are generally unable to identify a specific user associated with an IP, but only tie an IP address with an account holder for it.

Another interesting hypothetical from this opinion concerns graffiti, and a transportation company choosing to create a register with information about the circumstances of damage to its passenger vehicles "as well as the images of the damaged items and of the 'tags' or 'signatures' of the author." When the register is created, the creator of the graffiti is unknown and may never be known. Nonetheless, "the purpose of the processing is precisely to identify individuals to whom the information relates as the authors of the damage, so as to be able to exercise legal claims against them." Hence, the processing is to be made "subject to data protection rules, which allow such processing as legitimate under certain circumstances and subject to certain safeguards."

2. *The Underlying Philosophy of the EU Data Directive.* Consider the following argument by Joel Reidenberg:

> The background and underlying philosophy of the European Directive differs in important ways from that of the United States. While there is a consensus among democratic states that information privacy is a critical element of civil society, the United States has, in recent years, left the protection of privacy to markets rather than law. In contrast, Europe treats privacy as a political imperative anchored in fundamental human rights. European democracies approach information privacy from the perspective of social protection. In European democracies, public liberty derives from the community of individuals, and law is the fundamental basis to pursue norms of social and citizen protection. This vision of governance generally regards the state as the necessary player to frame the social community in which individuals develop and in which information practices must serve individual identity. Citizen autonomy, in this view, effectively depends on a backdrop of legal rights. Law

---

[45] Article 29 Data Protection Working Party, Opinion 2/2007 on the concept of personal data (June 20, 2007).

thus enshrines prophylactic protection through comprehensive rights and responsibilities. Indeed, citizens trust government more than the private sector with personal information.[46]

As you examine the various provisions of the EU Data Directive and the OECD Privacy Guidelines throughout this chapter, consider how the overall approach of European democracies toward protecting differs from that of the United States. Are there ways in which the approaches are similar? To the extent that the approaches are different, think about why such differences exist.

3. ***Electronic Communication and the Processing of Personal Data.*** Personal data processed in connection with electronic communications are the subject of the ePrivacy Directive (Directive 2002/58/EC concerning the processing of personal data and the protection of privacy in the electronic communications sector). In turn, this document has been subject to two important amending directives. The later directives are the 2006 Data Retention Directive (Directive 2006/24) and a 2009 Amendment Directive (Directive 2009/136).

The ePrivacy Directive establishes specific protections covering electronic mail, telephone communications, traffic data, calling line identification, and unsolicited communications. Member states were required to transpose the Directive before October 31, 2002. Like the EU Data Protection Directive, the ePrivacy Directive is intended to harmonize national law in Europe. Article 5 of this Directive sets out a strong presumption in favor of communications privacy:

> Member States shall ensure the confidentiality of communications and the related traffic data by means of a public communications network and publicly available electronic communications services, through national legislation. In particular, they shall prohibit listening, tapping, storage or other kinds of interception or surveillance of communications and the related traffic data by persons other than users, without the consent of the users concerned, except when legally authorised to do so in accordance with Article 15(1). This paragraph shall not prevent technical storage which is necessary for the conveyance of a communication without prejudice to the principle of confidentiality.

The ePrivacy Directive directs Member States to permit unsolicited commercial telephone calls, e-mails, and faxes only with the subject's opt-in consent. It gives subscribers to communication services the right to be informed before they are included in any subscriber directory.

The EU is now considering an ePrivacy Regulation (ePR) to replace this Directive. The precise dimensions of the ePR are still uncertain, and there has been considerable controversy and delay around this measure.[47]

---

[46] Joel R. Reidenberg, *E-Commerce and Trans-Atlantic Privacy,* 38 Hous. L. Rev. 717, 730-31 (2001).

[47] For information from the Commission on the ePR, see European Commission, *Proposal for a Regulation on Privacy and Electronic Communications* (Jan. 10, 2017).

CRIMINAL PROCEEDINGS AGAINST BODIL LINDQVIST

European Court of Justice, 11/6/2003

1. By order of 23 February 2001, received at the Court on 1 March 2001, the Gota hovratt (Gota Court of Appeal) referred to the Court for a preliminary ruling under Article 234 EC seven questions concerning *inter alia* the interpretation of Directive 95/46/EC of the European Parliament and of the Council of 24 October 1995 on the protection of individuals with regard to the processing of personal data and on the free movement of such data.

2. Those questions were raised in criminal proceedings before that court against Mrs. Lindqvist, who was charged with breach of the Swedish legislation on the protection of personal data for publishing on her internet site personal data on a number of people working with her on a voluntary basis in a parish of the Swedish Protestant Church. . . .

12. In addition to her job as a maintenance worker, Mrs. Lindqvist worked as a catechist in the parish of Alseda (Sweden). She followed a data processing course on which she had *inter alia* to set up a home page on the internet. At the end of 1998, Mrs. Lindqvist set up internet pages at home on her personal computer in order to allow parishioners preparing for their confirmation to obtain information they might need. At her request, the administrator of the Swedish Church's website set up a link between those pages and that site.

13. The pages in question contained information about Mrs. Lindqvist and 18 colleagues in the parish, sometimes including their full names and in other cases only their first names. Mrs. Lindqvist also described, in a mildly humorous manner, the jobs held by her colleagues and their hobbies. In many cases family circumstances and telephone numbers and other matters were mentioned. She also stated that one colleague had injured her foot and was on half-time on medical grounds.

14. Mrs. Lindqvist had not informed her colleagues of the existence of those pages or obtained their consent, nor did she notify the Datainspektionen (supervisory authority for the protection of electronically transmitted data) of her activity. She removed the pages in question as soon as she became aware that they were not appreciated by some of her colleagues.

15. The public prosecutor brought a prosecution against Mrs. Lindqvist charging her with breach of the PUL [Personuppgiftslag, Swedish law on personal data] on the grounds that she had:

- processed personal data by automatic means without giving prior written notification to the Datainspektionen (Paragraph 36 of the PUL);
- processed sensitive personal data (injured foot and half-time on medical grounds) without authorisation (Paragraph 13 of the PUL);
- transferred processed personal data to a third country without authorisation (Paragraph 33 of the PUL).

16. Mrs. Lindqvist accepted the facts but disputed that she was guilty of an offence. Mrs. Lindqvist was fined by the Eksjo tingsratt (District Court) (Sweden) and appealed against that sentence to the referring court.

17. The amount of the fine was SEK 4000,[48] which was arrived at by multiplying the sum of SEK 100, representing Mrs. Lindqvist's financial position, by a factor of 40, reflecting the severity of the offence. Mrs. Lindqvist was also sentenced to pay SEK 300[49] to a Swedish fund to assist victims of crimes. . . .

19. . . . [T]he referring court asks whether the act of referring, on an internet page, to various persons and identifying them by name or by other means, for instance by giving their telephone number or information regarding their working conditions and hobbies, constitutes the processing of personal data wholly or partly by automatic means within the meaning of Article 3(1) of Directive 95/46. . . .

24. The term personal data used in Article 3(1) of Directive 95/46 covers, according to the definition in Article 2(a) thereof, any information relating to an identified or identifiable natural person. The term undoubtedly covers the name of a person in conjunction with his telephone coordinates or information about his working conditions or hobbies.

25. According to the definition in Article 2(b) of Directive 95/46, the term processing of such data used in Article 3(1) covers any operation or set of operations which is performed upon personal data, whether or not by automatic means. That provision gives several examples of such operations, including disclosure by transmission, dissemination or otherwise making data available. It follows that the operation of loading personal data on an internet page must be considered to be such processing.

27. . . . [T]he act of referring, on an internet page, to various persons and identifying them by name or by other means, for instance by giving their telephone number or information regarding their working conditions and hobbies, constitutes the processing of personal data wholly or partly by automatic means within the meaning of Article 3(1) of Directive 95/46. . . .

[The court concludes that neither the exception for the processing of personal data or for charitable and religious organizations in Article 3(2) apply in this case. Hence, the court affirmed the convictions for illegal processing of information and illegal disclosure of health information.]

37. Article 3(2) of Directive 95/46 provides for two exceptions to its scope.

38. The first exception concerns the processing of personal data in the course of an activity which falls outside the scope of Community law, such as those provided for by Titles V and VI of the Treaty on European Union, and in any case processing operations concerning public security, defence, State security (including the economic well-being of the State when the processing operation relates to State security matters) and the activities of the State in areas of criminal law.

39. As the activities of Mrs. Lindqvist which are at issue in the main proceedings are essentially not economic but charitable and religious, it is necessary to consider whether they constitute the processing of personal data in the course of an activity which falls outside the scope of Community law within the meaning of the first indent of Article 3(2) of Directive 95/46. . . .

43. The activities mentioned by way of example in the first indent of Article 3(2) of Directive 95/46 (in other words, the activities provided for by Titles V and

---

[48] Editors' Note: This sum is approximately $670.
[49] Editors' Note: This sum is approximately $50.

VI of the Treaty on European Union and processing operations concerning public security, defence, State security and activities in areas of criminal law) are, in any event, activities of the State or of State authorities and unrelated to the fields of activity of individuals.

44. It must therefore be considered that the activities mentioned by way of example in the first indent of Article 3(2) of Directive 95/46 are intended to define the scope of the exception provided for there, with the result that that exception applies only to the activities which are expressly listed there or which can be classified in the same category (*ejusdem generis*).

45. Charitable or religious activities such as those carried out by Mrs. Lindqvist cannot be considered equivalent to the activities listed in the first indent of Article 3(2) of Directive 95/46 and are thus not covered by that exception.

46. As regards the exception provided for in the second indent of Article 3(2) of Directive 95/46, the 12th recital in the preamble to that directive, which concerns that exception, cites, as examples of the processing of data carried out by a natural person in the exercise of activities which are exclusively personal or domestic, correspondence and the holding of records of addresses.

47. That exception must therefore be interpreted as relating only to activities which are carried out in the course of private or family life of individuals, which is clearly not the case with the processing of personal data consisting in publication on the internet so that those data are made accessible to an indefinite number of people.

48. The answer to the third question must therefore be that processing of personal data such as that described in the reply to the first question is not covered by any of the exceptions in Article 3(2) of Directive 95/46.

49. By its fourth question, the referring court seeks to know whether reference to the fact that an individual has injured her foot and is on half-time on medical grounds constitutes personal data concerning health within the meaning of Article 8(1) of Directive 95/46.

50. In the light of the purpose of the directive, the expression data concerning health used in Article 8(1) thereof must be given a wide interpretation so as to include information concerning all aspects, both physical and mental, of the health of an individual.

51. The answer to the fourth question must therefore be that reference to the fact that an individual has injured her foot and is on half-time on medical grounds constitutes personal data concerning health within the meaning of Article 8(1) of Directive 95/46.

65. For its part, Article 25 of Directive 95/46 imposes a series of obligations on Member States and on the Commission for the purposes of monitoring transfers of personal data to third countries in the light of the level of protection afforded to such data in each of those countries. . . .

69. If Article 25 of Directive 95/46 were interpreted to mean that there is transfer [of data] to a third country every time that personal data are loaded onto an internet page, that transfer would necessarily be a transfer to all the third countries where there are the technical means needed to access the internet. The special regime provided for by Chapter IV of the directive would thus necessarily become a regime of general application, as regards operations on the internet. Thus, if the Commission found, pursuant to Article 25(4) of Directive 95/46, that

even one third country did not ensure adequate protection, the Member States would be obliged to prevent any personal data being placed on the internet.

70. Accordingly, it must be concluded that Article 25 of Directive 95/46 is to be interpreted as meaning that operations such as those carried out by Mrs. Lindqvist do not as such constitute a transfer [of data] to a third country. It is thus unnecessary to investigate whether an individual from a third country has accessed the internet page concerned or whether the server of that hosting service is physically in a third country. . . .

72. . . . [T]he referring court seeks to know whether the provisions of Directive 95/46, in a case such as that in the main proceedings, bring about a restriction which conflicts with the general principles of freedom of expression or other freedoms and rights, which are applicable within the European Union and are enshrined in inter alia Article 10 of the ECHR.

86. . . . [F]undamental rights have a particular importance, as demonstrated by the case in the main proceedings, in which, in essence, Mrs. Lindqvist's freedom of expression in her work preparing people for Communion and her freedom to carry out activities contributing to religious life have to be weighed against the protection of the private life of the individuals about whom Mrs. Lindqvist has placed data on her internet site.

87. Consequently, it is for the authorities and courts of the Member States not only to interpret their national law in a manner consistent with Directive 95/46 but also to make sure they do not rely on an interpretation of it which would be in conflict with the fundamental rights protected by the Community legal order or with the other general principles of Community law, such as inter alia the principle of proportionality. . . .

90. The answer to the sixth question must therefore be that the provisions of Directive 95/46 do not, in themselves, bring about a restriction which conflicts with the general principles of freedom of expression or other freedoms and rights, which are applicable within the European Union and are enshrined inter alia in Article 10 of the ECHR. It is for the national authorities and courts responsible for applying the national legislation implementing Directive 95/46 to ensure a fair balance between the rights and interests in question, including the fundamental rights protected by the Community legal order.

91. By its seventh question, the referring court essentially seeks to know whether it is permissible for the Member States to provide for greater protection for personal data or a wider scope than are required under Directive 95/46.

95. Directive 95/46 is intended, as appears from the eighth recital in the preamble thereto, to ensure that the level of protection of the rights and freedoms of individuals with regard to the processing of personal data is equivalent in all Member States. The tenth recital adds that the approximation of the national laws applicable in this area must not result in any lessening of the protection they afford but must, on the contrary, seek to ensure a high level of protection in the Community.

96. The harmonisation of those national laws is therefore not limited to minimal harmonisation but amounts to harmonisation which is generally complete. It is upon that view that Directive 95/46 is intended to ensure free movement of personal data while guaranteeing a high level of protection for the rights and interests of the individuals to whom such data relate.

97. It is true that Directive 95/46 allows the Member States a margin for manoeuvre in certain areas and authorises them to maintain or introduce particular rules for specific situations as a large number of its provisions demonstrate. However, such possibilities must be made use of in the manner provided for by Directive 95/46 and in accordance with its objective of maintaining a balance between the free movement of personal data and the protection of private life.

98. On the other hand, nothing prevents a Member State from extending the scope of the national legislation implementing the provisions of Directive 95/46 to areas not included within the scope thereof, provided that no other provision of Community law precludes it.

99. In the light of those considerations, the answer to the seventh question must be that measures taken by the Member States to ensure the protection of personal data must be consistent both with the provisions of Directive 95/46 and with its objective of maintaining a balance between freedom of movement of personal data and the protection of private life. However, nothing prevents a Member State from extending the scope of the national legislation implementing the provisions of Directive 95/46 to areas not included in the scope thereof provided that no other provision of Community law precludes it.

THE COURT, in answer to the questions referred to it by the Gota hovratt by order of 23 February 2001, hereby rules:

1. The act of referring, on an internet page, to various persons and identifying them by name or by other means, for instance by giving their telephone number or information regarding their working conditions and hobbies, constitutes the processing of personal data. . . .

4. There is no transfer [of data] to a third country within the meaning of Article 25 of Directive 95/46 where an individual in a Member State loads personal data onto an internet page which is stored on an internet site on which the page can be consulted and which is hosted by a natural or legal person who is established in that State or in another Member State, thereby making those data accessible to anyone who connects to the internet, including people in a third country. . . .

NOTES & QUESTIONS

1. *A Sweeping Decision.* The *Lindqvist* court found that Mrs. Lindqvist's posting of her website on the Internet constituted the processing of data. It found that she had illegally processed personal information as well as health information. It read the Directive's provisions about personal data about health to extend even to a mention of a foot injury. Without the data subject's permission, such personal information could not be subject to processing. The court also found that Member States could enact data privacy protections beyond the areas specified within the Directive. It stated that "nothing prevents a Member State from extending the scope of the national legislation implementing the provisions of Directive 95/46 to areas not included within the scope thereof, provided that no other provision of Community law precludes it."

In a negative reaction to this case, a student note in the United States argues: "The possibility of having each and every citizen claim that his or her privacy has been compromised by a use of information about him or her somewhere on the Internet is a monumental bureaucratic disaster, one which is difficult to imagine was the imagined intent of the drafters of the European Union's Data Protection Directive."[50] Do you agree that the decision is "draconian and abusive"?

2. **Lindqvist *in the United States?*** Imagine that Mrs. Lindqvist worked at the Lutheran Church in Lake Wobegon, Minnesota, and created a website similar to the one at stake in the above decision. Imagine you are an attorney and that an offended member of the church visits your office and seeks legal action against the Minnesota Mrs. Lindqvist. What are the available legal claims under U.S. law? Are they likely to be successful?

3. *No Transfer of Information.* The *Lindqvist* court also decided that she had not transferred the information on the site to a third country. Why did it reach this conclusion? Under what circumstances might a European court decide, to the contrary, that a website was transferring information to a third country? Would this decision have been decided differently if technology existed that could restrict access to a website based on the location of the viewer?

GOOGLE SPAIN SL, GOOGLE INC. V. AGENCIA ESPAÑOLA DE PROTECCIÓN DE DATOS (AEPD), MARIO COSTEJA GONZÁLEZ

European Court of Justice, Case C-131/12 (May 13, 2014)

---

14. On 5 March 2010, Mr Costeja González, a Spanish national resident in Spain, lodged with the AEPD a complaint against La Vanguardia Ediciones SL, which publishes a daily newspaper with a large circulation, in particular in Catalonia (Spain) ('La Vanguardia'), and against Google Spain and Google Inc. The complaint was based on the fact that, when an internet user entered Mr Costeja González's name in the search engine of the Google group ('Google Search'), he would obtain links to two pages of La Vanguardia's newspaper, of 19 January and 9 March 1998 respectively, on which an announcement mentioning Mr Costeja González's name appeared for a real-estate auction connected with attachment proceedings for the recovery of social security debts. . . .

Consideration of the questions referred

[Questions concerning material scope of the Directive]

26. As regards in particular the internet, the Court has already had occasion to state that the operation of loading personal data on an internet page must be considered to be such 'processing' within the meaning of Article 2(b) of Directive 95/46 (see Case C-101/01 *Lindqvist*). . . .

28. Therefore, it must be found that, in exploring the internet automatically, constantly and systematically in search of the information which is published there,

---

[50] Flora J. Garcia, *Bodil Lindqvist: A Swedish Churchgoer's Violation of the European Union's Data Protection Directive Should Be a Warning to U.S. Legislators*, 15 Fordham Intell. Prop. Media & Ent. L.J. 1206, 1232 (2005).

the operator of a search engine 'collects' such data which it subsequently 'retrieves', 'records' and 'organises' within the framework of its indexing programmes, 'stores' on its servers and, as the case may be, 'discloses' and 'makes available' to its users in the form of lists of search results. As those operations are referred to expressly and unconditionally in Article 2(b) of Directive 95/46, they must be classified as 'processing' within the meaning of that provision, regardless of the fact that the operator of the search engine also carries out the same operations in respect of other types of information and does not distinguish between the latter and the personal data.

29. Nor is the foregoing finding affected by the fact that those data have already been published on the internet and are not altered by the search engine. . . .

32. As to the question whether the operator of a search engine must be regarded as the 'controller' in respect of the processing of personal data that is carried out by that engine in the context of an activity such as that at issue in the main proceedings, it should be recalled that Article 2(d) of Directive 95/46 defines 'controller' as 'the natural or legal person, public authority, agency or any other body which alone or jointly with others determines the purposes and means of the processing of personal data'.

33. It is the search engine operator which determines the purposes and means of that activity and thus of the processing of personal data that it itself carries out within the framework of that activity and which must, consequently, be regarded as the 'controller' in respect of that processing pursuant to Article 2(d).

34. Furthermore, it would be contrary not only to the clear wording of that provision but also to its objective — which is to ensure, through a broad definition of the concept of 'controller', effective and complete protection of data subjects — to exclude the operator of a search engine from that definition on the ground that it does not exercise control over the personal data published on the web pages of third parties. . . .

36. Moreover, it is undisputed that that activity of search engines plays a decisive role in the overall dissemination of those data in that it renders the latter accessible to any internet user making a search on the basis of the data subject's name, including to internet users who otherwise would not have found the web page on which those data are published. . . .

[Questions concerning territorial scope of Directive]

42. . . . [T]he referring court seeks to establish whether it is possible to apply the national legislation transposing Directive 95/46 in circumstances such as those at issue in the main proceedings.

44   Specifically, the main issues raised by the referring court concern the notion of 'establishment', within the meaning of Article 4(1)(a) of Directive 95/46, and of 'use of equipment situated on the territory of the said Member State', within the meaning of Article 4(1)(c). . . .

55. In the light of that objective of Directive 95/46 and of the wording of Article 4(1)(a), it must be held that the processing of personal data for the purposes of the service of a search engine such as Google Search, which is operated by an undertaking that has its seat in a third State but has an establishment in a Member

State, is carried out 'in the context of the activities' of that establishment if the latter is intended to promote and sell, in that Member State, advertising space offered by the search engine which serves to make the service offered by that engine profitable.

56. In such circumstances, the activities of the operator of the search engine and those of its establishment situated in the Member State concerned are inextricably linked since the activities relating to the advertising space constitute the means of rendering the search engine at issue economically profitable and that engine is, at the same time, the means enabling those activities to be performed.

57. As has been stated in paragraphs 26 to 28 of the present judgment, the very display of personal data on a search results page constitutes processing of such data. Since that display of results is accompanied, on the same page, by the display of advertising linked to the search terms, it is clear that the processing of personal data in question is carried out in the context of the commercial and advertising activity of the controller's establishment on the territory of a Member State, in this instance Spanish territory.

58. That being so, it cannot be accepted that the processing of personal data carried out for the purposes of the operation of the search engine should escape the obligations and guarantees laid down by Directive 95/46, which would compromise the directive's effectiveness and the effective and complete protection of the fundamental rights and freedoms of natural persons which the directive seeks to ensure . . .

[Questions concerning the extent of the responsibility of the operator of a search engine under the Directive]

80. It must be pointed out at the outset that . . . processing of personal data, such as that at issue in the main proceedings, carried out by the operator of a search engine is liable to affect significantly the fundamental rights to privacy and to the protection of personal data when the search by means of that engine is carried out on the basis of an individual's name, since that processing enables any internet user to obtain through the list of results a structured overview of the information relating to that individual that can be found on the internet — information which potentially concerns a vast number of aspects of his private life and which, without the search engine, could not have been interconnected or could have been only with great difficulty — and thereby to establish a more or less detailed profile of him. Furthermore, the effect of the interference with those rights of the data subject is heightened on account of the important role played by the internet and search engines in modern society, which render the information contained in such a list of results ubiquitous . . . .

81. In the light of the potential seriousness of that interference, it is clear that it cannot be justified by merely the economic interest which the operator of such an engine has in that processing. However, inasmuch as the removal of links from the list of results could, depending on the information at issue, have effects upon the legitimate interest of internet users potentially interested in having access to that information, in situations such as that at issue in the main proceedings a fair balance should be sought in particular between that interest and the data subject's fundamental rights under Articles 7 and 8 of the Charter. Whilst it is true that the

data subject's rights protected by those articles also override, as a general rule, that interest of internet users, that balance may however depend, in specific cases, on the nature of the information in question and its sensitivity for the data subject's private life and on the interest of the public in having that information, an interest which may vary, in particular, according to the role played by the data subject in public life. . . .

84. Given the ease with which information published on a website can be replicated on other sites and the fact that the persons responsible for its publication are not always subject to European Union legislation, effective and complete protection of data users could not be achieved if the latter had to obtain first or in parallel the erasure of the information relating to them from the publishers of websites.

85. Furthermore, the processing by the publisher of a web page consisting in the publication of information relating to an individual may, in some circumstances, be carried out 'solely for journalistic purposes' and thus benefit, by virtue of Article 9 of Directive 95/46, from derogations from the requirements laid down by the directive, whereas that does not appear to be so in the case of the processing carried out by the operator of a search engine. It cannot therefore be ruled out that in certain circumstances the data subject is capable of exercising the rights referred to in Article 12(b) and subparagraph (a) of the first paragraph of Article 14 of Directive 95/46 against that operator but not against the publisher of the web page. . . .

87. Indeed, since the inclusion in the list of results, displayed following a search made on the basis of a person's name, of a web page and of the information contained on it relating to that person makes access to that information appreciably easier for any internet user making a search in respect of the person concerned and may play a decisive role in the dissemination of that information, it is liable to constitute a more significant interference with the data subject's fundamental right to privacy than the publication on the web page.

88. In the light of all the foregoing considerations, . . . the operator of a search engine is obliged to remove from the list of results displayed following a search made on the basis of a person's name links to web pages, published by third parties and containing information relating to that person, also in a case where that name or information is not erased beforehand or simultaneously from those web pages, and even, as the case may be, when its publication in itself on those pages is lawful.

[Questions concerning the scope of the data subject's
rights guaranteed by the Directive]

89. By Question 3, the referring court asks, in essence, whether Article 12(b) and subparagraph (a) of the first paragraph of Article 14 of Directive 95/46 are to be interpreted as enabling the data subject to require the operator of a search engine to remove from the list of results displayed following a search made on the basis of his name links to web pages published lawfully by third parties and containing true information relating to him, on the ground that that information may be prejudicial to him or that he wishes it to be 'forgotten' after a certain time. . . .

94. Therefore, if it is found, following a request by the data subject pursuant to Article 12(b) of Directive 95/46, that the inclusion in the list of results displayed following a search made on the basis of his name of the links to web pages published lawfully by third parties and containing true information relating to him personally is, at this point in time, incompatible with Article 6(1)(c) to (e) of the directive because that information appears, having regard to all the circumstances of the case, to be inadequate, irrelevant or no longer relevant, or excessive in relation to the purposes of the processing at issue carried out by the operator of the search engine, the information and links concerned in the list of results must be erased. . . .

96. In the light of the foregoing, when appraising such requests made in order to oppose processing such as that at issue in the main proceedings, it should in particular be examined whether the data subject has a right that the information relating to him personally should, at this point in time, no longer be linked to his name by a list of results displayed following a search made on the basis of his name. In this connection, it must be pointed out that it is not necessary in order to find such a right that the inclusion of the information in question in the list of results causes prejudice to the data subject.

97. As the data subject may, in the light of his fundamental rights under Articles 7 and 8 of the Charter, request that the information in question no longer be made available to the general public by its inclusion in such a list of results, it should be held, as follows in particular from paragraph 81 of the present judgment, that those rights override, as a rule, not only the economic interest of the operator of the search engine but also the interest of the general public in finding that information upon a search relating to the data subject's name. However, that would not be the case if it appeared, for particular reasons, such as the role played by the data subject in public life, that the interference with his fundamental rights is justified by the preponderant interest of the general public in having, on account of inclusion in the list of results, access to the information in question.

98. As regards a situation such as that at issue in the main proceedings, which concerns the display, in the list of results that the internet user obtains by making a search by means of Google Search on the basis of the data subject's name, of links to pages of the on-line archives of a daily newspaper that contain announcements mentioning the data subject's name and relating to a real-estate auction connected with attachment proceedings for the recovery of social security debts, it should be held that, having regard to the sensitivity for the data subject's private life of the information contained in those announcements and to the fact that its initial publication had taken place 16 years earlier, the data subject establishes a right that that information should no longer be linked to his name by means of such a list. Accordingly, since in the case in point there do not appear to be particular reasons substantiating a preponderant interest of the public in having, in the context of such a search, access to that information, a matter which is, however, for the referring court to establish, the data subject may, by virtue of Article 12(b) and subparagraph (a) of the first paragraph of Article 14 of Directive 95/46, require those links to be removed from the list of results.

NOTES & QUESTIONS

1. ***The Logic of* Google Spain.** Citing *Lindqvist*, the European Court of Justice in *Google Spain* declared that the operator of search engines was a "processor" of data under the Data Protection Directive. The operator of the search engine could not justify its activity simply through its "economic interest" in the processing, and it was not protected, as a publisher of a Web page might be, by the language regarding journalism in Article 9 of the Directive. The Court also found that even when publication of the information may be lawful, the operator of the search engine could be required to remove links from a person's name in its search results. Do you agree with all, some, or none of these conclusions?

2. ***The Duty of a Search Engine Operator and "the Right to be Forgotten."*** The *Google Spain* Court notes that the referring court had asked whether a data subject could require the operator of a search engine operator to remove truthful information relating to him because it was "prejudicial to him or that he wishes it to be 'forgotten' after a certain time." The Court found that even if the information did not cause "prejudice" to the data subject, a data subject's under Articles 7 and 8 of the Charter generally were weightier than the economic interest of the operator of the search engine and the interest of the general public in access to information. In the case at hand, it specifically found an interest in the data subject in not having the information linked to him. What are the duties of Google and other search engine operators under *Google Spain*?

3. ***International Reactions.*** The *Google Spain* decision was widely commented and reported on throughout the world. In the United Kingdom, Christopher Graham, the data protection commissioner, was unconcerned about the logistical challenges now facing Google. He told the BBC, "Google is a massive commercial organization making millions and millions out of processing people's personal information. They're going to have to do some tidying up."[51]

   In contrast, Jimmy Wales, the founder of Wikipedia, worried about Internet search engines now being placed in charge of "censoring history."[52] In Germany, Sigmar Gabriel, the Minister for Economic Affairs and Energy and Chairman of the Social Democratic Party, warned against the "Information capitalism" of a handful of American Internet companies.[53] In an essay in the *Frankfurt Allgemeine Zeitung* he wrote, "Europe stands for the opposite of this totalitarian idea of making every detail of human behavior, human emotions and human thought into the object of a capitalistic marketing strategy." According to Minister Gabriel, the European emphasis was on protection of human dignity by safeguarding of an interest in self-determination over personal data.

---

[51] Rowena Mason, *Right to Be Forgotten*, The Guardian (July 25, 2014).

[52] *Id.*

[53] Sigmar Gabriel, *Unsere politischen Konsequenzen aus der Google-Debatte*, FAZ (May 16, 2014).

4. *Commenting on Search Results*. Jonathan Zittrain considers the *Google Spain* decision to be a poor response to a significant policy issue: "[T]he Internet's ability to preserve indefinitely all its information about you" was a serious problem.[54] But Zittrain thought the decision "oddly narrow." It permitted the plaintiff to restrict the ability of search engines to list information, but not to have information removed from the Web or to restrict other Web pages— including articles about the decision itself—from listing the underlying information, such as the name of the plaintiff and the information that he viewed as objectionable. His proposed solution was for Google to re-introduce a feature, formerly found in its news aggregator, that allowed people to comment on information about them online. Such comments would provide context for search results.

5. *Website or Google Link?* In his analysis of *Google Spain*, Robert Post argues that this decision "fails to recognize that the circulation of texts of common interest among strangers makes possible the emergence of a "public" capable of forming the "public opinion" that is essential for democratic self-governance.[55]

   For Post, the Google Spain court should have looked first to the *La Vanguardia* website and its information about Costeja and whether this material concerned "a matter that is now newsworthy or of legitimate concern to the public." If so, remedies could include anonymization. If not, "we should ask whether a Google link to the website might nevertheless independently violate the right to be forgotten." This inquiry leads Post to conclude, "But if the *La Vanguardia* website does not violate the right to be forgotten, the Google link ought not be liable, and it does not matter whether it increases the circulation of the *La Vanguardia* website." Do you agree that it should be irrelevant that Costeja is more significantly harmed through the Google link than the publication on the web page of the newspaper?

6. *Google Responds to the Court of Justice.* In response to the decision, Google set up a Web page, "Search removal requests under data protection law in Europe."[56] It explains its approach there for compliance with the Court of Justice's opinion:

   > When you make . . . a request, we will balance rights of the individual with the public's interest to know and the right to distribute information. When evaluating your request, we will look at whether the results include outdated information about you, as well as whether there's a public interest in the information – for example, we may decline to remove certain information about financial scams, professional malpractice, criminal convictions or public conduct of government information.

   Does this language express the essence of the European Court of Justice's broad guidelines in the *Google Spain* decision?

---

[54] Jonathan Zittrain, *Don't Force Google to 'Forget,'* N.Y. Times (May 14, 2014).

[55] Robert C. Post, *Data Privacy and Dignitary Privacy:* Google Spain, *the Right to be Forgotten, and the Construction of the Public Sphere*, 67 Duke L.J. 981 (2018).

[56] https://support.google.com/legal/contact/lr_eudpa?product=websearch&hl=en-GB

In June 2014, Google then established an online form to allow those in the EU to request delisting of search requests that apply to them. It provides daily updates as to the statistics, country-by-country, regarding delisting requests and results.[57] By August 2020, it reported a total of requests to delist over 3.7 million URLs. It has received over 960,000 requests to delist. It approved delisting of 46.5% of the contested URL's. After first applying search result removals only to European domains, Google in 2016 began to apply these removal requests to all domains beyond Europe as long as the search engine was accessed within the EU. Google used the IP address to determine its location. Regarding its decisions not to delist, Google states:

> Determining whether content is in the public interest is complex and may mean considering many diverse factors, including—but not limited to—whether the content relates to the requester's professional life, a past crime, political office, position in public life, or whether the content is self-authored content, consists of government documents, or is journalistic in nature.

7. ***Geoblocking Not Worldwide Delisting.*** In 2019, Google won a follow up case before the CJEU, *Google v. Commission nationale de l'informatique et des libertés (CNIL)*, which established that it was not obliged to delist search result listings everywhere in the world.[58] After the *Google Spain* decision, Google used "geoblocking," which is based on a user's IP address and restricts access to delisted results for all users located in EU Member States. In *Google v. CNIL*, the CJEU reversed a 2015 order of the French data protection commission, the CNIL, requiring Google to remove search results that contained damaging or false information on a worldwide basis.

First, the CJEU decided that EU law did not create an obligation "to carry out such a de-referencing on all the versions of its search engine." Indeed, the Court acknowledged that "the balance between the right to privacy and the protection of personal data, on the one hand, and the freedom of information of internet users, on the other, is likely to vary significantly around the world." Second, the CJEU found that EU data protection commissioners could only order delisting in domains associated with other Member States after conferring with their counterpart regulators.

Finally, in an ambiguous passage the CJEU noted, near the end of its judgment, that there might be grounds, after all, for a global delisting:

> EU law does not currently require that the de-referencing granted concern all versions of the search engine in question, it also does not prohibit such a practice. Accordingly, a supervisory or judicial authority of a Member State remains competent to weigh up, in the light of national standards of protection of fundamental rights, a data subject's right to privacy and the protection of personal data concerning him or her, on the one hand, and the right to freedom of information, on the other, and, after weighing those rights against each other,

---

[57] Google, Requests to delist content under European privacy law, https://transparencyreport.google.com/eu-privacy/overview?hl=en

[58] Google v. Commission nationale de l'informatique et des libertés (CNIL), CJEU, C:2019:722 (2019).

to order, where appropriate, the operator of that search engine to carry out a de-referencing concerning all versions of that search engine.

In an attempt to interpret this language, the Electronic Frontier Foundation proposes that the CJEU might be preserving global delisting for extraordinary cases, or perhaps keeping it open whether global delisting might be permissible for the violation of other laws if not the right to be forgotten.[59]

8. ***Deleting Old Info at Cleveland.com.*** In a voluntary decision to allow deletion of information, Cleveland.com, the website associated with the Cleveland Plain Dealer, now permits people to remove accounts of their nonviolent crimes from its online stories. It explained: "If there's a dated story on our site that is causing you harm, we'll consider removing your name from it."[60] As a limitation on this policy, it stated: "We won't do this for stories about serious violent or sex crimes, nor will we entertain requests involving public corruption." Moving forward, cleveland.com also pledged to "greatly curtail our use of mug shots, restricting them to the most notorious of crimes."[61] The problem with mugshots is said to be that they reinforce "race stereotypes about crime" and are photographs "taken while people are in crisis." Finally, cleveland.com started a policy of ceasing to name "most people accused of most minor crimes."

How would you evaluate these policies? Do they distort the present or future, or protect people from answering for mistakes they made or minor crimes they committed many years earlier?

9. ***Beyond* Google Spain*: Visual Images and Autocomplete.*** As noted above, courts in France and Germany have found for Max Mosley and required Google to automate a procedure for blocking images in advance once a court finds a photograph to violate a legal interest in privacy. Another privacy issue concerns Google's Autocomplete function. As Google explains Autocomplete, "As you type in the search box, you can find information quickly by seeing search predictions that might be similar to the search terms you're typing."[62] Autocomplete is "a reflection of the search activity of users and the content of web pages."

Germany's highest court for civil matters, the Federal Court of Justice (*Bundesgerichtshof*)(BGH), has found that Google's Autocomplete can violate an individual's personality rights. In a 2013 case, the BGH found that the operator of a search engine was not generally required to check autocomplete suggestions in advance for violation of legal interests. BGH: Autocomplete, Az. VI ZR 269/12 (May 14, 2013). Rather, the search engine company became responsible once it had knowledge of a legal violation of a right of personality through an Autocomplete suggestion. Most importantly, the BGH found that an Autocomplete suggestion was Google's own content. Its software had

---

[59] David Greene, European Court's Decision in Right to Be Forgotten Case is a Win for Free Speech, Electronic Frontier Foundation (Sept. 26, 2019).

[60] Fill this form out for your Right to be Forgotten, cleveland.com (July 12, 2019), at https://www.cleveland.com/metro/2019/01/fill-this-form-out-for-your-right-to-be-forgotten.html.

[61] Chris Quinn, *Right to be forgotten: Cleveland.com rolls out process to remove mug shot, names from dated stories about minor crimes*, cleveland.com (June 12, 2019).

[62] https://support.google.com/websearch/answer/106230?hl=en.

generated the result. The Federal Court of Justice stated, "Untrue statements of facts do not have to be tolerated."

Once an affected party informed the software operator of an Autocomplete suggestion that violated a legal interest, the operator was required to prevent the software from generating this result. In its *Autocomplete* decision, the BGH had considered a plaintiff's claim that typing his first and last name in the Google search window lead to the search suggestion of "Scientology" and "Fraud." As the court noted, however, the plaintiff was neither a member of Scientology nor stood "in connection with a Fraud."

In a law review article published before this decision, Professor Niko Härtling argued against a finding against Google. In his view, no one who used a search engine on a regular basis would think that an Autocomplete search suggestion represented "the statement of a Google employee."[63] Rather, the suggestion was merely a truthful statement of already suggested language or concepts based on the activity of numerous Google users, who had typed certain words and not others into the search form.

How would you set a balance between freedom of expression and privacy when it comes to the matter of Autocomplete suggestions for search forms?

TELE2 SVERIGE AB V. POST- OCH TELESTYRELSEN & SEC'Y OF STATE FOR HOME DEPT V. WATSON (JOINED CASES)

European Court of Justice, Grand Chamber (Dec. 21, 2016)

[A few months before the European Court of Justice's *Google Spain* decision, the Court delivered another important privacy decision in *Digital Rights Ireland v. Minister for Communications*, Joined Cases C-293/12 and C-594/12 (April 8, 2014). In this decision, the European Court of Justice found that the Data Retention Directive failed to meet the necessary constitutional privacy standards.

The Directive did not create "any objective criterion by which to determine the limits of the access of the competent national authorities to the data and their subsequent us" of it. Moreover, it did not limit the access of the competent national authorities to "what is strictly necessary in the light of objective pursued" and did not require review of a request for access to a court or independent administrative entity. A final failing of the Data Retention Directive was its lack of sufficient safeguards for providers relating to the security of retained data.

In 2016 and 2017, the CJEU returned to the issue of data retention. First, in its *Tele2 Sverige* opinion, it considered the permissibility of national data retention legislation in light of the restrictions the ePrivacy Directive's Article 15 as well as the EU Charter's protections for privacy and data protection. It found the two national data retention laws before it in *Tele2 Sverige* to be invalid.

Second, in *Opinion 1/15*, the CJEU invalidated a proposed agreement between the EU and Canada to transfer passenger name record (PNR) data. The part of *Opinion 1/15* excerpted below concerns the agreement's data retention provisions. This opinion also develops the caselaw regarding the requirements of the EU for

---

[63] Niko Härting, *Rotlichtgerüchte: Haftet Google?*, 10 Kommunikation und Recht 633 (2012).

international data transfers, and this Chapter contains a further excerpt from *Opinion 1/15* in its section concerning that topic.]

62. By the first question in Case C 203/15, the Kammarrätten i Stockholm (Administrative Court of Appeal, Stockholm) seeks, in essence, to ascertain whether Article 15(1) of Directive 2002/58,[64] read in the light of Articles 7 and 8 and Article 52(1) of the Charter, must be interpreted as precluding national legislation such as that at issue in the main proceedings that provides, for the purpose of fighting crime, for general and indiscriminate retention of all traffic and location data of all subscribers and registered users with respect to all means of electronic communications.

63. That question arises, in particular, from the fact that Directive 2006/24,[65] which the national legislation at issue in the main proceedings was intended to transpose, was declared to be invalid by the *Digital Rights* judgment, though the parties disagree on the scope of that judgment and its effect on that legislation, given that it governs the retention of traffic and location data and access to that data by the national authorities.

102. Given the seriousness of the interference in the fundamental rights concerned represented by national legislation which, for the purpose of fighting crime, provides for the retention of traffic and location data, only the objective of fighting serious crime is capable of justifying such a measure

103. Further, while the effectiveness of the fight against serious crime, in particular organised crime and terrorism, may depend to a great extent on the use of modern investigation techniques, such an objective of general interest, however fundamental it may be, cannot in itself justify that national legislation providing for the general and indiscriminate retention of all traffic and location data . . .

104. In that regard, it must be observed, first, that the effect of such legislation, in the light of its characteristic features . . . , is that the retention of traffic and location data is the rule, whereas the system put in place by Directive 2002/58 requires the retention of data to be the exception.

105. Second, national legislation such as that at issue in the main proceedings, which covers, in a generalised manner, all subscribers and registered users and all means of electronic communication as well as all traffic data, provides for no differentiation, limitation or exception according to the objective pursued. It is comprehensive in that it affects all persons using electronic communication services, even though those persons are not, even indirectly, in a situation that is liable to give rise to criminal proceedings. It therefore applies even to persons for whom there is no evidence capable of suggesting that their conduct might have a link, even an indirect or remote one, with serious criminal offences. Further, it does not provide for any exception, and consequently it applies even to persons whose communications are subject, according to rules of national law, to the obligation of professional secrecy.

106. Such legislation does not require there to be any relationship between the data which must be retained and a threat to public security. In particular, it is not restricted to retention in relation to (i) data pertaining to a particular time period

---

[64] Editors' Note: This Directive is termed the ePrivacy Directive.

[65] Editors' Note: This Directive is termed the Data Retention Directive.

and/or geographical area and/or a group of persons likely to be involved, in one way or another, in a serious crime, or (ii) persons who could, for other reasons, contribute, through their data being retained, to fighting crime.

107. National legislation such as that at issue in the main proceedings therefore exceeds the limits of what is strictly necessary and cannot be considered to be justified, within a democratic society, as required by Article 15(1) of Directive 2002/58, read in the light of Articles 7, 8 and 11 and Article 52(1) of the Charter.

108. However, Article 15(1) of Directive 2002/58, read in the light of Articles 7, 8 and 11 and Article 52(1) of the Charter, does not prevent a Member State from adopting legislation permitting, as a preventive measure, the targeted retention of traffic and location data, for the purpose of fighting serious crime, provided that the retention of data is limited, with respect to the categories of data to be retained, the means of communication affected, the persons concerned and the retention period adopted, to what is strictly necessary.

109. In order to satisfy the requirements set out in the preceding paragraph of the present judgment, that national legislation must, first, lay down clear and precise rules governing the scope and application of such a data retention measure and imposing minimum safeguards, so that the persons whose data has been retained have sufficient guarantees of the effective protection of their personal data against the risk of misuse. That legislation must, in particular, indicate in what circumstances and under which conditions a data retention measure may, as a preventive measure, be adopted, thereby ensuring that such a measure is limited to what is strictly necessary

110. Second, as regards the substantive conditions which must be satisfied by national legislation that authorises, in the context of fighting crime, the retention, as a preventive measure, of traffic and location data, if it is to be ensured that data retention is limited to what is strictly necessary, it must be observed that, while those conditions may vary according to the nature of the measures taken for the purposes of prevention, investigation, detection and prosecution of serious crime, the retention of data must continue nonetheless to meet objective criteria, that establish a connection between the data to be retained and the objective pursued. In particular, such conditions must be shown to be such as actually to circumscribe, in practice, the extent of that measure and, thus, the public affected.

111. As regard the setting of limits on such a measure with respect to the public and the situations that may potentially be affected, the national legislation must be based on objective evidence which makes it possible to identify a public whose data is likely to reveal a link, at least an indirect one, with serious criminal offences, and to contribute in one way or another to fighting serious crime or to preventing a serious risk to public security. Such limits may be set by using a geographical criterion where the competent national authorities consider, on the basis of objective evidence, that there exists, in one or more geographical areas, a high risk of preparation for or commission of such offences.

112. Having regard to all of the foregoing, the answer to the first question referred in Case C 203/15 is that Article 15(1) of Directive 2002/58, read in the light of Articles 7, 8 and 11 and Article 52(1) of the Charter, must be interpreted as precluding national legislation which, for the purpose of fighting crime, provides for the general and indiscriminate retention of all traffic and location data

of all subscribers and registered users relating to all means of electronic communication.

The second question in Case C-203/15 and the first question in Case C-698/15

114. By the second question in Case C 203/15 and the first question in Case C 698/15, the referring courts seek, in essence, to ascertain whether Article 15(1) of Directive 2002/58, read in the light of Articles 7, 8 and Article 52(1) of the Charter, must be interpreted as precluding national legislation governing the protection and security of traffic and location data, and more particularly, the access of the competent national authorities to retained data, where that legislation does not restrict that access solely to the objective of fighting serious crime, where that access is not subject to prior review by a court or an independent administrative authority, and where there is no requirement that the data concerned should be retained within the European Union.

115. As regards objectives that are capable of justifying national legislation that derogates from the principle of confidentiality of electronic communications, it must be borne in mind that . . . . the list of objectives set out in the first sentence of Article 15(1) of Directive 2002/58 is exhaustive, access to the retained data must correspond, genuinely and strictly, to one of those objectives. Further, since the objective pursued by that legislation must be proportionate to the seriousness of the interference in fundamental rights that that access entails, it follows that, in the area of prevention, investigation, detection and prosecution of criminal offences, only the objective of fighting serious crime is capable of justifying such access to the retained data.

116. As regards compatibility with the principle of proportionality, national legislation governing the conditions under which the providers of electronic communications services must grant the competent national authorities access to the retained data must ensure . . . . that such access does not exceed the limits of what is strictly necessary.

117. Further, since the legislative measures referred to in Article 15(1) of Directive 2002/58 must, in accordance with recital 11 of that directive, 'be subject to adequate safeguards', a data retention measure must, as follows from the case-law cited in paragraph 109 of this judgment, lay down clear and precise rules indicating in what circumstances and under which conditions the providers of electronic communications services must grant the competent national authorities access to the data. Likewise, a measure of that kind must be legally binding under domestic law.

118. In order to ensure that access of the competent national authorities to retained data is limited to what is strictly necessary, it is, indeed, for national law to determine the conditions under which the providers of electronic communications services must grant such access. . . . That national legislation must also lay down the substantive and procedural conditions governing the access of the competent national authorities to the retained data

119. Accordingly, and since general access to all retained data, regardless of whether there is any link, at least indirect, with the intended purpose, cannot be regarded as limited to what is strictly necessary, the national legislation concerned must be based on objective criteria in order to define the circumstances and

conditions under which the competent national authorities are to be granted access to the data of subscribers or registered users. In that regard, access can, as a general rule, be granted, in relation to the objective of fighting crime, only to the data of individuals suspected of planning, committing or having committed a serious crime or of being implicated in one way or another in such a crime. However, in particular situations, where for example vital national security, defence or public security interests are threatened by terrorist activities, access to the data of other persons might also be granted where there is objective evidence from which it can be deduced that that data might, in a specific case, make an effective contribution to combating such activities.

120. In order to ensure, in practice, that those conditions are fully respected, it is essential that access of the competent national authorities to retained data should, as a general rule, except in cases of validly established urgency, be subject to a prior review carried out either by a court or by an independent administrative body, and that the decision of that court or body should be made following a reasoned request by those authorities submitted, inter alia, within the framework of procedures for the prevention, detection or prosecution of crime

121. Likewise, the competent national authorities to whom access to the retained data has been granted must notify the persons affected, under the applicable national procedures, as soon as that notification is no longer liable to jeopardise the investigations being undertaken by those authorities. That notification is, in fact, necessary to enable the persons affected to exercise, inter alia, their right to a legal remedy, expressly provided for in Article 15(2) of Directive 2002/58, read together with Article 22 of Directive 95/46, where their rights have been infringed

122. . . . . Given the quantity of retained data, the sensitivity of that data and the risk of unlawful access to it, the providers of electronic communications services must, in order to ensure the full integrity and confidentiality of that data, guarantee a particularly high level of protection and security by means of appropriate technical and organisational measures. In particular, the national legislation must make provision for the data to be retained within the European Union and for the irreversible destruction of the data at the end of the data retention period.

123. In any event, the Member States must ensure review, by an independent authority, of compliance with the level of protection guaranteed by EU law with respect to the protection of individuals in relation to the processing of personal data, that control being expressly required by Article 8(3) of the Charter and constituting, in accordance with the Court's settled case-law, an essential element of respect for the protection of individuals in relation to the processing of personal data. If that were not so, persons whose personal data was retained would be deprived of the right, guaranteed in Article 8(1) and (3) of the Charter, to lodge with the national supervisory authorities a claim seeking the protection of their data.

125. Having regard to all of the foregoing, the answer to the second question in Case C 203/15 and to the first question in Case C 698/15 is that Article 15(1) of Directive 2002/58, read in the light of Articles 7, 8 and 11 and Article 52(1) of the Charter, must be interpreted as precluding national legislation governing the protection and security of traffic and location data and, in particular, access of the

competent national authorities to the retained data, where the objective pursued by that access, in the context of fighting crime, is not restricted solely to fighting serious crime, where access is not subject to prior review by a court or an independent administrative authority, and where there is no requirement that the data concerned should be retained within the European Union.

OPINION 1/15 OF THE COURT

European Court of Justice, Grand Chamber (July 26, 2017)

[A year after the *TeleSverige 2* decision, the CJEU in 2017 returned to the topic of data retention in its *Opinion 1/15*. This opinion considers the conditions under which international agreements with the EU may legalize international data transfers. As part of this assessment, it applied its caselaw regarding data retention to a situation in which the personal data of an EU citizen would be transferred and stored in a non-EU nation. The proposed EU-Canada agreement would permit storage of the data in Canada for five years. Under it, the PNR data of all passengers from the EU to Canada would be collected and retained.

As for the PNR data covered by the envisaged agreement, it was to includes "the name(s) of the air passenger(s), information necessary to the reservation, such as the dates of intended travel and the travel itinerary, information relating to tickets, groups of persons checked-in under the same reservation number, passenger contact information, information relating to the means of payment or billing, information concerning baggage and general remarks regarding the passengers."]

(6)   The retention and use of PNR data

190. In order to ensure that the retention of the PNR data transferred, the access to that data by the Canadian authorities referred to in the envisaged agreement and the use of that data by those authorities is limited to what is strictly necessary, the envisaged agreement should, in accordance with the settled case-law of the Court cited in . . . this Opinion, lay down clear and precise rules indicating in what circumstances and under which conditions those authorities may retain, have access to and use such data.

191. So far as the retention of personal data is concerned, it must be pointed out that the legislation in question must, inter alia, continue to satisfy objective criteria that establish a connection between the personal data to be retained and the objective pursued (see, to that effect, judgments of 6 October 2015, Schrems, . . . and of 21 December 2016, Tele2 Sverige and Watson and Others).

(i)   The retention and use of PNR data before the arrival of air passengers, during their stay in Canada and on their departure

196. The envisaged agreement accordingly permits, throughout the retention period, the use of the PNR data of all air passengers for the purposes referred to in Article 3 thereof.

197. As regards the retention of PNR data and its use up to the air passengers' departure from Canada, it should be noted that PNR data, inter alia, facilitates security checks and border control checks. Its retention and use for that purpose may not, on account of its very nature, be restricted to a particular circle of air passengers, nor can it be subject to prior authorisation by a court or by an independent administrative body. Consequently, . . . it must be held that, for as long as the air passengers are in Canada or are due to leave that non-member country, the necessary connection between that data and the objective pursued by that agreement exists, and the agreement therefore does not exceed the limits of what is strictly necessary merely because it permits the systematic retention and use of the PNR data of all air passengers.

198. Similarly, the systematic use of PNR data for the purpose of verifying the reliability and topicality of the pre-established models and criteria on which the automated processing of that data is based, . . . or of defining new models and criteria for such processing, is directly related to carrying out the checks referred to in the preceding paragraph of this Opinion, and must, therefore, also be considered to not exceed the limits of what is strictly necessary.

199. Furthermore, it must be pointed out that, during the air passengers' stay in Canada and irrespective of the results of the automated analysis of the PNR data carried out prior to their arrival in that non-member country, cases may arise in which the Canadian Competent Authority has information, collected during that stay, indicating that use of their data might be necessary in order to combat terrorism and serious transnational crime.

200. As regards the use of PNR data in the situations referred to in the preceding paragraph, however, it should be pointed out that, since the air passengers have been allowed to enter the territory of that non-member country, following verification of their PNR data, the use of that data during their stay in Canada must be based on new circumstances justifying that use. That use therefore requires . . . rules laying down the substantive and procedural conditions governing that use in order, inter alia, to protect that data against the risk of abuse. Such rules must be based on objective criteria in order to define the circumstances and conditions under which the Canadian authorities referred to in the envisaged agreement are authorised to use that data.

201. In this connection, where there is objective evidence from which it may be inferred that the PNR data of one or more air passengers might make an effective contribution to combating terrorist offences and serious transnational crime, the use of that data does not exceed the limits of what is strictly necessary.

202. Furthermore, in order to ensure that, in practice, the conditions set out in the two preceding paragraphs are fully respected, it is essential that the use of retained PNR data, during the air passengers' stay in Canada, should, as a general rule, except in cases of validly established urgency, be subject to a prior review carried out either by a court, or by an independent administrative body, and that the decision of that court or body be made following a reasoned request by the competent authorities submitted, inter alia, within the framework of procedures for the prevention, detection or prosecution of crime.

203. In so far as the envisaged agreement does not meet the requirements set out in the two preceding paragraphs, that agreement does not ensure that the use

of the PNR data of air passengers during their stay in Canada, by the Canadian authorities referred to in the agreement, will be limited to what is strictly necessary.

(ii) The retention and use of PNR data after the air passengers' departure from Canada

204. Air passengers who have left Canada have, as a general rule, been subject to checks on entry to and on departure from Canada. Similarly, their PNR data has been verified before their arrival in Canada and, as the case may be, during their stay and on their departure from that non-member country. . . . In any event, it is not apparent that all air passengers who have travelled to Canada would present, after their departure from that country, a higher risk than other persons who have not travelled to that country during the previous five years and in respect of whom Canada does not therefore hold PNR data.

205. Consequently, as regards air passengers in respect of whom no such risk has been identified on their arrival in Canada and up to their departure from that non-member country, there would not appear to be, once they have left, a connection — even a merely indirect connection — between their PNR data and the objective pursued by the envisaged agreement which would justify that data being retained. The considerations put forward before the Court, inter alia, by the Council and the Commission regarding the average lifespan of international serious crime networks and the duration and complexity of investigations relating to those networks, do not justify the continued storage of the PNR data of all air passengers after their departure from Canada for the purposes of possibly accessing that data, regardless of whether there is any link with combating terrorism and serious transnational crime.

206. The continued storage of the PNR data of all air passengers after their departure from Canada is not therefore limited to what is strictly necessary.

207. However, in so far as, in specific cases, objective evidence is identified from which it may be inferred that certain air passengers may present a risk in terms of the fight against terrorism and serious transnational crime even after their departure from Canada, it seems permissible to store their PNR data beyond their stay in Canada.

208. As regards the use of PNR data so stored, such use should . . . be based on objective criteria in order to define the circumstances and conditions under which the Canadian authorities referred to in the envisaged agreement may have access to that data in order to use it. Similarly, that use should, except in cases of validly established urgency, be subject to a prior review carried out either by a court, or by an independent administrative body; the decision of that court or body authorising the use being made following a reasoned request by those authorities submitted, inter alia, within the framework of procedures for the prevention, detection or prosecution of crime.

209. As regards the period during which the PNR data of the air passengers . . . may be retained, it should be observed that the general period, provided for in Article 16(1) of the envisaged agreement, has been extended by one and a half years by comparison with the period provided for in the 2006 Agreement. In this connection, it must nevertheless be accepted, in the light, inter alia, of the considerations put forward, in particular, by the Council and the Commission,

mentioned in paragraph 205 of this Opinion, that the five-year retention period provided for in Article 16(1) of that agreement does not exceed the limits of what is strictly necessary for the purposes of combating terrorism and serious transnational crime.

210. Lastly, in so far as Article 9(2) of the envisaged agreement, which provides that Canada is to hold PNR data 'in a secure physical environment that is protected with access controls', means that that data has to be held in Canada, and in so far as Article 16(6) of that agreement, under which Canada is to destroy the PNR data at the end of the PNR data retention period, must be understood as requiring the irreversible destruction of that data, those provisions may be regarded as meeting the requirements as to clarity and precision.

211. Having regard to the considerations set out in paragraphs 204 to 206 and 208 of this Opinion, that agreement does not ensure that the retention and use of PNR data by the Canadian authorities after the air passengers' departure from Canada is limited to what is strictly necessary.

NOTES & QUESTIONS

1. *The Holding:* **Tele2 Sverige.** The *Tele2 Sverige* opinion invalidated national legislation on the grounds that these laws provided for general and indiscriminate data retention. Such an approach was incompatible with the ePrivacy Directive as interpreted in light of EU Charter rights. More specifically, the CJEU in *Tele2 Sverige* found that legislation could not permit "retention of traffic and location data" as the rule since the ePrivacy Directive "requires the retention of data to be the exception. *Tele2 Sverige,* ¶104. This opinion required "a relationship between the data which must be retained and a threat to public security." Id. at ¶106.

2. *The Holding:* **Opinion 1/15.** In this judgment, the CJEU was responding to a request from the European Parliament to assess a proposed agreement with Canada that set conditions for transfer of PNR data. Regarding its provisions for data retention, the Court found in principle that the agreement's five-year retention period did not exceed the limits of what was strictly necessary. *Opinion 1/15* at ¶209. At the same time, it found numerous problematic aspects of the data retention aspects of the agreement. For example, the retention and use of PNR information after a passenger left Canada were not strictly necessary. Such data may only be stored in Canada where certain passengers present a risk of terrorism or serious transnational criminal activities. Moreover, it required that the use of the retained data would be subject to prior review by an independent body, such as a court. Id. at ¶¶202, 208.

3. *Strictly Necessary Data Retention.* What steps would national legislation have to take to meet the CJEU's standards set out in *Tele2 Sverige and Opinion 1/15*? How can a statute limit data retention to that which is "strictly necessary" under EU law? What are the critical benchmarks for the CJEU? *Opinion 1/15* speaks of a requirement for "rules laying down the substantive and procedural conditions government" use of data, such as how that data is to be used during a passenger's stay in Canada. *Opinion 1/15,* ¶200. What elements must such

rules contain?

4. ***Post-Departure Storage of PNR.*** In *Opinion 1/15,* the CJEU found that PNR data of *all* EU passengers to Canada could not be retained in a blanket fashion post-departure. *Opinion 1/15,* ¶205. In particular, a justification regarding "the average lifespan of international serious crime networks" did not justify storage of information regarding all air passengers. In contrast, it would be permissible to store information post-departure about EU voyagers if "in specific cases," there was an identification of "objective evidence" relating to these individuals presenting "a risk in terms of the fight against terrorism and serious transnational crime even after their departure from Canada. Id. Do you agree with this approach? Should the CJEU defer to the assessment about blanket data retention from the Canadian and European negotiators of the PNR Agreement?

5. ***Data Localization.*** Among its mandated safeguards, the CJEU found it necessary, as part of a data retention law's protection of data security, that "the national legislation must make provision for the data to be retained within the European Union." *Tele2 Sverige,* ¶122. This part of the decision represents an important EU data localization requirement.

(c) The General Data Protection Regulation

The main reference point for European data protection law is now the General Data Protection Regulation (GDPR) of 2016. The GDPR took effect on May 25, 2018, which marked a decisive moment for international privacy law. The GDPR's influence is now felt throughout the world. As Jan Albrecht and Florian Jotzo observe, the GDPR on that date will "represent without any doubt the most important legal source for data protection."[66] In proof of this significance, Albrecht and Jotzo point to the Regulation's central role in "the largest domestic market in the world," the EU, as well as its future international impact.[67] Albrecht is in a good position to comment on the GDPR; a member of the Green party, he served for the EU Parliament as the influential Rapporteur of the Regulation.

The press in the United States marked the occasion of the GDPR taking effect in May 2018 with numerous stories about its significance. For the *N.Y. Times*, the GDPR made Europe into the "World's Leading Tech Watchdog."[68] It observed, "Europe has set the regulatory standard in reining in the immense power of tech giants." The *Washington Post* proposed, "The rules are significant because they are some of the most robust since the dawn of the Internet exceeding consumer protection in the United States."[69] *Wired* proclaimed: "Avoidance isn't an option."[70]

The GDPR replaced the European Data Protection Directive of 1995. The GDPR marks an important policy shift from a directive to a regulation. In EU law,

---

[66] Jan Philipp Albrecht & Florian Jotzo, *Das neue Datenschutzrecht der EU* 7 (2017).

[67] *Id.*

[68] Adam Satariano, *G.D.P.R, a New Privacy Law, Makes Europe World's Leading Tech Watchdog,* N.Y. Times (May 25, 2018).

[69] Hamza Shaban, *Facebook braces for new E.U. privacy law,* Washington Post (Jan. 29, 2018).

[70] Nitasha Tiku, *Europe's New Privacy Law Will Change the Web, and More,* Wired (March 19, 2018).

while a directive requires harmonizing legislation, a regulation establishes directly enforceable standards. As Christopher Kuner explains, "a regulation leads to a greater degree of harmonization, since it immediately becomes part of a national legal system, without the need for adoption of separate national legislation; has legal effect independent of national law; and overrides contrary national laws."[71]

The EU's recourse to a regulation follows from its recognition of both privacy as a human right and the high status of the individual. As already noted in this Chapter, cornerstone documents of European integration safeguard privacy and data protection as human rights. In a reflection of the data subject's high status, the GDPR provides directly binding statutory protection in EU law. This choice marks a notable change with the established path of EU consumer protection law, where the usual path has been to enact directives and not regulations to protect citizens.

There was another reason for the EU's choice of a regulation instead of taking the path of a Data Protection Directive 2.0. The Directive was widely considered to have fallen short in harmonizing data protection throughout the EU. According to the Commission, for example, Member States were interpreting the rules for consent differently, and the Directive's grant of "room for manoeuvre in certain areas" and its permitting member states to issue "particular rules for specific situations" had created "additional cost[s] and administrative burden[s]" for private stakeholders.[72] Due to this absence of uniformity under the Directive, a regulation was needed to create legal certainty within the internal market and to assure a continuing role for the EU "in promoting high data protection standards worldwide."[73]

Like the Directive, the GDPR contains strong protections for individual rights. It limits the sweep of individual content and restricts the processing of sensitive data and the use of "automated decision-making." Finally, it greatly increases the available enforcement tools, including fines, for violations of EU data protection law.

Extraterritorial Reach. In its Article 3, the GDPR sets out its jurisdictional sweep. As Dan Svantesson explains, "Article 3 outlines what types of contact with the EU's territory will activate the application of the GDPR, and it does so in a manner that is partly territoriality-dependent and partly territoriality-independent."[74]

First, the GDPR reaches all processing of personal data "in the context of the activities of an establishment of a controller or processor in the Union, regardless of whether the processing takes place in the Union or not." The idea of "an establishment" is far-reaching. As the GDPR's recital 22 states, "Establishment implies the effective and real exercise of activity through stable arrangements."

---

[71] Christopher Kuner, *The European Commission's Proposed Data Protection Regulation: A Copernican Revolution in European Data Protection Law*, 11 Privacy & Security L. Rep. 215, 217 (2012).

[72] Communication from the Commission to the European Parliament, the Council, the Economic and Social Committee and the Committee of the Regions, at 2, 8 COM (2010) 609 final (Nov. 11, 2010).

[73] *Id.* at 10.

[74] Dan Jerker B. Svantesson, *Article 3. Territorial Scope*, in The EU General Data Protection Regulation (GDPR): A Commentary 74, 76 (Christopher Kuner et al., eds. 2020).

The European Data Protection Board also notes that Article 3(1) can reach data processing regarding individuals who are not in the EU. In its view, "any personal data in the context of the activities of an establishment of a controller or processor in the Union would fall under the GDPR, regardless of the location or the nationality of the data subject whose personal data are being processed."

Second, the GDPR applies to two situations regarding the processing of personal data of data subjects by a controller or processor who is not established in the Union. The initial situation regulated by Article 3(2) concerns "the offering of goods or services in the Union," and "irrespective of whether a payment of the data subject is required." This provision relies on the "principle of market location," or, as the concept is expressed in German, the "*Marktortprinzip.*" The further circumstance covered by Article 3(2) is when a data subject's behavior within the Union is being monitored by the controller. This means, for example, that "the temporary physical presence of a foreign citizen . . . in the EU may trigger the application of the GDPR."

Limits on Data Processing. As an initial step in protecting individual rights, the GDPR requires a legal basis for the processing of personal data. The principles of the GDPR begin by requiring that information be: (1) "processed lawfully, fairly and in a transparent manner" (lawfulness, fairness, and transparency) and that it be (2) "collected for specified, explicit and legitimate purposes and not further processed in a manner that is incompatible with those purposes" (purpose limitation). Art. 5(1). The list continues with requirements of (3) data minimization; (4) data accuracy; (5) limited storage; (6) integrity; (7) data security; and (8) accountability for the data controller. Finally, in Article 51, the GDPR contains strong protections for (9) independent data protection authorities.

The Rights to Rectification and Erasure ("The Right to be Forgotten"). The GDPR provides a right of correction, termed a rectification interest, and imposes temporal limits on data use. The first interest permits the individual "to obtain from the controller without undue delay the rectification of inaccurate personal data concerning him or her." Art. 16. The controller is a person who or an organization which "determines the purposes and means of the processing of personal data." Art. 4(7). In addition, the individual shall have the right to have incomplete personal data completed." Art. 16.

As a second important personal interest, the Regulation creates a "right to erasure." Art. 17. In a parenthesis in its heading for this section, it refers to this individual interest as a "right to be forgotten." The right to erasure sets out a number of grounds that will trigger the controller's obligation to erase personal data. These begin with when "the personal data are no longer necessary in relation to the purposes for which they were collected or otherwise processed." Another erasure justification is when the individual withdraws her consent "and where there is no other legal ground for the processing." Other grounds for erasure include when the personal data are unlawfully processed, when a legal obligation in EU or Member State law require erasure, and when the data subject objects to processing and "there are no overriding legitimate grounds for the processing."

Consent. The GDPR strengthens individual rights in other ways. Among the most important of these measures are those that put in place strong restrictions on the use of consent requirements as a basis for processing personal data. As Christopher Kuner has observed, consent is an especially important concept in the EU because it is in "widespread use . . . as a legal basis for data processing."[75] The Directive required consent to be given "unambiguously." Directive, Art. 7(a). Strengthening this language, the GDPR requires that consent be "freely given, specific, informed and unambiguous."[76] GDPR, Recital 32 notes: "Silence, pre-ticked boxes or inactivity should not . . . constitute consent." Thus, the GDPR clearly favors the use of affirmative steps to constitute consent, and disfavors inaction as indicating consent.

Mechanisms for gathering consent must also be understandable and transparent. If the data subject provides consent in a written declaration that concerns other matters, "the request for consent" must be made "in a manner which is clearly distinguishable from the other matters, in an intelligible and easily accessible form, using clear and plain language." Art. 7(2). Where consent involves the personal data of a child or sensitive data, there are additional enumerated conditions that must be met. Art. 8(1).

As a further restriction, consent can be withdrawn at any time. The GDPR states: "It shall be as easy to withdraw as to give consent." Moreover, the burden of demonstrating consent is placed squarely on "the controller."[77] Art. 12(5). The GDPR requires the controller to be able "to demonstrate that the data subject has consented to a processing of his or her personal data." Art. 7(1). "Data subject" is an EU term of art that refers to "an identified or identifiable natural person." Art 4(1).

Finally, the GDPR introduces an importance ban on "tying" in its Article 7(4). The idea is that the terms within a single contractual agreement cannot be extended, or "tied," to include processing of personal data beyond that which is necessary to the purpose of the contract.[78] Article 7(4) states that agreement to the "performance of a contract, including the provision of a service" is invalid if made "conditional on consent to the processing of personal data that is not necessary for the performance of that contract."[79] In other words, a contract cannot tie consent for an initial data processing operation to a second one. Indeed, Recital 43, GDPR notes, "Consent is presumed not to be freely given . . . if the performance of a contract, including the provision of a service, is dependent on the consent despite such consent not being necessary for such performance." The ban on tying consolidates restrictions in the GDPR regarding necessity and purpose limitation; in doing so, it takes aim at myriad new digital business models based around data

---

[75] Christopher Kuner, *The European Commission's Proposed Data Protection Regulation: A Copernican Revolution in European Data Protection Law*, 11 Privacy & Security L. Rep. 215, 220 (2012).

[76] *Id.*

[77] *Id.* at art. 12(5).

[78] Ulrich Dammann, *Erfolge und Defizite der EU-Datenschutzgrundverordnung* 307, 311 ZEITSCHRIFT FÜR DATENSCHUTZ (2016).

[79] 2016 O.J. (L 119), art. 7.

trade. In the assessment of Ulrich Dammann, the GDPR's ban on tying is "unique in the entire world."[80]

Controllers and Processors. One of the most important points of terminology in the GDPR concerns the distinction between "controllers" and "processors." Article 4(7) contains the key definitions of these terms. A "controller" is the person or entity which "alone or jointly with others, determines the purposes and means of the processing of personal data." In contrast, a "processor" is the person or entity which "processes personal data on behalf on the controller." The GDPR then assigns greater responsibilities to the data controller than the data processor. For example, the controller is responsible for the lawfulness, fairness, and transparency of information. Art. 5(1). The obligations of data processors are set out in Article 28, and include processing personal data "only on documented instructions from the controller" and ensuring that "persons authorised to process the personal data have committed themselves to confidentiality or are under an appropriate statutory obligation of confidentiality."

Limits on Processing of Sensitive Data and Automated Decision-Making. The GDPR heightens the protections of the Directive for sensitive data and strengthens existing restrictions on automated decision-making. Article 9 provides a list of kinds of sensitive data, which it terms "special categories of personal data." The EU's attention to its "special categories" does not focus on risks from specific data processing operations, but singles out areas as being ex ante problematic for data processing. Following the Directive's approach, Article 9 flatly forbids the processing of "special categories" unless one of its specific exceptions is applicable.

The special categories in the GDPR are more extensive than in the Directive. The GDPR prohibits processing of personal data revealing: "racial or ethnic original political opinions, religious or philosophical beliefs, or trade union membership, and the processing of genetic data, biometric data for the purpose of uniquely identifying a natural person, data concerning health or data concerning a natural person's sex life or sexual orientation." Among the exceptions for processing such data are when the data subject has given "explicit consent" or the "processing is necessary for reasons of substantial public interest, on the basis of Union or Member State law." The latter exception further specifies that the law must "be proportionate to the aim pursued, respect the essence of the right to data protection and provide for suitable and specific measures to safeguard the fundamental rights and the interests of the data subject." Art. 9(2)(g).

As for automated processing, the Regulation relates this concept to concerns about profiling. Article 22 states:

The data subject shall have the right not to be subject to a decision based solely on automated processing, including profiling, which produces legal effects concerning him or her or similarly significantly affects him or her. Art. 22(1).

An open question under the GDPR concerns the impact of this provision on certain contemporary forms of "automated processing," most notably analytics and "Big Data."

---

[80] Dammann, *supra* note 155, at 311.

Monetary Fines. The GDPR increases the protection of individual rights by greatly increasing the size of monetary sanctions that are available for violations of it. Overall, administrative fines issued pursuant to the Regulation are to be "effective, proportionate and dissuasive." Art. 83(1). The Regulation grants to the power to levy such fines to the "supervisory authorities" of Member States. These entities are also called data protection commissions or commissioners.

Article 83(2) sets out a multi-factor test for calculation of administrative fines by the national data protection commissioners. The amount of the administrative fine in individual cases is required to take into account a long list of factors, including: "the nature, gravity and duration of the infringement taking into account the nature, scope, or purpose of the processing concerned as well as the number of data subjects affected and the level of damage suffered by them; [and] the intentional or negligent character of the infringement." The resulting yardstick provides a great measure of flexibility for a data protection commission in assessing penalties in individual cases.

Of special note, moreover, is that the GDPR permits fines under certain circumstances to reach as much as four percent of a company's worldwide revenues. Art. 83(6). At least on paper, this provision would permit penalties of as much as several hundred million dollars against companies. A fine of such magnitude might run afoul, however, of the Regulation's requirement that fines be "proportionate." Art. 83(1). Nonetheless, these penalty provisions demonstrate the EU's intention of ensuring compliance with its data protection rules.

Independent Supervisory Authorities. Much of the Regulation concerns the organization and practice of data protection within the EU. As Gerrit Hornung already noted of the draft GDPR: "Institutional and organizational arrangements make up a significant part" of it.[81] Some of these measures have been received with general approval, such as the steps that the GDPR takes to guarantee the independence of data protection commissions within their member states.

Article 52 requires that each supervisory authority "act with complete independence in performing its tasks and exercising its powers in accordance with this Regulation." Art. 52(1). The Regulation further specifies that the members of each supervisory authority are to "remain free from external influence, whether direct or indirect, and shall neither seek nor take instructions from anybody." Art. 52(2). The GDPR also requires the Member States to provide each supervisory authority "with the human, technical and financial resources, premises and infrastructure necessary for the effective performance of its tasks and exercise of its powers." Art. 52(4).

The European Data Protection Board's Consistency Mechanism. The Regulation creates a new institution, the European Data Protection Board (EDPB). Art. 68. In so doing, the Regulation upgrades the status of the Article 29 Working Party, the existing panel of national supervisory authorities. The EDPB provides a useful forum in which national supervisory authorities can reach a consensus about important issues. The EDPB has the power to make both non-binding

---

[81] Gerrit Hornung, *Eine Datenschutz-Grundverordnung für Europa? Licht und Schatten im Kommissionsentwurf vom 25.1.2012*, 2012 Zeitschrift für Datenschutz 99, 104.

recommendations and binding decisions in individual cases. Art. 65. Its decision-making power extends, for example, to cases of conflict where multiple supervisory authorities are involved and are unable to reach consensus. Art. 65(1)(a); Art. 60(4).

The Adequacy Standard. Like the Directive, the Regulation requires "an adequate level of protection" before a transfer of data to a non-EU country. This Chapter examines the issue of international data transfers below. Art. 45.

BUNDESVERBAND DER VERBRAUCHERZENTRALEN UND VERBRAUCHERVERBÄNDE V. PLANET 49 GMBH

European Court of Justice (Grand Chamber)(Oct. 1, 2019)

---

25. On 24 September 2013, Planet49 organised a promotional lottery on the website www.dein-macbook.de.

26. Internet users wishing to take part in that lottery were required to enter their postcodes, which redirected them to a web page where they were required to enter their names and addresses. Beneath the input fields for the address were two bodies of explanatory text accompanied by checkboxes. The first body of text with a checkbox without a preselected tick ('the first checkbox') read:

'I agree to certain sponsors and cooperation partners providing me with information by post or by telephone or by email/SMS about offers from their respective commercial sectors. I can determine these myself here; otherwise, the selection is made by the organiser. I can revoke this consent at any time. Further information about this can be found here.'

27. The second set of text with a checkbox containing a preselected tick ('the second checkbox') read:

'I agree to the web analytics service Remintrex being used for me. This has the consequence that, following registration for the lottery, the lottery organiser, [Planet49], sets cookies, which enables Planet49 to evaluate my surfing and use behaviour on websites of advertising partners and thus enables advertising by Remintrex that is based on my interests. I can delete the cookies at any time. You can read more about this here.'

28. Participation in the lottery was possible only if at least the first checkbox was ticked.

29. The hyperlink associated with the words 'sponsors and cooperation partners' and 'here' next to the first checkbox opened a list of 57 companies, their addresses, the commercial sector to be advertised and the method of communication used for the advertising (email, post or telephone). The underlined word 'Unsubscribe' was contained after the name of each company. The following statement preceded the list:

'By clicking on the "Unsubscribe" link, I am deciding that no advertising consent is permitted to be granted to the partner/sponsor in question. If I have not unsubscribed from any or a sufficient number of partners/sponsors, Planet49 will choose partners/sponsors for me at its discretion (maximum number: 30 partners/sponsors).'

30. When the hyperlink associated with the word 'here' next to the second checkbox was clicked on, the following information was displayed:

'The cookies named ceng_cache, ceng_etag, ceng_png and gcr are small files which are stored in an assigned manner on your hard disk by the browser you use and by means of which certain information is supplied which enables more user-friendly and effective advertising. The cookies contain a specific randomly generated number (ID), which is at the same time assigned to your registration data. If you then visit the website of an advertising partner which is registered for Remintrex (to find out whether a registration exists, please consult the advertising partner's data protection declaration), Remintrex automatically records, by virtue of an iFrame which is integrated there, that you (or the user with the stored ID) have visited the site, which product you have shown interest in and whether a transaction was entered into.

Subsequently, [Planet49] can arrange, on the basis of the advertising consent given during registration for the lottery, for advertising emails to be sent to you which take account of your interests demonstrated on the advertising partner's website. After revoking the advertising consent, you will of course not receive any more email advertising.

The information communicated by these cookies is used exclusively for the purposes of advertising in which products of the advertising partner are presented. The information is collected, stored and used separately for each advertising partner. User profiles involving multiple advertising partners will not be created under any circumstances. The individual advertising partners do not receive any personal data.

If you have no further interest in using the cookies, you can delete them via your browser at any time. You can find a guide in your browser's ["help"] function.

No programs can be run or viruses transmitted by means of the cookies.

You of course have the option to revoke this consent at any time. You can send the revocation in writing to [Planet49] [address]. However, an email to our customer services department [email address] will also suffice.'

31. According to the order for reference, cookies are text files which the provider of a website stores on the website user's computer which that website provider can access again when the user visits the website on a further occasion, in order to facilitate navigation on the internet or transactions, or to access information about user behaviour.

Consideration of the questions referred

43. The questions referred must . . . be answered having regard to both Directive 95/46 and Regulation 2016/679.

Question 1(a) and (c)

44. By Question 1(a) and (c), the referring court asks, in essence, whether Article 2(f) and Article 5(3) of Directive 2002/58, read in conjunction with Article 2(h) of Directive 95/46 and Article 6(1)(a) of Regulation 2016/679, must be interpreted as meaning that the consent referred to in those provisions is validly constituted if, in the form of cookies, the storage of information or access to information already stored in a website user's terminal equipment is permitted by

way of a pre-checked checkbox which the user must deselect to refuse his or her consent.

45. As a preliminary matter, it is important to note that, according to the order for reference, the cookies likely to be placed on the terminal equipment of a user participating in the promotional lottery organised by Planet49 contain a number which is assigned to the registration data of that user, who must enter his or her name and address in the registration.form for the lottery. The referring court adds that, by linking that number with that data, a connection between a person to the data stored by the cookies arises if the user uses the internet, such that the collection of that data by means of cookies is a form of processing of personal data. Those statements were confirmed by Planet49, which noted in its written observations that the consent to which the second checkbox refers is intended to authorise the collection and processing of personal data, not anonymous data.

46. On the basis of those explanations, it should be noted that, in accordance with Article 5(3) of Directive 2002/58, Member States are to ensure that the storing of information, or the gaining of access to information already stored, in the terminal equipment of a user is only allowed on condition that the user concerned has given his or her consent, having been provided with clear and comprehensive information, in accordance with Directive 95/46, inter alia, about the purposes of the processing.

49. As regards the wording of Article 5(3) of Directive 2002/58, it should be made clear that, although that provision states expressly that the user must have 'given his or her consent' to the storage of and access to cookies on his or her terminal equipment, that provision does not, by contrast, indicate the way in which that consent must be given. The wording 'given his or her consent' does, however, lend itself to a literal interpretation according to which action is required on the part of the user in order to give his or her consent. In that regard, it is clear from recital 17 of Directive 2002/58 that, for the purposes of that directive, a user's consent may be given by any appropriate method enabling a freely given specific and informed indication of the user's wishes, including 'by ticking a box when visiting an internet website'.

51. Article 2(h) of Directive 95/46 defines 'the data subject's consent' as being 'any freely given specific and informed indication of his wishes by which the data subject signifies his agreement to personal data relating to him being processed'.

52. Thus, as the Advocate General stated in point 60 of his Opinion, the requirement of an 'indication' of the data subject's wishes clearly points to active, rather than passive, behaviour. However, consent given in the form of a preselected tick in a checkbox does not imply active behaviour on the part of a website user.

53. That interpretation is borne out by Article 7 of Directive 95/46, which sets out an exhaustive list of cases in which the processing of personal data can be regarded as lawful.

54. In particular, Article 7(a) of Directive 95/46 provides that the data subject's consent may make such processing lawful provided that the data subject has given his or her consent 'unambiguously'. Only active behaviour on the part of the data subject with a view to giving his or her consent may fulfil that requirement.

55. In that regard, it would appear impossible in practice to ascertain objectively whether a website user had actually given his or her consent to the processing of his or her personal data by not deselecting a pre-ticked checkbox

nor, in any event, whether that consent had been informed. It is not inconceivable that a user would not have read the information accompanying the preselected checkbox, or even would not have noticed that checkbox, before continuing with his or her activity on the website visited.

57. As regards the foregoing, the consent referred to in Article 2(f) and Article 5(3) of Directive 2002/58, read in conjunction with Article 2(h) of Directive 95/46, is therefore not validly constituted if the storage of information, or access to information already stored in an website user's terminal equipment, is permitted by way of a checkbox pre-ticked by the service provider which the user must deselect to refuse his or her consent.

58. It should be added that the indication of the data subject's wishes referred to in Article 2(h) of Directive 95/46 must, inter alia, be 'specific' in the sense that it must relate specifically to the processing of the data in question and cannot be inferred from an indication of the data subject's wishes for other purposes.

59. In the present case, contrary to what Planet49 claims, the fact that a user selects the button to participate in the promotional lottery organised by that company cannot therefore be sufficient for it to be concluded that the user validly gave his or her consent to the storage of cookies.

60. A fortiori, the preceding interpretation applies in the light of Regulation 2016/679.

61. As the Advocate General stated, in essence, in point 70 of his Opinion, the wording of Article 4(11) of Regulation 2016/679, which defines the 'data subject's consent' for the purposes of that regulation and, in particular, of Article 6(1)(a) thereof, to which Question 1(c) refers, appears even more stringent than that of Article 2(h) of Directive 95/46 in that it requires a 'freely given, specific, informed and unambiguous' indication of the data subject's wishes in the form of a statement or of 'clear affirmative action' signifying agreement to the processing of the personal data relating to him or her.

62. Active consent is thus now expressly laid down in Regulation 2016/679. It should be noted in that regard that, according to recital 32 thereof, giving consent could include ticking a box when visiting an internet website. On the other hand, that recital expressly precludes 'silence, pre-ticked boxes or inactivity' from constituting consent.

63. It follows that the consent referred to in Article 2(f) and in Article 5(3) of Directive 2002/58, read in conjunction with Article 4(11) and Article 6(1)(a) of Regulation 2016/679, is not validly constituted if the storage of information, or access to information already stored in the website user's terminal equipment, is permitted by way of a pre-ticked checkbox which the user must deselect to refuse his or her consent.

Question 1(b)

66. By Question 1(b), the referring court wishes to know, in essence, whether Article 2(f) and Article 5(3) of Directive 2002/58, read in conjunction with Article 2(h) of Directive 95/46 and Article 6(1)(a) of Regulation 2016/679, must be interpreted differently according to whether or not the information stored or accessed on a website user's terminal equipment is personal data within the meaning of Directive 95/46 and Regulation 2016/679.

67. As stated in paragraph 45 above, according to the order for reference, the storage of cookies at issue in the main proceedings amounts to a processing of personal data.

68. That being the case, the Court notes, in any event, that Article 5(3) of Directive 2002/58 refers to 'the storing of information' and 'the gaining of access to information already stored', without characterising that information or specifying that it must be personal data.

70. That interpretation is borne out by recital 24 of Directive 2002/58, according to which any information stored in the terminal equipment of users of electronic communications networks are part of the private sphere of the users requiring protection under the European Convention for the Protection of Human Rights and Fundamental Freedoms. That protection applies to any information stored in such terminal equipment, regardless of whether or not it is personal data, and is intended, in particular, as is clear from that recital, to protect users from the risk that hidden identifiers and other similar devices enter those users' terminal equipment without their knowledge.

71. In the light of the foregoing considerations, the answer to Question 1(b) is that Article 2(f) and Article 5(3) of Directive 2002/58, read in conjunction with Article 2(h) of Directive 95/46 and Article 4(11) and Article 6(1)(a) of Regulation 2016/679, are not to be interpreted differently according to whether or not the information stored or accessed on a website user's terminal equipment is personal data within the meaning of Directive 95/46 and Regulation 2016/679.

Question 2

72. By Question 2, the referring court asks, in essence, whether Article 5(3) of Directive 2002/58 must be interpreted as meaning that the information that the service provider must give to a website user includes the duration of the operation of cookies and whether or not third parties may have access to those cookies.

73. As has already been made clear in paragraph 46 above, Article 5(3) of Directive 2002/58 requires that the user concerned has given his or her consent, having been provided with clear and comprehensive information, 'in accordance with Directive [95/46]', inter alia, about the purposes of the processing.

74. As the Advocate General stated in point 115 of his Opinion, clear and comprehensive information implies that a user is in a position to be able to determine easily the consequences of any consent he or she might give and ensure that the consent given is well informed. It must be clearly comprehensible and sufficiently detailed so as to enable the user to comprehend the functioning of the cookies employed.

75. In a situation such as that at issue in the main proceedings, in which, according to the file before the Court, cookies aim to collect information for advertising purposes relating to the products of partners of the organiser of the promotional lottery, the duration of the operation of the cookies and whether or not third parties may have access to those cookies form part of the clear and comprehensive information which must be provided to the user in accordance with Article 5(3) of Directive 2002/58.

78. Although the duration of the processing of the data is not included as part of that information, it is, however, clear from the words 'at least' in Article 10 of Directive 95/46 that that information is not listed exhaustively. Information on the

duration of the operation of cookies must be regarded as meeting the requirement of fair data processing provided for in that article in that, in a situation such as that at issue in the main proceedings, a long, or even unlimited, duration means collecting a large amount of information on users' surfing behaviour and how often they may visit the websites of the organiser of the promotional lottery's advertising partners.

79. That interpretation is borne out by Article 13(2)(a) of Regulation 2016/679, which provides that the controller must, in order to ensure fair and transparent processing, provide the data subject with information relating, inter alia, to the period for which the personal data will be stored, or if that is not possible, to the criteria used to determine that period.

80. As to whether or not third parties may have access to cookies, that is information included within the information referred to in Article 10(c) of Directive 95/46 and in Article 13(1)(e) of Regulation 2016/679, since those provisions expressly refer to the recipients or categories of recipients of the data.

81. In the light of the foregoing considerations, the answer to Question 2 is that Article 5(3) of Directive 2002/58 must be interpreted as meaning that the information that the service provider must give to a website user includes the duration of the operation of cookies and whether or not third parties may have access to those cookies.

NOTES & QUESTIONS

1. **Planet 49.** In its *Planet49* opinion, the European Court of Justice made three important determinations in interpreting the Data Protection Directive and the GDPR, both of which applied to the matter before it due to the case's timeline. Planet49 had organized an online promotional lottery, which required users first to enter in their postcode and then their names and addresses. At that point, Planet49 sought separate consent for users being contacted by third parties and for cookies being placed on users' browsers in exchange for participating in the online lottery. Consent for the third-party promotional offers was sought through the use of an unchecked box, and consent for the use of cookies through a pre-checked box.

   First, the CJEU found that the consent to cookies was not valid if gathered through the use of "a pre-checked checkbox which the user must deselect to refuse his or her consent." Consent, whether pursuant to the Directive or GDPR, had to be "freely given" and "informed." The CJEU noted, "It is not inconceivable that a user would not have read the information accompanying the preselected checkbox, or even would not have noticed that checkbox, before continuing with his or her activity on the website visited."

   Second, the Court found that as regards the question of consent, it did not matter whether or not cookies could be characterized as "personal data." The Directive and GDPR alike intended "to protect users from the risk that hidden identifiers and other similar devices enter those users' terminal equipment without their knowledge." Finally, the CJEU found that under the Directive 2002/58, the ePrivacy Directive, and the GDPR, Planet49 had to provide information to users regarding duration of the period for storage of the cookies and whether or not third parties have access to the cookies.

How do these requirements compare with those under U.S. law?

2. ***Fundamental Protections Versus Consent and Contract?*** The GDPR's fundamental protections cannot be overcome through individual consent or contract. Individuals cannot choose to "opt out" from core protections, such as purpose limitation, data minimization, data accuracy, limited storage, and so on. In the analysis of Niko Härting, for example, "Even if consent makes data processing legitimate," the "data minimization" principle of Article 6 "may make it unlawful."[82] Orla Lynskey has tied this result to the fundamental rights charter of the EU. She writes, "[T]he EU sought to enact a data protection regime which could not be circumvented by private agreements due to its fundamental rights charter."[83] As a result, "an individual cannot choose to privately contract away his or her rights."

Christopher Kuner makes a similar point in analyzing the EU's regulation of international transfers of data. These rules are secondary to the requirement of a legal basis for the processing of information. Kuner observes that "companies become almost mesmerized with the mechanism to provide an adequate legal basis for the transfer, while neglecting to ask themselves what the legal basis is for the processing in the first place."[84] He adds: "Providing a legal basis for data processing is not a specific action, but rather an important principle that should be kept in mind at all stages of the company's compliance program."

3. ***Contracts and Consumer Law.*** In evaluating the permissibility of contracts involving personal data, the GDPR draws on its consumer protection law. The GDPR requires a policing of the substantive terms of the contract as well as the form of its presentation. Concerning substance, the GDPR's Recital 42 references the Council Directive of 1993 on Unfair Terms in Consumer Contracts, which includes an expansive "black list" of unfair terms.[85] Its sweeping rule is that any contractual term which has not been individually negotiated is unfair if "it causes a significant imbalance in the parties' rights and obligations under the contract, to the detriment of the consumer."[86] The GDPR makes these protections part of the future DNA of EU privacy law.

4. ***Controllers, Processers, and a Uniform Terminology.*** The GDPR assigns different responsibilities to parties that are "controllers" and those that are "processors." In the United States, the law makes a similar distinction between the chief entity that collects and processes personal information and a range of outside entities, which it refers to using a non-standardized terminology. The *Data Privacy Principles* of the American Law Association has adopted the

---

[82] Niko Härting, *Datenschutz-Grundverordnung* 26 (2016).

[83] Orla Lynskey, *The Foundations of EU Data Protection Law* 40 (2015).

[84] Christopher Kuner, *European Data Protection Law* 242 (2d ed. 2007) (emphasis removed).

[85] 2016 O.J. (L 119), ¶ 42.

[86] 1993 O.J. (L 95). *See* Jane K. Winn & Mark Webber, *The Impact of EU Unfair Contract Terms Law on U.S. Business-to-Consumer Internet Merchants*, 62 Bus. Lawyer 6, 9 (2006) (analyzing the Unfair Terms Directive and its "non-exclusive list of terms that may be deemed unfair.").

terms "processors" and "controllers" and advocates for their use in American information privacy law. It explains the rationale behind this decision in Comment g, §2:

> There are many different terms for data controllers and data: processors in various privacy laws. For example, under HIPAA, data controllers are called "covered entities" and data processors are called "business associates." For the sake of consistency, and because the GDPR terminology is the most precise and descriptive, the Principles adopt "data controllers" and "data processors" when referring to these critical concepts. Having one set of terms is more understandable and easier to follow than having dozens of differing terms with varying definitions. Additionally, these terms facilitate greater harmonization of the law between the United States and the EU, as well as other countries, most of which follow an EU-style approach in their privacy law.

Would adoption of the EU's terminology advance U.S. privacy law? How do you think legal responsibilities should be apportioned between controllers and processors? What should the role be for contractual agreements between controllers and processors?

5. *What About the Cloud?* The GDPR raises complex questions concerning its territorial scope. For example, Article 3(1) states that it "applies to the processing of personal data in the context of the activities of an establishment of a controller or processor in the Union, regardless of whether the processing takes place in the Union or not." As under the Directive, the key test, as the CJEU found in its *Weltimo* decision, is whether the controller or processor had "stable arrangements in the territory of a member state."[87] Under Article 3(2), in contrast, the key issue is whether a controller or processor is "offering goods or services" to data subjects in the EU, or engaging in the "monitoring of their behavior as far as their behavior takes place within the Union."

How does one decide whether a Cloud provider has an "establishment" in the sense of Article 3(1)? Note, too, that under Article 3(1), the persons whose data are being processed need not be a resident or even located in the EU; the key issue is where the data processor is located. Does this provision mean that an EU-based data processing center with customers in India, China, or Chile will be required to follow the GDPR? Is such a result problematic in your judgment?

6. *What About the Right to Erasure?* In its Article 17, the GDPR creates a "right to erasure." According to Jef Ausloos, the merit of this right is "how it emphasizes, clarifies, and centralizes key data protection safeguards into one provision."[88] Ausloos would have us think of Article 17 not as "an autonomous provision that data subjects can invoke against a controller," but more so as "a convenient proxy through which individuals can 'exercise control.'" In functioning as "a central hub for data subject empowerment in the GDPR," this right also "constitutes a critical check on whether the GDPR is safeguarded through the processing lifecycle."

---

[87] Weltimmo s. r. o. v. Nemzeti Adatvédelmi és Információszabadság Hatóság, CJEU (Oct. 1, 2015).

[88] Jef Ausloos, *The Right to Erasure in EU Data Protection Law* 476 (2020).

Does the right to erasure place too much responsibility on individuals to defend their privacy interests? Are there risks to other interests through the GDPR's right to erasure? How do you think it should be balanced against these other interests, including freedom of expression?

C. INTERNATIONAL TRANSFERS OF DATA

We live today in a global economy that is becoming increasingly dependent upon information. The Internet has enabled a dramatic increase in international communication and commerce. As a result, personal information increasingly flows across the borders of different nations around the world. International data transfers can also occur pursuant to discovery requests in litigation in the United States that involves foreign parties.

Each nation has its own set of privacy laws and regulations. These differences raise at least two difficulties. First, differing levels of protection might interfere with the smooth and efficient flow of personal information between countries. Thus, there is a need for harmonization or convergence of approaches to regulating the processing of personal data. Second, countries seeking to protect the privacy of their citizens must depend upon the protections accorded by other countries since a vast amount of personal data flows out of its borders to these other countries.

The data flow can occur under many circumstances: One of the most important is when transnational litigation takes place. Gil Keteltas has pointed to significant underlying differences in the way that litigation takes place in most jurisdictions outside the United States as opposed to within it.[89] In non-American court systems, "[p]retrial discovery is limited, with few documents changing hands." In contrast, "discovery in U.S. litigation is a right, and key information must be provided to an opponent even without a request from the opponent." Moreover, the Federal Rules of Civil Procedure permit discovery of all information relevant to a claim or defense and define relevancy broadly. Not surprisingly, the U.S. approach to discovery has led to collisions with the privacy laws in other jurisdictions.

1. INTERNATIONAL DATA TRANSFERS IN LITIGATION

VOLKSWAGEN, A.G. V. VALDEZ

909 S.W.2d 900 (Tex. 1995)

This mandamus action involves a conflict between Texas' discovery rules and Germany's privacy laws. We conclude that the trial court abused its discretion in failing to balance the competing interests of the parties and disregarding German law in its entirety. After balancing the respective parties' interests, we further

---

[89] Gil Keteltas, *US E-discovery*, in *E-Discovery and Data Privacy: A Practical Guide* 3, 6 (2011).

conclude that the information sought should not be produced. Accordingly, we conditionally grant the writ of mandamus. . . .

The real parties in interest sued both Volkswagen of America and its German parent company, Volkswagen A.G. (VWAG), in products liability for personal injuries resulting from an accident involving their 1970 model Volkswagen. The real parties sought production of VWAG's current corporate telephone book to identify individuals who might have relevant information concerning defects in the automobile's door latches. This book contains the names, job titles, position within the company, and direct dial work numbers of more than 20,000 employees as well as the private home numbers of individuals in management positions. VWAG objected to this request on the basis of the German Federal Data Protection Act, which prohibits the dissemination of private information without the consent of the individuals. *Bundesdatenschutzgesetz*, BGBl, I, 2954 (1990) (FRG) (BDSG). The trial court overruled VWAG's objection and ordered it to produce the phone book.

When information sought for production is located in a foreign country, guidance is provided by the Restatement (Third) of Foreign Relations Law § 442 (1987). Section 442(1)(a) states:

> A court or agency in the United States, when authorized by statute or rule of court, may order a person subject to its jurisdiction to produce documents, objects, or other information relevant to an action or investigation, even if the information or the person in possession of the information is outside the United States.

However, when the laws of the foreign sovereign protect relevant information from discovery, the interests of the domestic court or agency must be balanced with those of the foreign sovereign. The Restatement suggests:

> In deciding whether to issue an order directing production of information located abroad, and in framing such an order, a court or agency in the United States should take into account the importance to the investigation or litigation of the documents or other information requested; the degree of specificity of the request; whether the information originated in the United States; the availability of alternative means of securing the information; and the extent to which noncompliance with the request would undermine important interests of the United States, or compliance with the request would undermine important interests of the state [or country] where the information is located.

Restatement (Third) of Foreign Relations Law § 442(1)(c) (1987). Accordingly, only after a careful balancing of these interests should the trial court rule on a party's request for production.

Before the Restatement's balancing test may be applied, we must determine whether German and U.S. laws actually conflict. That a conflict exists is readily apparent after examination. Texas discovery rules allow an opposing party to discover evidence relevant to the subject matter in the pending action. Tex. R. Civ. P. 166b(2)(a). Germany's privacy laws protect from dissemination "personal data," which is defined as "information concerning the personal or material circumstances of an identified or identifiable individual." BDSG § 3(1). VWAG produced a plethora of authorities confirming its allegation that information contained in its current corporate phone book is, in fact, personal data. The affidavit of Horst-Gunther Bens explicitly acknowledges that VWAG's production of the book would violate the BDSG, while also explaining that privacy rights under German law are "equal in rank to the right of freedom of speech." Likewise, Paul Schwartz, a professor at the University of Arkansas School of Law and expert on German data protection law, opined that production of the book would be violative. This fact is also confirmed by Dr. Gerard Dronsch, the state commissioner for data protection for Lower Saxony, and the German Federal Ministry of Labor and Social Order. Additionally, the country of Germany submitted an amicus curiae brief, explicitly stating that production of the book would violate the BDSG. In the face of such overwhelming evidence, we have little doubt that German privacy laws conflict with the discovery laws of Texas.

As mentioned, the Restatement balancing test involves five factors. Two of the five factors are undisputed. First, as to the degree of specificity of the request, we note that the real parties' request is specific. All they seek is production of the one easily identifiable current corporate directory. Second, regarding where the document originated, VWAG is a German company and the book contains the names and other information of its German employees employed at its Wolfsburg plant and its facilities located in Brunswick, Emden, Kassel and Salzgitter, all within the country of Germany. The real parties do not contest that this book originated in Germany.

The remaining three factors deserve careful consideration. One, we must look to alternative discovery sources that are available. There are numerous alternative means that the real parties can and have used to obtain information which is the substantial equivalent of VWAG's current corporate phone book. VWAG produced its 1969 corporate phone book, and its United States subsidiary, Volkswagen of America, produced its current corporate phone book. Additionally, Erich Unterreiner, a current engineer for VWAG who also worked there in 1969, identified 29 past and present employees knowledgeable in the design of the 1970 model Volkswagen. He also provided a great deal of information about VWAG's organizational structure and identified Ernst Nockemann as "the man who did most of the design and development work in door latches." Therefore, there are adequate alternatives the real parties may use to discover the names of VWAG employees knowledgeable about the design of the subject vehicle.

Two, as to whether important interests of either this country or Germany are undermined, we conclude that, as asserted by Germany in its amicus curiae brief, its interests would be undermined if VWAG complied with the real parties' request for production. As we discussed, production of the book would violate German privacy laws. And, there is no evidence in the record suggesting that VWAG's failure to produce this phone book would undermine any important interest of this country, particularly when the record shows that alternative methods for obtaining the information exist.

Finally, VWAG's current corporate phone book bears little importance to the present litigation. The real parties already possess VWAG's 1969 corporate phone book that contains the names of the people who worked on the 1970 model Volkswagen. They have Volkswagen of America's current corporate phone book. And, they have the names of many VWAG employees directly responsible for the design and construction of the 1970 model Volkswagen. The plaintiffs simply desire to have the telephone book produced so they might double check the information provided in previous requests.

The trial court failed to balance the interests of the foreign sovereign with those of the real parties in any respect. In fact, the trial court rejected any consideration of German law. This was an abuse of discretion. Further, based on the record, we conclude that the trial court abused its discretion in ordering production of the book in question. VWAG's current corporate phone book should not be produced in contravention of German law. . . .

NOTES & QUESTIONS

1. ***The Effects of Foreign Data Protection Law on the United States.*** The *Valdez* case shows another way in which foreign data protection law can affect the United States. Prior to this opinion, a Texas trial court had ordered Volkwagen A.G. to turn over information located in Germany. In *Valdez*, the Texas Supreme Court reversed this lower court because its order would violate the legal obligation under U.S. Foreign Relations law to balance the interest of a foreign sovereign with those of the U.S. court. How well do you think the Texas High Court balanced the different interests involved? Why was the information in the corporate phone book considered to be personal data?

2. ***Privacy Logs.*** In *In re Vitamins Antitrust Litigation*, 2001 WL 1049433 (D.D.C. 2001), a U.S. district court allowed German defendants to maintain a "privacy log detailing exactly what requested information would be covered by the German privacy laws." This court felt that the protective order in the case provided some privacy protection, and also believed that the German defendants should "not be allowed to withhold information based upon minor inequivalencies between the Protective Order in this case and the [Federal Data Protection statute of Germany]." But the court also noted that the German defendants appeared "to have some legitimate privacy law concerns and that the Protective Order in this case may not be sufficiently detailed to shield them for criminal liability in their own country." Hence, to gain a better understanding of the information that was at stake and how necessary it would be to plaintiffs' claims, the court decided to allow the use of a privacy log, which would allow a determination of the importance of the information that was sought and "whether there was a way to amend the Protective Order to safeguard defendants from liability in the production of this information."

3. ***The Sedona Conference.*** A nonpartisan, nonprofit educational institute, the Sedona Conference has developed a guidance on cross-border transfers.[90] It identifies six principles to guide jurisdictional conflicts in this area. These are:

> (1) nonexclusive jurisdiction for the country or countries where data subjects live and organizations engage in their economic activities;
> (2) nonexclusive jurisdiction to any country "inextricably linked" to the contested data processing;
> (3) for "commercial transactions in which the contracting parties have comparable bargaining power," the "informed choice" of parties to a contract

---

[90] The Sedona Conference, *Commentary and Principles on Jurisdictional Conflicts over Transfers of Personal Data Across Borders* (June 2019).

is to "determine the jurisdiction or applicable law with respect to the processing of personal data in connection with the respective commercial transaction, and such choice should be respected so long as it bears a reasonable nexus to the parties and the transaction;

(4) other than in "commercial transactions, in which the natural person freely makes a choice, a person's choice of jurisdiction or law should not deprive him or her of protections that would otherwise be applicable to his or her data"; (5) "data in transit" should be treated as if were located in its place or origin "absent extraordinary circumstances"; and

(6) when personal data subject to the jurisdiction of a sovereign nation is material to "a litigation, investigation, or other legal proceeding" in another nation, such data is to be provided if subject to "appropriate safeguards."

Do these principles adequately protect the diverse interests present in cross-border transfers of personal data?

2. ADEQUATE LEVEL OF PROTECTION

Transborder Data Flows: An Adequacy Finding. Chapter V, Articles 44-50 of the GDPR establishes the rules for when Member States may permit the transfer of personal data to non-EU countries, or so-called "third countries." The GDPR sets out the same "adequacy standard" as found in the Data Protection Directive's Article 25. One path to adequacy is through a formal adequacy finding by the Commission. At Article 45, the GDPR states:

1. A transfer of personal data to a third country or an international organisation may take place where the Commission has decided that the third country, a territory or one or more specified sectors within that third country, or the international organisation in question ensures an adequate level of protection. Such a transfer shall not require any specific authorisation.

2. When assessing the adequacy of the level of protection, the Commission shall, in particular, take account of the following elements:

(a) the rule of law, respect for human rights and fundamental freedoms, relevant legislation, both general and sectoral, including concerning public security, defence, national security and criminal law and the access of public authorities to personal data, as well as the implementation of such legislation, data protection rules, professional rules and security measures, including rules for the onward transfer of personal data to another third country or international organisation which are complied with in that country or international organisation, case-law, as well as effective and enforceable data subject rights and effective administrative and judicial redress for the data subjects whose personal data are being transferred;

(b) the existence and effective functioning of one or more independent supervisory authorities in the third country or to which an international organisation is subject, with responsibility for ensuring and enforcing compliance with the data protection rules, including adequate enforcement powers, for assisting and advising the data subjects in exercising their rights and for cooperation with the supervisory authorities of the Member States; and

(c) the international commitments the third country or international organisation concerned has entered into, or other obligations arising from legally binding conventions or instruments as well as from its participation in multilateral or regional systems, in particular in relation to the protection of personal data.

As under the Directive, the GDPR blocks the transfer of personal information over which it has jurisdiction when the data are processed in a third-party country that fails to meet the requirements of "adequacy." What do you think the reason is behind this requirement? Is this an example of an "extraterritorial" application of European law?

Transfers Subject to Appropriate Safeguards. Even without a formal finding of adequacy, the GDPR foresees other paths to ensure a data transfer with an adequate level of protection. These are set out in Article 46, and include Binding Corporate Rules (BCRs) and Standard Contract Clauses (SCCs). BCRs are to apply within an entire organization and must be legally binding as well as approved by the appropriate data protection commission. The GDPR's Article 47 sets out detailed requirements for this path to adequacy. As for the SCCs, the GDPR requires the Commission to approve these arrangements. Art. 46(2)(c).

Exceptions to the Adequacy Requirement. The GDPR provides for certain derogations, or exceptions, to its adequacy requirement. Transfers of personal data to a third-party country that do not ensure an adequate level of protection may still take place on condition that the data subject has explicitly consented; the transfer of data is "necessary for the performance of a contract between the data subject and the controller"; and the transfer is necessary for "important reasons of public interest." Article 49. There are several additional exceptions.

Adequate Level of Protection. As the CJEU's *Schrems* decision makes clear, adequate protection means "essentially equivalent" protection. The full list of adequacy determinations of the EU (with the date of the finding) are as follows:

- Andorra (2010)
- Argentina (2003)
- Australia: Passenger Name Records Agreement (2008)
- Canada (2001) (commercial organizations only)
- Balliwick of Guersney (2003)
- Balliwick of Jersey (2008)
- The Faeroe Islands (2010)
- Isle of Man (2004)
- Israel (2011)
- Japan (2019)
- New Zealand (2012)
- Switzerland (2000)
- Uruguay (2012)

This list consists of the names of countries or otherwise autonomous areas and covers the entire country or autonomous area with two exceptions. First, Australia concluded an agreement to permit information from passengers on flights from the EU to the Australian Customs and Border Protection Service. Second, Canada has received an adequacy determination but only for those organizations that fall under Canada's Personal Information Protection and Electronic Documents Act (PIPEDA), which regulates commercial organizations.

The United States has never formally sought an adequacy determination from the European Commission for its entire legal system, as opposed to the more limited EU recognition of the Passenger Name Records Agreement and the Safe Harbor Principles. This reticence is likely due, according to Christopher Wolf, a leading D.C.-based privacy lawyer, "because of the well-understood outcome: request denied."[91] The Privacy Shield supplies an adequate level of data protection for U.S. companies that comply with its requirements.

Three countries are considered adequate due to their membership in the European Economic Area (EEA): Norway, Liechtenstein, and Iceland. Currently, the EU Commission is engaged in talks regarding an adequacy determination with South Korea.

3. FROM SAFE HARBOR TO PRIVACY SHIELD TO BEYOND

By the late 1980s, European policymakers realized that their efforts to create strong safeguards for data protection necessitated transborder policies for the data of EU citizens. Because of global data flows already present in that pre-Internet age, legal regulatory efforts in the EU were doomed to failure if their reach ended at the territorial borders of Europe. From the EU perspective, moreover, permitting an abuse of European citizens' personal information *outside* of Europe would make a mockery out of the decades of work to create high levels of privacy *inside* Europe. Important efforts followed at the trans-European level and within member states to fashion a legal response to the perceived threat to privacy of international data transfers.

The resulting EU policy requirement then and now is an "adequate level of protection" in any non-EU recipient nation before a transfer of personal data from an EU member state. Both the Directive (1995) and the GDPR (2016) contain this "adequacy" requirement.[92] In consequence, data transfers from the EU to the U.S. have a questionable legal status.

This legal uncertainty follows from EU skepticism about the sufficiency of U.S. information privacy law. In 1999, the Article 29 Working Party, the influential group of national data protection commissioners, summed up the European view of the matter. It declared that the "current patchwork of narrowly focused sectoral laws and voluntary self-regulation in the U.S. is not adequate."[93] Yet, with so much valuable data trade between the EU and U.S., both sides had considerable incentives to find policy solutions to bridge their different legal approaches to data privacy. The most significant first-generation outcome of this

---

[91] Christopher Wolf, *Delusions of Adequacy*, 43 Washington Univ. J.L. & Policy 227, 229 (2013).

[92] Directive, art. 56; GDPR, at art. 45.

[93] Working Party on the Protection of Individuals with regard to the Processing of Personal Data, *Opinion 1/99*, 2 DG MARKT Doc. 5092/98, WP 15 (Jan. 26, 1999).

policy effort was the Safe Harbor Agreement, a treaty negotiated by the U.S. Department of Commerce and the Commission of the EU.

In 1998, the U.S. Department of Commerce began negotiations with the EU Commission to formulate a "safe harbor" agreement to ensure that the United States met the EU Data Directive's "adequacy" requirement in Article 25. In July 2000, the negotiations yielded the Safe Harbor Arrangement as well as other supportive documents elaborating on the principles, such as letters and a list of Frequently Asked Questions.

The process for EU approval of the Safe Harbor agreement began with the EU Parliament, which issued a negative non-binding resolution about it. In this resolution, the EU Parliament condemned the Safe Harbor by a vote of 279 to 259 because of concerns over the adequacy of U.S. protections and the perception that the agreement had numerous loopholes.[94] The ultimate decision on whether the EU would approve the Safe Harbor agreement rested with the EU Commission, and on July 26, 2000, this entity approved it.

Decisions by organization to qualify for the Safe Harbor were voluntary, but once they joined it, they were required to publicly declare their compliance and to do so on a Department of Commerce website. The Safe Harbor represented a bold policy innovation: it transplanted EU data protection concepts into U.S. law in a fashion beyond the willingness of Congress or the ability of the FTC and other regulatory agencies. Its Principles were intended to be close enough to those of EU data protection so that the U.S. companies in following them would provide "adequate" data protection. Although U.S. companies needed only apply the Safe Harbor Principles to the personal data of Europeans, they were also free to bring all their data systems into compliance with it and apply these standards to U.S. citizens. In some instances, U.S. organizations decided to do so for reasons varying from managerial simplicity to policy leadership. In turn, the transplantation by the Safe Harbor of EU data protection onto U.S. territory proved politically palatable because decisions by U.S. companies to qualify for it were voluntary.

Another factor made the Safe Harbor acceptable in the U.S. As Paul Schwartz and Karl-Nikolaus Peifer have argued, "The Safe Harbor's negotiated standards weakened classic EU principles just enough to make the agreement tolerable on the American side of the Atlantic, but not too much to make them indefensible in Brussels."[95] At least, the EU at first did not view these standards as excessively watered down.[96]

Despite grumblings in the EU about the Safe Harbor, this treaty's future success seemed assured for the twenty-first century with over 5,000 U.S.

---

[94] Steven R. Salbu, The European Union Data Privacy Directive and International Relations, 35 Vand. J. Transnat'l L. 655, 678-79 (2002). There were 22 abstentions.

[95] Paul M. Schwartz & Karl-Nikolaus Peifer, Transatlantic Data Privacy, 106 Georgetown L.J. 115 (2017).

[96] Over time, the unhappiness in the EU with the Safe Harbor grew. For an indication of this evolving attitude see its commissioned reports from Galexia—an Australia consulting company—on the framework's weaknesses, Chris Connolly, *EU/US Safe Harbor—Effectiveness of the Framework in relation to National Security Surveillance*, GALEXIA (Oct 7, 2013), http://www.europarl.europa.eu/document/activities/cont/201310/20131008ATT72504/20131008A TT72504EN.pdf (testimony before the EU Parliament summarizing the 2008 and 2010 Galexia studies). For an analysis of the Galexia studies' strengths and weaknesses and further reflections on the "Unsafe Harbor," see THORSTEN HENNRICH, CLOUD COMPUTING 180–86 (2016).

companies entering it.[97] When the Commission and the Commerce Department began to consider improvements in a "Safe Harbor 2.0" in 2012, many in the U.S. expected only tinkering with the accepted formula. This expectation was, in turn, dashed by the Edward Snowden revelations, which began in June 2013. A former government analyst, Snowden leaked documents that detailed widespread collaboration by American companies with the NSA and called into doubt the "adequacy" of the protection in the U.S.

Then on October 6, 2015, the European Court of Justice's opinion in *Schrems v. Data Protection Commissioner* (*Schrems I*) ended any hope of only minor changes to the Safe Harbor. This judgment voided the Safe Harbor agreement and, thereby, strengthened the hand of EU negotiators in the ongoing discussions that would lead to the Privacy Shield. The European Commission gave its final approval to this new agreement in February 2016. Over 5,300 U.S. companies joined this agreement before the CJEU invalidated it in its Schrems II decision on July 16, 2020. At the same time, however, the EU Court upheld the validity of the standard contractual clauses, an alternate way for organization in non-adequate countries to receive personal information from the EU.

SCHREMS V. DATA PROTECTION COMMISSIONER (JOINED BY DIGITAL RIGHTS IRELAND) [SCHREMS I]

European Court of Justice, Case C-362/14 (6 October 2015)

---

2. The request has been made in proceedings between Mr Schrems and the Data Protection Commissioner ('the Commissioner') concerning the latter's refusal to investigate a complaint made by Mr Schrems regarding the fact that Facebook Ireland Ltd ('Facebook Ireland') transfers the personal data of its users to the United States of America and keeps it on servers located in that country.

The dispute in the main proceedings and the questions referred for a preliminary ruling

26. Mr Schrems, an Austrian national residing in Austria, has been a user of the Facebook social network ('Facebook') since 2008.

27. Any person residing in the European Union who wishes to use Facebook is required to conclude, at the time of his registration, a contract with Facebook Ireland, a subsidiary of Facebook Inc. which is itself established in the United States. Some or all of the personal data of Facebook Ireland's users who reside in the European Union is transferred to servers belonging to Facebook Inc. that are located in the United States, where it undergoes processing.

28. On 25 June 2013 Mr Schrems made a complaint to the Commissioner by which he in essence asked the latter to exercise his statutory powers by prohibiting Facebook Ireland from transferring his personal data to the United States. He contended in his complaint that the law and practice in force in that country did not ensure adequate protection of the personal data held in its territory against the

---

[97] The Department of Commerce continues to maintain the Safe Harbor List with its 5,457 entries. *See* U.S.–EU Safe Harbor List, Export, https://safeharbor.export.gov/list.aspx.

surveillance activities that were engaged in there by the public authorities. Mr Schrems referred in this regard to the revelations made by Edward Snowden concerning the activities of the United States intelligence services, in particular those of the National Security Agency ('the NSA').

29. Since the Commissioner took the view that he was not required to investigate the matters raised by Mr Schrems in the complaint, he rejected it as unfounded. The Commissioner considered that there was no evidence that Mr Schrems' personal data had been accessed by the NSA. He added that the allegations raised by Mr Schrems in his complaint could not be profitably put forward since any question of the adequacy of data protection in the United States had to be determined in accordance with Decision 2000/520 and the Commission had found in that decision that the United States ensured an adequate level of protection.

30. Mr Schrems brought an action before the High Court challenging the decision at issue in the main proceedings. After considering the evidence adduced by the parties to the main proceedings, the High Court found that the electronic surveillance and interception of personal data transferred from the European Union to the United States serve necessary and indispensable objectives in the public interest. However, it added that the revelations made by Edward Snowden had demonstrated a 'significant over-reach' on the part of the NSA and other federal agencies.

32. The High Court stated that Irish law precludes the transfer of personal data outside national territory save where the third country ensures an adequate level of protection for privacy and fundamental rights and freedoms. The importance of the rights to privacy and to inviolability of the dwelling, which are guaranteed by the Irish Constitution, requires that any interference with those rights be proportionate and in accordance with the law.

34. . . . . [T]he High Court considers that this case concerns the implementation of EU law as referred to in Article 51 of the Charter and that the legality of the decision at issue in the main proceedings must therefore be assessed in the light of EU law. . . . .

35. The High Court further observes that in his action Mr Schrems in reality raises the legality of the safe harbour regime which was established by Decision 2000/520 and gives rise to the decision at issue in the main proceedings. . . .

Consideration of the questions referred

The powers of the national supervisory authorities, within the meaning of Article 28 of Directive 95/46, when the Commission has adopted a decision pursuant to Article 25(6) of that directive.

38. It should be recalled first of all that the provisions of Directive 95/46, inasmuch as they govern the processing of personal data liable to infringe fundamental freedoms, in particular the right to respect for private life, must necessarily be interpreted in the light of the fundamental rights guaranteed by the Charter.

41. The guarantee of the independence of national supervisory authorities is intended to ensure the effectiveness and reliability of the monitoring of compliance

with the provisions concerning protection of individuals with regard to the processing of personal data and must be interpreted in the light of that aim. It was established in order to strengthen the protection of individuals and bodies affected by the decisions of those authorities. The establishment in Member States of independent supervisory authorities is therefore, as stated in recital 62 in the preamble to Directive 95/46, an essential component of the protection of individuals with regard to the processing of personal data.

53. [A] Commission decision adopted pursuant to Article 25(6) of Directive 95/46, such as Decision 2000/520, cannot prevent persons whose personal data has been or could be transferred to a third country from lodging with the national supervisory authorities a claim, within the meaning of Article 28(4) of that directive, concerning the protection of their rights and freedoms in regard to the processing of that data. Likewise, ... , a decision of that nature cannot eliminate or reduce the powers expressly accorded to the national supervisory authorities by Article 8(3) of the Charter and Article 28 of the directive.

57. . . . . Article 28 of Directive 95/46 applies, by its very nature, to any processing of personal data. Thus, even if the Commission has adopted a decision pursuant to Article 25(6) of that directive, the national supervisory authorities, when hearing a claim lodged by a person concerning the protection of his rights and freedoms in regard to the processing of personal data relating to him, must be able to examine, with complete independence, whether the transfer of that data complies with the requirements laid down by the directive.

58. If that were not so, persons whose personal data has been or could be transferred to the third country concerned would be denied the right, guaranteed by Article 8(1) and (3) of the Charter, to lodge with the national supervisory authorities a claim for the purpose of protecting their fundamental rights.

59. A claim, within the meaning of Article 28(4) of Directive 95/46, by which a person whose personal data has been or could be transferred to a third country contends, as in the main proceedings, that, notwithstanding what the Commission has found in a decision adopted pursuant to Article 25(6) of that directive, the law and practices of that country do not ensure an adequate level of protection must be understood as concerning, in essence, whether that decision is compatible with the protection of the privacy and of the fundamental rights and freedoms of individuals.

66. Having regard to the foregoing considerations, the answer to the questions referred is that Article 25(6) of Directive 95/46, read in the light of Articles 7, 8 and 47 of the Charter, must be interpreted as meaning that a decision adopted pursuant to that provision, such as Decision 2000/520, by which the Commission finds that a third country ensures an adequate level of protection, does not prevent a supervisory authority of a Member State, within the meaning of Article 28 of that directive, from examining the claim of a person concerning the protection of his rights and freedoms in regard to the processing of personal data relating to him which has been transferred from a Member State to that third country when that person contends that the law and practices in force in the third country do not ensure an adequate level of protection.

The validity of Decision 2000/520

73. The word 'adequate' in Article 25(6) of Directive 95/46 admittedly signifies that a third country cannot be required to ensure a level of protection identical to that guaranteed in the EU legal order. However, as the Advocate General has observed in point 141 of his Opinion, the term 'adequate level of protection' must be understood as requiring the third country in fact to ensure, by reason of its domestic law or its international commitments, a level of protection of fundamental rights and freedoms that is essentially equivalent to that guaranteed within the European Union by virtue of Directive 95/46 read in the light of the Charter. If there were no such requirement, the objective referred to in the previous paragraph of the present judgment would be disregarded. Furthermore, the high level of protection guaranteed by Directive 95/46 read in the light of the Charter could easily be circumvented by transfers of personal data from the European Union to third countries for the purpose of being processed in those countries.

74. It is clear from the express wording of Article 25(6) of Directive 95/46 that it is the legal order of the third country covered by the Commission decision that must ensure an adequate level of protection. . . .

75. Accordingly, when examining the level of protection afforded by a third country, the Commission is obliged to assess the content of the applicable rules in that country resulting from its domestic law or international commitments and the practice designed to ensure compliance with those rules, since it must, under Article 25(2) of Directive 95/46, take account of all the circumstances surrounding a transfer of personal data to a third country.

76. Also, in the light of the fact that the level of protection ensured by a third country is liable to change, it is incumbent upon the Commission, after it has adopted a decision pursuant to Article 25(6) of Directive 95/46, to check periodically whether the finding relating to the adequacy of the level of protection ensured by the third country in question is still factually and legally justified. Such a check is required, in any event, when evidence gives rise to a doubt in that regard.

78. In this regard, it must be stated that, in view of, first, the important role played by the protection of personal data in the light of the fundamental right to respect for private life and, secondly, the large number of persons whose fundamental rights are liable to be infringed where personal data is transferred to a third country not ensuring an adequate level of protection, the Commission's discretion as to the adequacy of the level of protection ensured by a third country is reduced, with the result that review of the requirements stemming from Article 25 of Directive 95/46, read in the light of the Charter, should be strict.

86. Thus, Decision 2000/520 lays down that 'national security, public interest, or law enforcement requirements' have primacy over the safe harbour principles, primacy pursuant to which self-certified United States organisations receiving personal data from the European Union are bound to disregard those principles without limitation where they conflict with those requirements and therefore prove incompatible with them.

87. In the light of the general nature of the derogation set out in the fourth paragraph of Annex I to Decision 2000/520, that decision thus enables interference, founded on national security and public interest requirements or on domestic legislation of the United States, with the fundamental rights of the

persons whose personal data is or could be transferred from the European Union to the United States. To establish the existence of an interference with the fundamental right to respect for private life, it does not matter whether the information in question relating to private life is sensitive or whether the persons concerned have suffered any adverse consequences on account of that interference.

88. In addition, Decision 2000/520 does not contain any finding regarding the existence, in the United States, of rules adopted by the State intended to limit any interference with the fundamental rights of the persons whose data is transferred from the European Union to the United States, interference which the State entities of that country would be authorised to engage in when they pursue legitimate objectives, such as national security.

89. Nor does Decision 2000/520 refer to the existence of effective legal protection against interference of that kind. . . .

92. Furthermore and above all, protection of the fundamental right to respect for private life at EU level requires derogations and limitations in relation to the protection of personal data to apply only in so far as is strictly necessary.

93. Legislation is not limited to what is strictly necessary where it authorises, on a generalised basis, storage of all the personal data of all the persons whose data has been transferred from the European Union to the United States without any differentiation, limitation or exception being made in the light of the objective pursued and without an objective criterion being laid down by which to determine the limits of the access of the public authorities to the data, and of its subsequent use, for purposes which are specific, strictly restricted and capable of justifying the interference which both access to that data and its use entail . . . .

94. In particular, legislation permitting the public authorities to have access on a generalised basis to the content of electronic communications must be regarded as compromising the essence of the fundamental right to respect for private life, as guaranteed by Article 7 of the Charter.

95. Likewise, legislation not providing for any possibility for an individual to pursue legal remedies in order to have access to personal data relating to him, or to obtain the rectification or erasure of such data, does not respect the essence of the fundamental right to effective judicial protection, as enshrined in Article 47 of the Charter. The first paragraph of Article 47 of the Charter requires everyone whose rights and freedoms guaranteed by the law of the European Union are violated to have the right to an effective remedy before a tribunal in compliance with the conditions laid down in that article. The very existence of effective judicial review designed to ensure compliance with provisions of EU law is inherent in the existence of the rule of law . . . .

102. The first subparagraph of Article 3(1) of Decision 2000/520 must . . . be understood as denying the national supervisory authorities the powers which they derive from Article 28 of Directive 95/46, where a person, in bringing a claim under that provision, puts forward matters that may call into question whether a Commission decision that has found, on the basis of Article 25(6) of the directive, that a third country ensures an adequate level of protection is compatible with the protection of the privacy and of the fundamental rights and freedoms of individuals.

103. The implementing power granted by the EU legislature to the Commission in Article 25(6) of Directive 95/46 does not confer upon it

competence to restrict the national supervisory authorities' powers referred to in the previous paragraph of the present judgment

106. Having regard to all the foregoing considerations, it is to be concluded that Decision 2000/520 is invalid.

NOTES & QUESTIONS

1. *The* **Shrems I** *Holding.* In *Schrems*, the CJEU struck down the Safe Harbor arrangement. This opinion also takes decisive steps to develop the EU constitutional law of data protection. First, the CJEU identified a violation of Article 7 of the Charter by the Safe Harbor's providing access to the U.S. government of the data of EU citizens. Second, it provided a constitutional analysis regarding the "adequacy" standard of the Directive. In *Schrems*, the Luxembourg Court observed that "an adequate level of protection" in any international data transfer meant "a level of protection of fundamental rights and freedoms that is *essentially equivalent* to that guaranteed within the European Union" (emphasis supplied). Finally, it found that the Charter's Article 8(1) and (3) safeguarded the "complete independence" of data protection commissioners.

2. *Standard Contractual Clauses and Binding Corporate Rules.* Beyond the Safe Harbor, the EU has approved two sets of Standard Contract Clauses (SCCs) to allow data transfers. Companies that follow these "off-the-rack" terms for a given data transfer will be considered to have met the EU's adequacy standard. In addition to the SCCs, the EU permits the use of Binding Corporate Rules (BCRs) as a means to meet the Directive's "adequacy test." BCRs can be used only when international data transfers occur within a single company or a group of affiliated companies. Companies that have gone through the EU approval process for a BCR include Accenture, BP, e-Bay, General Electric, HP, and Michelin.[98] The GDPR permits the use of BCRs as a way for a company to demonstrate adequate data protection for an international data transfer. Its Article 47 contains detailed rules for approval of BCRs by a supervisory authority.

3. *The Same Fate for SCCs and BCRs?* Soon after the *Schrems I* decision, observers began to wonder if the same objections raised to Safe Harbor adequacy might not be made to SCCs and BCR's. The CJEU had found, after all, that the Safe Harbor did not provide adequate protection against access to information by U.S. intelligence agencies. The CJEU also called for a standard of "essentially equivalent" protection in looking at the totality of protection in the third-party nation.

In follow-up litigation in Ireland, Max Schrems challenged the SCCs before the CJEU. In *Schrems II*, which we excerpt below, the CJEU upheld the SCCs, placed some new obligations regarding their use, and invalidated the Privacy Shield, the successor agreement to the Safe Harbor. As in *Schrems I*, the issue

---

[98] Francoise Gilbert, Binding Corporate Rules 451, 463-64 in I Eighth Annual Institute on Privacy and Security Law (Francoise Gilbert et al. eds., 2007).

before the Court was a transfer by Facebook from its Dublin headquarters to the U.S. Before turning to *Schrems II*, we will first examine the Privacy Shield.

U.S. DEPARTMENT OF COMMERCE, EU-U.S. PRIVACY SHIELD FRAMEWORK PRINCIPLES

(July 7, 2016)

I. OVERVIEW

1. While the United States and the European Union share the goal of enhancing privacy protection, the United States takes a different approach to privacy from that taken by the European Union. The United States uses a sectoral approach that relies on a mix of legislation, regulation, and self-regulation. Given those differences and to provide organizations in the United States with a reliable mechanism for personal data transfers to the United States from the European Union while ensuring that EU data subjects continue to benefit from effective safeguards and protection as required by European legislation with respect to the processing of their personal data when they have been transferred to non-EU countries, the Department of Commerce is issuing these Privacy Shield Principles, including the Supplemental Principles (collectively 'the Principles') under its statutory authority to foster, promote, and develop international commerce (15 U.S.C. § 1512). The Principles were developed in consultation with the European Commission, and with industry and other stakeholders, to facilitate trade and commerce between the United States and European Union. They are intended for use solely by organizations in the United States receiving personal data from the European Union for the purpose of qualifying for the Privacy Shield and thus benefitting from the European Commission's adequacy decision. . . .

2. In order to rely on the Privacy Shield to effectuate transfers of personal data from the EU, an organization must self-certify its adherence to the Principles to the Department of Commerce (or its designee) ('the Department'). While decisions by organizations to thus enter the Privacy Shield are entirely voluntary, effective compliance is compulsory: organizations that self-certify to the Department and publicly declare their commitment to adhere to the Principles must comply fully with the Principles. In order to enter the Privacy Shield, an organization must (a) be subject to the investigatory and enforcement powers of the Federal Trade Commission (the 'FTC'), the Department of Transportation or another statutory body that will effectively ensure compliance with the Principles (other U.S. statutory bodies recognized by the EU may be included as an annex in the future); (b) publicly declare its commitment to comply with the Principles; (c) publicly disclose its privacy policies in line with these Principles; and (d) fully implement them. An organization's failure to comply is enforceable under Section 5 of the Federal Trade Commission Act prohibiting unfair and deceptive acts in or affecting commerce (15 U.S.C. § 45(a)) or other laws or regulations prohibiting such acts.

3. The Department of Commerce will maintain and make available to the public an authoritative list of U.S. organizations that have self-certified to the Department

and declared their commitment to adhere to the Principles ('the Privacy Shield List'). . . .

4. The Department will also maintain and make available to the public an authoritative record of U.S. organizations that had previously self-certified to the Department, but that have been removed from the Privacy Shield List. . . .

5. Adherence to these Principles may be limited: (a) to the extent necessary to meet national security, public interest, or law enforcement requirements; (b) by statute, government regulation, or case law that creates conflicting obligations or explicit authorizations, provided that, in exercising any such authorization, an organization can demonstrate that its non-compliance with the Principles is limited to the extent necessary to meet the overriding legitimate interests furthered by such authorization; or (c) if the effect of the Directive or Member State law is to allow exceptions or derogations, provided such exceptions or derogations are applied in comparable contexts. Consistent with the goal of enhancing privacy protection, organizations should strive to implement these Principles fully and transparently, including indicating in their privacy policies where exceptions to the Principles permitted by (b) above will apply on a regular basis. For the same reason, where the option is allowable under the Principles and/or U.S. law, organizations are expected to opt for the higher protection where possible.

8. Definitions:

   a. 'Personal data' and 'personal information' are data about an identified or identifiable individual that are within the scope of the Directive, received by an organization in the United States from the European Union, and recorded in any form.
   b. 'Processing' of personal data means any operation or set of operations which is performed upon personal data, whether or not by automated means, such as collection, recording, organization, storage, adaptation or alteration, retrieval, consultation, use, disclosure or dissemination, and erasure or destruction.
   c. 'Controller' means a person or organization which, alone or jointly with others, determines the purposes and means of the processing of personal data.

II. PRINCIPLES

1. Notice

   a. An organization must inform individuals about:
      i.   its participation in the Privacy Shield and provide a link to, or the web address for, the Privacy Shield List,
      ii. the types of personal data collected and, where applicable, the entities or subsidiaries of the organization also adhering to the Principles,
      iii. its commitment to subject to the Principles all personal data received from the EU in reliance on the Privacy Shield,

iv. the purposes for which it collects and uses personal information about them,

v. how to contact the organization with any inquiries or complaints, including any relevant establishment in the EU that can respond to such inquiries or complaints,

vi. the type or identity of third parties to which it discloses personal information, and the purposes for which it does so,

vii. the right of individuals to access their personal data,

viii. the choices and means the organization offers individuals for limiting the use and disclosure of their personal data,

ix. the independent dispute resolution body designated to address complaints and provide appropriate recourse free of charge to the individual, and whether it is: (1) the panel established by DPAs, (2) an alternative dispute resolution provider based in the EU, or (3) an alternative dispute resolution provider based in the United States,

x. being subject to the investigatory and enforcement powers of the FTC, the Department of Transportation or any other U.S. authorized statutory body,

xi. the possibility, under certain conditions, for the individual to invoke binding arbitration,

xii. the requirement to disclose personal information in response to lawful requests by public authorities, including to meet national security or law enforcement requirements, and

xiii. its liability in cases of onward transfers to third parties.

b. This notice must be provided in clear and conspicuous language when individuals are first asked to provide personal information to the organization or as soon thereafter as is practicable, but in any event before the organization uses such information for a purpose other than that for which it was originally collected or processed by the transferring organization or discloses it for the first time to a third party.

2. Choice

a. An organization must offer individuals the opportunity to choose (opt out) whether their personal information is (i) to be disclosed to a third party or (ii) to be used for a purpose that is materially different from the purpose(s) for which it was originally collected or subsequently authorized by the individuals. Individuals must be provided with clear, conspicuous, and readily available mechanisms to exercise choice.

b. By derogation to the previous paragraph, it is not necessary to provide choice when disclosure is made to a third party that is acting as an agent to perform task(s) on behalf of and under the instructions of the organization. However, an organization shall always enter into a contract with the agent.

c. For sensitive information (i.e., personal information specifying medical or health conditions, racial or ethnic origin, political opinions, religious or philosophical beliefs, trade union membership or information specifying the sex life of the individual), organizations must obtain affirmative express consent (opt in) from individuals if such information is to be (i) disclosed to a third party or (ii) used for a purpose other than those for which it was originally collected or subsequently authorized by the individuals through the exercise of opt-in choice. . . .

3. Accountability for Onward Transfer

    a. To transfer personal information to a third party acting as a controller, organizations must comply with the Notice and Choice Principles. Organizations must also enter into a contract with the third-party controller that provides that such data may only be processed for limited and specified purposes consistent with the consent provided by the individual and that the recipient will provide the same level of protection as the Principles and will notify the organization if it makes a determination that it can no longer meet this obligation. . . .

    b. To transfer personal data to a third party acting as an agent, organizations must: (i) transfer such data only for limited and specified purposes; (ii) ascertain that the agent is obligated to provide at least the same level of privacy protection as is required by the Principles; (iii) take reasonable and appropriate steps to ensure that the agent effectively processes the personal information transferred in a manner consistent with the organization's obligations under the Principles; (iv) require the agent to notify the organization if it makes a determination that it can no longer meet its obligation to provide the same level of protection as is required by the Principles; (v) upon notice, including under (iv), take reasonable and appropriate steps to stop and remediate unauthorized processing; and (vi) provide a summary or a representative copy of the relevant privacy provisions of its contract with that agent to the Department upon request.

4. Security

    a. Organizations creating, maintaining, using or disseminating personal information must take reasonable and appropriate measures to protect it from loss, misuse and unauthorized access, disclosure, alteration and destruction, taking into due account the risks involved in the processing and the nature of the personal data.

5. Data integrity and purpose limitation

    a. Consistent with the Principles, personal information must be limited to the information that is relevant for the purposes of processing. An organization may not process personal information in a way that is incompatible with the purposes for which it has been collected or subsequently authorized by the individual. To the extent necessary for those purposes, an organization must take reasonable steps to ensure that personal data is reliable for its intended use, accurate, complete, and current. An organization must adhere to the Principles for as long as it retains such information.

b. Information may be retained in a form identifying or making identifiable the individual only for as long as it serves a purpose of processing within the meaning of 5a. This obligation does not prevent organizations from processing personal information for longer periods for the time and to the extent such processing reasonably serves the purposes of archiving in the public interest, journalism, literature and art, scientific or historical research, and statistical analysis. . . .

6. Access

a. Individuals must have access to personal information about them that an organization holds and be able to correct, amend, or delete that information where it is inaccurate, or has been processed in violation of the Principles, except where the burden or expense of providing access would be disproportionate to the risks to the individual's privacy in the case in question, or where the rights of persons other than the individual would be violated.

7. Recourse, enforcement and liability

a. Effective privacy protection must include robust mechanisms for assuring compliance with the Principles, recourse for individuals who are affected by non-compliance with the Principles, and consequences for the organization when the Principles are not followed. At a minimum such mechanisms must include:
   i. readily available independent recourse mechanisms by which each individual's complaints and disputes are investigated and expeditiously resolved at no cost to the individual and by reference to the Principles, and damages awarded where the applicable law or private-sector initiatives so provide;
   ii. follow-up procedures for verifying that the attestations and assertions organizations make about their privacy practices are true and that privacy practices have been implemented as presented and, in particular, with regard to cases of non-compliance; and
   iii. obligations to remedy problems arising out of failure to comply with the Principles by organizations announcing their adherence to them and consequences for such organizations. Sanctions must be sufficiently rigorous to ensure compliance by organizations. . . .

d. In the context of an onward transfer, a Privacy Shield organization has responsibility for the processing of personal information it receives under the Privacy Shield and subsequently transfers to a third party acting as an agent on its behalf. The Privacy Shield organization shall remain liable under the Principles if its agent processes such personal information in a manner inconsistent with the Principles, unless the organization proves that it is not responsible for the event giving rise to the damage. . . .

III. SUPPLEMENTAL PRINCIPLES

1. Sensitive Data
   a. An organization is not required to obtain affirmative express consent (opt in) with respect to sensitive data where the processing is:
      i. in the vital interests of the data subject or another person;
      ii. necessary for the establishment of legal claims or defenses;
      iii. required to provide medical care or diagnosis;
      iv. carried out in the course of legitimate activities by a foundation, association or any other non-profit body with a political, philosophical, religious or trade-union aim and on condition that the processing relates solely to the members of the body or to the persons who have regular contact with it in connection with its purposes and that the data are not disclosed to a third party without the consent of the data subjects;
      v. necessary to carry out the organization's obligations in the field of employment law; or
      vi. related to data that are manifestly made public by the individual.

2. Journalistic Exceptions

   a. Given U.S. constitutional protections for freedom of the press and the Directive's exemption for journalistic material, where the rights of a free press embodied in the First Amendment of the U.S. Constitution intersect with privacy protection interests, the First Amendment must govern the balancing of these interests with regard to the activities of U.S. persons or organizations.
   b. Personal information that is gathered for publication, broadcast, or other forms of public communication of journalistic material, whether used or not, as well as information found in previously published material disseminated from media archives, is not subject to the requirements of the Privacy Shield Principles. . . .
8. Access

   a. The Access Principle in Practice
      i. Under the Privacy Shield Principles, the right of access is fundamental to privacy protection. In particular, it allows individuals to verify the accuracy of information held about them. The Access Principle means that individuals have the right to:
         1. obtain from an organization confirmation of whether or not the organization is processing personal data relating to them;
         2. have communicated to them such data so that they could verify its accuracy and the lawfulness of the processing; and
         3. have the data corrected, amended or deleted where it is inaccurate or processed in violation of the Principles. . . .
   b. Burden or Expense of Providing Access
      i. The right of access to personal data may be restricted in exceptional circumstances where the legitimate rights of persons other than the individual would be violated or where the burden or expense of

providing access would be disproportionate to the risks to the individual's privacy in the case in question. Expense and burden are important factors and should be taken into account but they are not controlling factors in determining whether providing access is reasonable.

PAUL M. SCHWARTZ & KARL-NIKOLAUS PEIFER, TRANSATLANTIC DATA PRIVACY LAW

106 Georgetown L.J. 115 (2017)

Like the Safe Harbor, the Privacy Shield is best understood as a mixture of EU and U.S. standards. Post-Snowden and *Schrems*, the EU could tug the resulting agreement closer to its fundamental principles. At the same time, the U.S. could sign it because it contained weaker versions of some of the core EU principles of data privacy. Moreover, many elements of the framework depend on future decisions as oversight mechanisms are deployed. Hence, U.S. negotiators could in good conscience agree to it and trust in future collaborative decision making with the EU. The four core Privacy Shield Principles concern "data integrity and purpose limitation," "choice," enforcement, and oversight. In assessing the Privacy Shield, we concentrate on those principles.

Data Integrity and Choice

The first key standard of the Privacy Shield is the "Data Integrity and Purpose Limitation Principle," which revisits the Safe Harbor's "Data Integrity Principle." The Privacy Shield adds language, front and center, regarding a requirement of "Purpose Limitation," which telegraphs its increased requirements around compatibility. The Principle also adds specific language, not found in the Safe Harbor, that emphasizes the existence of an "express prohibition on incompatible processing." U.S. companies must now pay greater attention to collection of personal information from EU citizens and the creation of limits to make only compatible uses of it. Moreover, the increased enforcement mechanisms of the Privacy Shield suggest greater pressure in the future from the EU on companies regarding incompatible uses of information.

"Data integrity and purpose limitation" are also bolstered within the Privacy Shield by a new requirement that restricts "onward transfers" of information. Such transfers to a third party must be for a limited and specified purpose and expressed in business-to-business agreements that provide the same level of protection as the Privacy Shield Principles. In this fashion, the European idea of a state protecting its citizens against bad decisions has been transplanted into international law and U.S. legal mechanisms. Here is a collective mechanism that places limits on individual privacy decision making.

From the perspective of U.S. negotiators, there is mixed news in this result. On the plus side, the language regarding a ban on incompatibility amounts to less than the full-blown EU concept. In EU law, a compatible use must be "specified, explicit, and legitimate."[99] Yet, the language of the Privacy Shield nonetheless moves U.S. companies, if taken seriously and enforced strongly, in a decisive direction towards the idea of "purpose specification."

The second key standard is "choice." The Privacy Shield establishes both opt-out and opt-in rights for the EU data subject whose personal information is being transferred to the U.S. It handles opt-in largely in the same fashion as the Safe Harbor. Before the processing of "sensitive data" of an EU citizen, organizations in the U.S. must obtain "the data subject's affirmative express consent." In other words, the Privacy Shield requires opt-in before processing such information. The concept of sensitive data is a long-established idea in EU data protection law, and a category that the GDPR expands further.[100] U.S. companies must make correct use of stringent EU consent mechanisms. In some instances, such as data processing involving sensitive information, the high requirements for consent will make problematic certain kinds of data transfers.[101]

As for opt-out, the Privacy Shield makes an important change to the Safe Harbor's regime. It creates a new category within compatibility, and one otherwise unknown to EU data protection law. It envisions a "materially changed, but still compatible" processing operation, which is made subject to an opt-out. This language represents an EU concession to the U.S.; it accepts the possibility that a "material" change in purpose may nonetheless still be close enough to the original purpose of collection not to require another round of individual consent. As for an *incompatible* use of information, the Privacy Shield explicitly forbids it without new consent. Under EU law, such consent must be specific, collected separately from the initial agreement to processing, and subject to a strict tying restriction.

The Privacy Shield brings the "choice" principle into closer alignment with EU protections for the data subject than the Safe Harbor had done.[102] At the same time, the U.S. negotiators could craft a new category for opt-out, namely that of a material, yet compatible, change in use. Here is a source for future EU–U.S. discussions and possible conflict. The two data privacy regimes are far apart on questions regarding compatibility and purpose specification. In resolving disputes around this issue, mechanisms for enforcement and oversight are critical. They are critical because through these new processes the EU and U.S. will create new shared concepts regarding compatibility and purpose specification. We now turn to enforcement and oversight.

---

[99] GDPR, at art. 5(1)(b).

[100] The GDPR refers to categories that include "personal data revealing racial or ethnic origin, political opinions, religious or philosophical beliefs, or trade union membership, and the processing of genetic data, biometric data for the purpose of uniquely identifying a natural person, data concerning health or data concerning a natural person's sex life or sexual orientation." GDPR, at art. 9(1).

[101] The health care sector in the U.S., for example, will face considerable challenges to use of the Privacy Shield and may choose to process personal data of EU citizens solely within the EU. This result follows in part from the strict standards for protecting sensitive data.

[102] From the U.S. perspective, the Safe Harbor contained weaker and, hence, more desirable language regarding consent.

Enforcement

The third set of core principles regards enforcement, and, here, the Privacy Shield marks a considerable change from the Safe Harbor. Enforcement represents the area in the Privacy Shield with the greatest American concessions and the strongest moves in the EU direction. In the words of the European Commission, the Privacy Shield contains strong supervision mechanisms "to ensure that companies follow the rules that they submitted themselves to."[103] The new section concerning redress is termed, "Recourse, Enforcement and Liability Principle." Redress under the Privacy Shield consists of both general enforcement mechanisms and a subset relating only to U.S. intelligence agencies. The general enforcement mechanisms are extensive; the data subject may place a complaint with a Privacy Shield company in the U.S.; complain to their national data protection authority; use alternative dispute resolution if the U.S. company signs up for it; and make use of the "Privacy Shield Panel," an arbitration mechanism that permits binding decisions against U.S. companies.

After the Snowden revelations and the *Schrems* decision, the issue of U.S. government access to the data of EU citizens became a critical issue in Privacy Shield negotiations. The Privacy Shield creates important safeguards regarding U.S. government access to personal data of EU citizens. Among the important changes relating to enforcement is the creation of a U.S. Ombudsperson, who is independent from U.S. intelligence services. The Ombudsperson will respond to individual complaints from individuals who believe that their personal data has been misused by U.S. national security agencies. The Privacy Shield agreement also references important congressional and Executive Branch changes regarding regulation of foreign intelligence surveillance by U.S. agencies. The aim is to document factual changes compared to the record that had been before the *Schrems* court in 2015. The step is a prudent one, taken in anticipation of future litigation in the EU.

Oversight

The fourth set of core principles regards oversight. There is now supervision of enforcement procedures by the FTC and the Department of Commerce as well as a specified process to remove companies with insufficient procedures from the Privacy Shield list and to subject them to sanctions. There is also an annual joint review of the Privacy Shield by EU and U.S. officials. Although the Safe Harbor included a limited number of these concepts, the Privacy Shield adds to the oversight list and heightens the overall requirements. To be sure, however, these requirements take the form of political commitments in an agreement with the EU rather than firm statutory obligations through U.S. law. Nonetheless, in the aftermath of *Schrems*, the Privacy Shield necessarily provides strong oversight of the NSA and U.S. intelligence community and provides new ways for EU citizens

---

[103] Communication from the Commission to the European Parliament and the Council—Transatlantic Data Flows: Restoring Trust through Strong Safeguards, COM (2016) 117 final (Feb. 29, 2016) [hereinafter Transatlantic Data Flows].

to obtain redress from the U.S. government as well as private organizations. By comparison, the Safe Harbor did not address national security surveillance.

In sum, the Privacy Shield displays concessions by both sides regarding their own legal models for data privacy. Above all, the document moves the system for data transfers more in the direction of EU data protection law than the Safe Harbor did. At the same time, from the U.S. perspective, the bottom line for the free flow of data was acceptable. At the press conference in Brussels announcing the Privacy Shield, U.S. Commerce Secretary Penny Pritzker declared that a "free flow of data" was assured "[f]or businesses."[104] Secretary Pritzker added, "For consumers, the free flow of data means that you can take advantage of the latest, most innovative digital products and services, no matter where they originate."[105]

NOTES & QUESTIONS

1. *FTC Enforcement.* The FTC brought its first enforcement action based on a company's entering into the Safe Harbor in 2009. By the time of the demise of the Safe Harbor, it had brought thirty-nine enforcement actions pursuant to this agreement. These actions fall roughly into two groups.

   First, the FTC includes an allegation of violation of the Safe Harbor in a complaint that also claims violations of Section 5 of the FTC Act. Examples of such an enforcement action include the actions against Myspace (2012), Facebook (2011), and Google (2012).

   Second, the FTC has acted against companies who made false Safe Harbor certification claims. These actions do not allege substantive violations of the Safe Harbor principles, but rather that a company falsely, deceptively, or misleadingly claimed that it held a valid certification. Companies make these claims either through statements in a privacy policy or a Safe Harbor certification mark on their Website. Some of these organizations joined the Safe Harbor, but failed to renew their annual certification while continuing to represent themselves as current members.

   In October 2009, for example, the FTC announced settlement agreements with six companies over charges that they falsely claimed membership in the Safe Harbor. In January 2014, the FTC announced Safe Harbor settlements with 12 companies over the same kind of charges. These companies include three professional football teams: the Atlanta Falcons, Denver Broncos, and Tennessee Titans. The 2014 settlements were also with BitTorrent, Inc., a provider of the peer-to-peer file -sharing protocol; DataMotion, Inc, a provider of an encrypted e-mail platform; and Reynolds Consumer Products, Inc., the maker of aluminum foil and other consumer products.

   As under the Safe Harbor, the FTC had important enforcement powers pursuant to the Privacy Shield. It has stated a commitment to four key areas:

---

[104] *Remarks by U.S. Secretary of Commerce Penny Pritzker at EU–U.S. Privacy Shield Framework Press Conference*, U.S. Dep't of Com. (July 12, 2016), https://www.commerce.gov/news/secretary-speeches/2016/07/remarks-us-secretary-commerce-penny-pritzker-eu-us-privacy-shield.

[105] *Id.*

(1) referral prioritization and investigations; (2) addressed false or deceptive Privacy Shield claims; (3) continued order monitoring; and (4) enhanced engagement and enforcement cooperation with EU data protection authorities.[106]

DATA PROTECTION COMMISSIONER V. FACEBOOK IRELAND LTD, AND MAXIMILLIAN SCHREMS [SCHREMS II]

CJEU , Case C-311/18 (July 16, 2020) (Grand Chamber)

42. In the judgment of 6 October 2015, *Schrems*, the Court declared Commission Decision 2000/520/EC of 26 July 2000 pursuant to Directive 95/46/EC of the European Parliament and of the Council on the adequacy of the protection provided by the safe harbour privacy principles and related frequently asked questions issued by the US Department of Commerce, in which the Commission had found that that third country ensured an adequate level of protection, invalid.

43. Following the delivery of that judgment, the Commission adopted the Privacy Shield Decision, after having, for the purposes of adopting that decision, assessed the US legislation, as stated in recital 65 of the decision:

'The Commission has assessed the limitations and safeguards available in U.S. law as regards access and use of personal data transferred under the EU-U.S. Privacy Shield by U.S. public authorities for national security, law enforcement and other public interest purposes. In addition, the U.S. government, through its Office of the Director of National Intelligence (ODNI) . . . , has provided the Commission with detailed representations and commitments that are contained in Annex VI to this decision. By letter signed by the Secretary of State and attached as Annex III to this decision the U.S. government has also committed to create a new oversight mechanism for national security interference, the Privacy Shield Ombudsperson, who is independent from the Intelligence Community. Finally, a representation from the U.S. Department of Justice, contained in Annex VII to this decision, describes the limitations and safeguards applicable to access and use of data by public authorities for law enforcement and other public interest purposes. In order to enhance transparency and to reflect the legal nature of these commitments, each of the documents listed and annexed to this decision will be published in the U.S. Federal Register.'

The dispute in the main proceedings and the questions referred for a preliminary ruling

50. Mr Schrems, an Austrian national residing in Austria, has been a user of the Facebook social network ('Facebook') since 2008.

51 Any person residing in the European Union who wishes to use Facebook is required to conclude, at the time of his or her registration, a contract with Facebook Ireland, a subsidiary of Facebook Inc. which is itself established in the United States. Some or all of the personal data of Facebook Ireland's users who reside in

---

[106] Letter from Chairwoman Edith Ramirez to Věra Jourová, Commissioner for Justice, Consumers and Gender Equality of the European Commission, Describing Federal Trade Commission Enforcement of the New EU-U.S. Privacy Shield Framework (July 7, 2016).

the European Union is transferred to servers belonging to Facebook Inc. that are located in the United States, where it undergoes processing.

55. In his reformulated complaint lodged on 1 December 2015, Mr Schrems claimed, inter alia, that United States law requires Facebook Inc. to make the personal data transferred to it available to certain United States authorities, such as the National Security Agency (NSA) and the Federal Bureau of Investigation (FBI). He submitted that, since that data was used in the context of various monitoring programmes in a manner incompatible with Articles 7, 8 and 47 of the Charter, the SCC Decision[107] cannot justify the transfer of that data to the United States. In those circumstances, Mr Schrems asked the Commissioner to prohibit or suspend the transfer of his personal data to Facebook Inc.

Consideration of the questions referred

The first question

80. By its first question, the referring court wishes to know, in essence, whether Article 2(1) and Article 2(2)(a), (b) and (d) of the GDPR, read in conjunction with Article 4(2) TEU,[108] must be interpreted as meaning that that regulation applies to the transfer of personal data by an economic operator established in a Member State to another economic operator established in a third country, in circumstances where, at the time of that transfer or thereafter, that data is liable to be processed by the authorities of that third country for the purposes of public security, defence and State security.

86. The possibility that the personal data transferred between two economic operators for commercial purposes might undergo, at the time of the transfer or thereafter, processing for the purposes of public security, defence and State security by the authorities of that third country cannot remove that transfer from the scope of the GDPR.

87. Indeed, by expressly requiring the Commission, when assessing the adequacy of the level of protection afforded by a third country, to take account, inter alia, of 'relevant legislation, both general and sectoral, including concerning public security, defence, national security and criminal law and the access of public authorities to personal data, as well as the implementation of such legislation', it is patent from the very wording of Article 45(2)(a) of that regulation that no processing by a third country of personal data for the purposes of public security, defence and State security excludes the transfer at issue from the application of the regulation.

---

[107] [The SCC Decision refers to the Commission's formal finding that the standard contractual clauses provided adequate protection. Commission Implementing Decision (EU) 2016/2297 of 16 December 2016 (OJ 2016 L 344, p. 100) ("the SCC Decision").]

[108] [TEU refers to the Treaty on the European Union. Article 4(2) TEU requires the EU to "respect the equality of Member States before the Treaties as well as their national identities." It further calls for the Union to respect "essential State functions, including . . . maintaining law and order and safeguarding national security. In particular, national security remains the sole responsibility of each Member State."]

The second, third and sixth questions

90. [T]he referring court asks the Court to specify which factors need to be taken into consideration for the purpose of determining whether that level of protection is ensured in the context of . . . a [data] transfer [to a country outside of the EU].

91. [I]n the absence of an adequacy decision under Article 45(3) of that regulation, a controller or processor may transfer personal data to a third country only if the controller or processor has provided 'appropriate safeguards', and on condition that 'enforceable data subject rights and effective legal remedies for data subjects' are available, such safeguards being able to be provided . . . by the standard data protection clauses adopted by the Commission.

95. [T]he GDPR states that, where 'a third country, a territory or a specified sector within a third country . . . no longer ensures an adequate level of data protection. . . . the transfer of personal data to that third country . . . should be prohibited, unless the requirements [of that regulation] relating to transfers subject to appropriate safeguards . . . are fulfilled'. . . . [I]n the absence of an adequacy decision, the appropriate safeguards to be taken by the controller or processor in accordance with Article 46(1) of the regulation must 'compensate for the lack of data protection in a third country' in order to 'ensure compliance with data protection requirements and the rights of the data subjects appropriate to processing within the Union'.

105. [T]he answer to the second, third and sixth questions is that Article 46(1) and Article 46(2)(c) of the GDPR must be interpreted as meaning that the appropriate safeguards, enforceable rights and effective legal remedies required by those provisions must ensure that data subjects whose personal data are transferred to a third country pursuant to standard data protection clauses are afforded a level of protection essentially equivalent to that guaranteed within the European Union by that regulation, read in the light of the Charter. To that end, the assessment of the level of protection afforded in the context of such a transfer must, in particular, take into consideration both the contractual clauses agreed between the controller or processor established in the European Union and the recipient of the transfer established in the third country concerned and, as regards any access by the public authorities of that third country to the personal data transferred. . . .

The eighth question

106. By its eighth question, the referring court wishes to know . . . [whether the] supervisory authority is required to suspend or prohibit a transfer of personal data to a third country pursuant to standard data protection clauses adopted by the Commission, if, in the view of that supervisory authority, those clauses are not or cannot be complied with in that third country . . .

107. [T]he national supervisory authorities are responsible for monitoring compliance with the EU rules concerning the protection of natural persons with regard to the processing of personal data. Each of those authorities is therefore vested with the power to check whether a transfer of personal data from its own

Member State to a third country complies with the requirements laid down in that regulation.

108. It follows from those provisions that the supervisory authorities' primary responsibility is to monitor the application of the GDPR and to ensure its enforcement. The exercise of that responsibility is of particular importance where personal data is transferred to a third country since, as is clear from recital 116 of that regulation, 'when personal data moves across borders outside the Union it may put at increased risk the ability of natural persons to exercise data protection rights in particular to protect themselves from the unlawful use or disclosure of that information'. . . .

110. Article 78(1) and (2) of the GDPR recognises the right of each person to an effective judicial remedy, in particular, where the supervisory authority fails to deal with his or her complaint. . . .

111. In order to handle complaints lodged, Article 58(1) of the GDPR confers extensive investigative powers on each supervisory authority. If a supervisory authority takes the view, following an investigation, that a data subject whose personal data have been transferred to a third country is not afforded an adequate level of protection in that country, it is required, under EU law, to take appropriate action in order to remedy any findings of inadequacy, irrespective of the reason for, or nature of, that inadequacy. . . .

113. [T]he supervisory authority is required . . . to suspend or prohibit a transfer of personal data to a third country if . . . the standard data protection clauses are not or cannot be complied with in that third country and the protection of the data transferred that is required by EU law cannot be ensured by other means, where the controller or a processor has not itself suspended or put an end to the transfer.

119. [A] Commission adequacy decision adopted pursuant to Article 45(3) of the GDPR cannot prevent persons whose personal data has been or could be transferred to a third country from lodging a complaint, within the meaning of Article 77(1) of the GDPR, with the competent national supervisory authority concerning the protection of their rights and freedoms in regard to the processing of that data. . . .

120. Thus, even if the Commission has adopted a Commission adequacy decision, the competent national supervisory authority, when a complaint is lodged by a person concerning the protection of his or her rights and freedoms in regard to the processing of personal data relating to him or her, must be able to examine, with complete independence, whether the transfer of that data complies with the requirements laid down by the GDPR and, where relevant, to bring an action before the national courts in order for them, if they share the doubts of that supervisory authority as to the validity of the Commission adequacy decision, to make a reference for a preliminary ruling for the purpose of examining its validity.

121. In the light of the foregoing considerations, the answer to the eighth question is that Article 58(2)(f) and (j) of the GDPR must be interpreted as meaning that, unless there is a valid Commission adequacy decision, the competent supervisory authority is required to suspend or prohibit a transfer of data to a third country pursuant to standard data protection clauses adopted by the Commission, if, in the view of that supervisory authority and in the light of all the circumstances of that transfer, those clauses are not or cannot be complied with in that third

country and the protection of the data transferred that is required by EU law . . . and by the Charter.

The 7th and 11th questions

122. By its 7th and 11th questions, which it is appropriate to consider together, the referring court seeks clarification from the Court, in essence, on the validity of the [Standard Contractual Clauses ("SCC")] Decision in the light of Articles 7, 8 and 47 of the Charter.

123. [T]he referring court asks whether the SCC Decision is capable of ensuring an adequate level of protection of the personal data transferred to third countries given that the standard data protection clauses provided for in that decision do not bind the supervisory authorities of those third countries.

125. [A]lthough those clauses are binding on a controller established in the European Union and the recipient of the transfer of personal data established in a third country where they have concluded a contract incorporating those clauses, it is common ground that those clauses are not capable of binding the authorities of that third country, since they are not party to the contract.

126. Therefore, although there are situations in which, depending on the law and practices in force in the third country concerned, the recipient of such a transfer is in a position to guarantee the necessary protection of the data solely on the basis of standard data protection clauses, there are others in which the content of those standard clauses might not constitute a sufficient means of ensuring, in practice, the effective protection of personal data transferred to the third country concerned. That is the case, in particular, where the law of that third country allows its public authorities to interfere with the rights of the data subjects to which that data relates.

127. Thus, the question arises whether a Commission decision concerning standard data protection clauses . . . is invalid in the absence, in that decision, of guarantees which can be enforced against the public authorities of the third countries to which personal data is or could be transferred pursuant to those clauses.

128. Article 46(1) of the GDPR provides that, in the absence of an adequacy decision, a controller or processor may transfer personal data to a third country only if the controller or processor has provided appropriate safeguards, and on condition that enforceable data subject rights and effective legal remedies for data subjects are available. . . .

132. Since by their inherently contractual nature standard data protection clauses cannot bind the public authorities of third countries, . . . it may prove necessary to supplement the guarantees contained in those standard data protection clauses. In that regard, recital 109 of the regulation states that 'the possibility for the controller . . . to use standard data-protection clauses adopted by the Commission ... should [not] prevent [it] . . . from adding other clauses or additional safeguards' and states, in particular, that the controller 'should be encouraged to provide additional safeguards . . . that supplement standard [data] protection clauses'.

133. It follows that the standard data protection clauses adopted by the Commission on the basis of Article 46(2)(c) of the GDPR are solely intended to provide contractual guarantees that apply uniformly in all third countries to

controllers and processors established in the European Union and, consequently, independently of the level of protection guaranteed in each third country. In so far as those standard data protection clauses cannot . . . provide guarantees beyond a contractual obligation to ensure compliance with the level of protection required under EU law, they may require . . . the adoption of supplementary measures by the controller in order to ensure compliance with that level of protection.

135. Where the controller or a processor established in the European Union is not able to take adequate additional measures to guarantee such protection, the controller or processor or, failing that, the competent supervisory authority, are required to suspend or end the transfer of personal data to the third country concerned. That is the case, in particular, where the law of that third country imposes on the recipient of personal data from the European Union obligations which are contrary to those clauses and are, therefore, capable of impinging on the contractual guarantee of an adequate level of protection against access by the public authorities of that third country to that data.

142. It follows that a controller established in the European Union and the recipient of personal data are required to verify, prior to any transfer, whether the level of protection required by EU law is respected in the third country concerned. The recipient is, where appropriate, under an obligation . . . to inform the controller of any inability to comply with those clauses, the latter then being, in turn, obliged to suspend the transfer of data and/or to terminate the contract.

147. [T]he task of enforcing that regulation is conferred, in principle, on each supervisory authority on the territory of its own Member State. . . . [I]n order to avoid divergent decisions, Article 64(2) of the GDPR provides for the possibility for a supervisory authority . . . to refer the matter to the European Data Protection Board (EDPB) for an opinion, which may, under Article 65(1)(c) of the GDPR, adopt a binding decision, in particular where a supervisory authority does not follow the opinion issued.

The 4th, 5th, 9th and 10th questions

150. By its ninth question, the referring court wishes to know, in essence, whether and to what extent findings in the Privacy Shield Decision to the effect that the United States ensures an adequate level of protection are binding on the supervisory authority of a Member State. . . .

164. [T]he Privacy Shield Decision . . . states. . . that adherence to those principles may be limited, inter alia, 'to the extent necessary to meet national security, public interest, or law enforcement requirements'. . . . .

165. [T]he Privacy Shield Decision thus enables interference, based on national security and public interest requirements or on domestic legislation of the United States, with the fundamental rights of the persons whose personal data is or could be transferred from the European Union to the United States. More particularly, as noted in the Privacy Shield Decision, such interference can arise from access to, and use of, personal data transferred from the European Union to the United States by US public authorities through the PRISM and UPSTREAM surveillance programmes under Section 702 of the FISA and E.O. 12333.

The finding of an adequate level of protection

168. In the light of the factors mentioned by the Commission in the Privacy Shield Decision and the referring court's findings in the main proceedings, the referring court harbours doubts as to whether US law in fact ensures the adequate level of protection. . . . In particular, that court considers that the law of that third country does not provide for the necessary limitations and safeguards with regard to the interferences authorised by its national legislation and does not ensure effective judicial protection against such interferences. As far as concerns effective judicial protection, it adds that the introduction of a Privacy Shield Ombudsperson cannot, in its view, remedy those deficiencies since an ombudsperson cannot be regarded as a tribunal within the meaning of Article 47 of the Charter.

171. The Court has held that the communication of personal data to a third party, such as a public authority, constitutes an interference with the fundamental rights enshrined in Articles 7 and 8 of the Charter, whatever the subsequent use of the information communicated. The same is true of the retention of personal data and access to that data with a view to its use by public authorities, irrespective of whether the information in question relating to private life is sensitive or whether the persons concerned have been inconvenienced in any way on account of that interference.

173. [U]nder Article 8(2) of the Charter, personal data must . . . be processed 'for specified purposes and on the basis of the consent of the person concerned or some other legitimate basis laid down by law'.

174. Furthermore, . . . any limitation on the exercise of the rights and freedoms recognised by the Charter must be provided for by law and respect the essence of those rights and freedoms. . . . [S]ubject to the principle of proportionality, limitations may be made to those rights and freedoms only if they are necessary and genuinely meet objectives of general interest recognised by the Union or the need to protect the rights and freedoms of others.

175. [A]ny limitation on the exercise of fundamental rights must be provided for by law implies that the legal basis which permits the interference with those rights must itself define the scope of the limitation on the exercise of the right concerned.

176. Lastly, in order to satisfy the requirement of proportionality according to which derogations from and limitations on the protection of personal data must apply only in so far as is strictly necessary, the legislation in question which entails the interference must lay down clear and precise rules governing the scope and application of the measure in question and imposing minimum safeguards, so that the persons whose data has been transferred have sufficient guarantees to protect effectively their personal data against the risk of abuse. . . .

177. Article 45(2)(a) of the GDPR states that, in its assessment of the adequacy of the level of protection in a third country, the Commission is, in particular, to take account of 'effective and enforceable data subject rights' for data subjects whose personal data are transferred.

179. [Regarding] the surveillance programmes based on Section 702 of the FISA, the Commission found, in recital 109 of the Privacy Shield Decision, that, according to that article, 'the FISC does not authorise individual surveillance measures; rather, it authorises surveillance programs (like PRISM, UPSTREAM)

on the basis of annual certifications prepared by the Attorney General and the Director of National Intelligence (DNI)'. As is clear from that recital, the supervisory role of the FISC is thus designed to verify whether those surveillance programmes relate to the objective of acquiring foreign intelligence information, but it does not cover the issue of whether 'individuals are properly targeted to acquire foreign intelligence information'.

180. It is thus apparent that Section 702 of the FISA does not indicate any limitations on the power it confers to implement surveillance programmes for the purposes of foreign intelligence or the existence of guarantees for non-US persons potentially targeted by those programmes. In those circumstances . . . , that article cannot ensure a level of protection essentially equivalent to that guaranteed by the Charter. . . .

181. [T]he US Government has accepted, in reply to a question put by the Court, that PPD-28 does not grant data subjects actionable rights before the courts against the US authorities. Therefore, the Privacy Shield Decision cannot ensure a level of protection essentially equivalent to that arising from the Charter. . . ,

182. As regards the monitoring programmes based on E.O. 12333, it is clear from the file before the Court that that order does not confer rights which are enforceable against the US authorities in the courts either.

183. It should be added that PPD-28 . . . allows for '"bulk" collection . . . of a relatively large volume of signals intelligence information or data under circumstances where the Intelligence Community cannot use an identifier associated with a specific target ... to focus the collection.' That possibility, which allows, in the context of the surveillance programmes based on E.O. 12333, access to data in transit to the United States without that access being subject to any judicial review, does not, in any event, delimit in a sufficiently clear and precise manner the scope of such bulk collection of personal data.

185. In those circumstances, the limitations on the protection of personal data arising from the domestic law of the United States on the access and use by US public authorities of such data transferred from the European Union to the United States, which the Commission assessed in the Privacy Shield Decision, are not circumscribed in a way that satisfies requirements that are essentially equivalent to those required, under EU law, by the second sentence of Article 52(1) of the Charter.

192. [A]s regards both the surveillance programmes based on Section 702 of the FISA and those based on E.O. 12333, it has been noted in paragraphs 181 and 182 above that neither PPD-28 nor E.O. 12333 grants data subjects rights actionable in the courts against the US authorities, from which it follows that data subjects have no right to an effective remedy.

193. The Commission found, however, in recitals 115 and 116 of the Privacy Shield Decision, that, as a result of the Ombudsperson Mechanism introduced by the US authorities, . . . the United States can be deemed to ensure a level of protection essentially equivalent to that guaranteed by Article 47 of the Charter.

194. [D]ata subjects must have the possibility of bringing legal action before an independent and impartial court in order to have access to their personal data, or to obtain the rectification or erasure of such data.

195. [T]he Ombudsperson is appointed by the Secretary of State and is an integral part of the US State Department, [and] the dismissal or revocation of the

appointment of the Ombudsperson is [not] accompanied by any particular guarantees, which is such as to undermine the Ombudsman's independence from the executive.

196. Similarly, . . . the Privacy Shield Decision refers to a commitment from the US Government that the relevant component of the intelligence services is required to correct any violation of the applicable rules detected by the Privacy Shield Ombudsperson, there is nothing in that decision to indicate that that ombudsperson has the power to adopt decisions that are binding on those intelligence services and does not mention any legal safeguards that would accompany that political commitment on which data subjects could rely.

197. Therefore, the ombudsperson mechanism to which the Privacy Shield Decision refers does not provide any cause of action before a body which offers the persons whose data is transferred to the United States guarantees essentially equivalent to those required by Article 47 of the Charter.

199. It follows that Article 1 of the Privacy Shield Decision is incompatible with Article 45(1) of the GDPR, read in the light of Articles 7, 8 and 47 of the Charter, and is therefore invalid.

201. In the light of all of the foregoing considerations, it is to be concluded that the Privacy Shield Decision is invalid.

202. As to whether it is appropriate to maintain the effects of that decision for the purposes of avoiding the creation of a legal vacuum, the Court notes that, in any event, in view of Article 49 of the GDPR, the annulment of an adequacy decision such as the Privacy Shield Decision is not liable to create such a legal vacuum. That article details the conditions under which transfers of personal data to third countries may take place in the absence of an adequacy decision under Article 45(3) of the GDPR or appropriate safeguards under Article 46 of the GDPR.

NOTES & QUESTIONS

1. *The Holding.* In *Schrems II*, the European Court of Justice (CJEU) issued a pathbreaking opinion. In a nutshell, it upheld the Standard Contractual Clauses (SCC) and invalidated the Privacy Shield. But this decision is highly complex and reached important matters in addition to these two elements.

   First, the CJEU noted that the GDPR applied to the matter before it and rejected the argument that the Treaty on the European Union (TEU) changed this result. The TEU places national security matters within the sole responsibility of the Member States. But GDPR Art. 45 explicitly discusses processing by national security authorities, and, therefore, the CJEU decided that the GDPR was squarely on point in this case.

   Second, it examined the Standard Contractual Clauses (SCC) Decision of the Commission, which approved this means for transferring personal data from EU member states to third countries. According to the CJEU, a transfer of data pursuant to the SCC had to provide "a level of protection essentially equivalent to that guaranteed in the European Union" by the GDPR and the Charter of Human Rights. It stated that any evaluation of the level of protection under the

SCC would have to include scrutiny of "any access by the public authorities of [a] third country to the personal data transferred."

Third, each member state's national supervisory authority was required to suspend or prohibit a transfer of data to the third state pursuant to an SCC if an investigation showed that the transfer did not meet the required level of protection.

Fourth, the CJEU placed important responsibilities on the controller or processor who made use of the SCC. In particular, the controller must "verify, prior to any transfer, whether the level of protection required by EU law is respected in the third country concerned." If there are concerns about the level of protection due to potential government surveillance, "supplementary measures" can be taken to address these concerns – though the CJEU did not specify what these measures would entail. If supplementary measures cannot address the concerns, the transfer of data cannot occur.

Finally, the CJEU invalidated the Privacy Shield. In the Court's view, the relevant law in the United States law regarding foreign surveillance did not meet EU standards, including the principle of proportionality. Among the flaws noted by the CJEU were the lack of limits on the scope of bulk collection of personal data; the lack of an effective remedy for a data subject from the EU, including the inability to bring legal action before an independent court; and the insufficiency of the ombudsperson mechanism.

2. ***Privacy Shield 2.0.*** Trying to find the lighter side of *Schrems II*, Omer Tene of the International Association of Privacy Professionals started a poll on Twitter immediately after *Schrems II* for the best name for the next agreement between the EU and U.S. The winner? "Last Chance." Another strong contender was "Pirate Bay," which was considered a fitting successor to the Safe Harbor and Privacy Shield.

   In a more somber reaction to the *Schrems II* decision, Secretary of Commerce Wilbur Ross noted that that the Department of Commerce was "deeply disappointed" in the decision and that it remained "in close contact with the European Commission and European Data Protection Board on this matter" and that it hoped "to be able to limit the negative consequences" of it.[109]

   Will it be feasible for the U.S. and EU to negotiate a Privacy Shield 2.0.?

   Looking at the *Schrems II* decision, what would be the elements of a Privacy Shield 2.0 if it is to fulfill the requirements of the CJEU? What changes, for example, will be required to U.S. foreign intelligence law? Would firming up the status and powers of the Ombudsperson position be enough? What kind of judicial appeal would FISA need to grant to EU residents? Would such a statutorily guaranteed interest fulfill the constitutional requirements for standing that the Supreme Court articulated in its *Clapper* decision?

3. ***New Controller Responsibilities.*** *Schrems II* places a significant responsibility on controllers to supplement the guarantees of the SCC and to verify, prior to a transfer, whether the protections required by EU law will be met. This part of

---

[109] U.S. Secretary of Commerce Wilbur Ross Statement on Schrems II Ruling and the Importance of EU-U.S. Data Flows, U.S. Department of Commerce (July 16, 2020), at https://www.commerce.gov/news/press-releases/2020/07/us-secretary-commerce-wilbur-ross-statement-schrems-ii-ruling-and.

the decision has worldwide applicability. How feasible is it for controllers to verify the level of foreign intelligence surveillance in any third country anywhere in the world before a transfer information? Will encryption provide an adequate supplement to SCC?

4. *Data Localization*. Would it help non-EU organizations to meet the requirements of *Schrems II* by storing their information in EU-based clouds? Two shortcomings appear in this approach. First, the stored data will still have to be transferable to the third countries to be useful for a global enterprise. Hence, the problem of insuring "essentially equivalent protection" remains. Second, to the extent that data localization also means centralization, it may lead to the perverse result of making it easier for outside intelligence agencies to engage in surveillance of it. Anupam Chander and Uyên Lê call this issue, the "Jackpot" problem. As they point out, "Centralizing information about users in a locality might actually ease the logistical burdens of foreign intelligence agencies, which can now concentrate their surveillance of a particular nation's citizens more easily."[110]

5. *National Security Data Processing and Brexit.* The Treaty on the European Union generally exempts national security matters from Union competence. But *Schrems II* found that the GDPR did apply to post-transfer processing by national security authorities in a third country. As a result, data processing by national security authorities of third countries will be subject to types of scrutiny under the GDPR from which the same kinds of entities in member states are exempt. This result has significant implications for the United Kingdom (U.K.), which is exiting the EU on December 31, 2020. The UK is now seeking a formal adequacy assessment from the EU.

   The U.K. has a tradition of vigorous international surveillance activities through the General Communications Headquarters (GCHQ), its equivalent to the National Security Agency in the U.S. It is also part of the Five Eyes, an anglophone intelligence community. The other members of this alliance are Australia, Canada, New Zealand, and the U.S. As a member of the EU, however, the U.K.'s intelligence collection was largely excluded by review by the European Commission, the European Data Protection Board, and the Data Protection Authorities of other Member States. Indeed, its activities were helpful for other members of the European security community, who benefitted from the U.K.'s data gathering through data sharing arrangements. Peter Schaar, a former Data Protection Commissioner of Germany, termed such techniques within the European security community as "competency hopping," or the practice of routing around internal limits set in national law through data sharing arrangements with other countries.[111]

   Post-Brexit, a different set of EU institutions will evaluate the U.K.'s data collection as part of its adequacy evaluation. From this perspective, the U.K.'s departure for the EU represents a potential shift in power in the EU and the U.K. to institutions and advocates that are privacy-oriented rather security-

---

[110] Anupam Chander and Uyên Lê, *Data Nationalism*, 64 Emory L.J. 677, 717 (2015).

[111] For a discussion, see Paul M. Schwartz, *Systematic Government Access to Private-Sector Data in Germany*, 61, 88-89 in Bulk Collection (James X. Dempsey & Fred Cate, eds.) (2017).

oriented. Moreover, it means that the CJEU will have the last word on the permissibility of an adequacy finding from the Commission for the U.K.

6. *The FTC Speaks.* Over 5,000 U.S. companies entered into it the Privacy Shield prior to its invalidation by the CJEU. To what extent should these companies keep following the Privacy Shield and keep referring to it in their Privacy Policies? The FTC has advised companies to continue to follow Privacy Shield; its update post-*Schrems II* is: "We continue to expect companies to comply with their ongoing obligations with respect to transfers made under the Privacy Shield Framework."[112] To avoid being unfair or deceptive, however, do these companies have to update their Privacy Policies to indicate that the Privacy Shield no longer exists?

7. *Plan B for Organizations?* Alternate mechanisms are available for companies located outside the EU to maintain their international data flows. These include: (1) the SCC plus additional safeguards as *Schrems II* requires; (2) non-standard contractual clauses, which, however, have to approved by the lead Data Protection Authority with jurisdiction over a company; and (3) Binding Corporate Rules. Based on the material in this chapter, what do you think are the strengths and weaknesses of each of these mechanisms?

8. *European Data Protection Board Guidance.* A few days after the *Schrems II* decision, the European Data Protection Board (EDPB) published a FAQ on it.[113] The FAQs stated that there would not be a "grace period" after the decision, which meant that the CJEU's decision had to be "taken into account for any transfer to the U.S." on an immediate basis. Regarding the further use of SCCs, the EDPB placed the onus on the data importer. It observed:

> Whether or not you can transfer personal data on the basis of SCCs will depend on the result of your assessment, taking into account the circumstances of the transfers, and supplementary measures you could put in place. The supplementary measures along with SCCs, following a case-by-case analysis of the circumstances surrounding the transfer, would have to ensure that U.S.law does not impinge on the adequate level of protection they guarantee.

To what extent can a data importer in the United States assess the impact of U.S. law, such as Section 702 FISA and Executive Order 12333, on a particular data transfer?

9. **The CJEU as Ultimate Decisionmaker:** *Opinion 1/15.* In between *Schrems I* and *Schrems II*, the CJEU invalidated a proposed agreement between the EU and Canada concerning the transfer of passenger (PNR) data between the EU and Canada. Parts of this decision, *Opinion 1/15* (2017), concerning data retention were excerpted above. The CJEU declared that the proposed PNR agreement failed to meet the adequacy standard. For the CJEU, the proposed international agreement was unacceptable in its then current form. Several of

---

[112] FTC, Update on the Privacy Shield Framework (July 21, 2020), at https://www.ftc.gov/tips-advice/business-center/privacy-and-security/privacy-shield.

[113] EDPB, Frequently Asked Questions on the Court of Justice of the European Union in Case C-311/18 – Data Protection Commissioner v. Facebook Ireland Ltd and Maximillian Schrems (July 23, 2020).

its elements failed to comport with the requirements of EU data protection. These included its failure to provide sufficient protections for the transfer of sensitive data; to require non-automated individual re-examination of automated decisions that would adversely affect an air passenger; to limit transfers of data within the Canadian government or to governments in other third countries; and to safeguard the individual privacy rights of air passengers.

CHAPTER **2**

GDPR: SELECTED PROVISIONS

REGULATION (EU) 2016/679 OF THE EUROPEAN PARLIAMENT AND OF THE COUNCIL

of 27 April 2016

on the protection of natural persons with regard to the processing of personal data and on the free movement of such data, and repealing Directive 95/46/EC (General Data Protection Regulation)

(Text with EEA relevance)

THE EUROPEAN PARLIAMENT AND THE COUNCIL OF THE EUROPEAN UNION,

Having regard to the Treaty on the Functioning of the European Union, and in particular Article 16 thereof,

Having regard to the proposal from the European Commission,

After transmission of the draft legislative act to the national parliaments,

Having regard to the opinion of the European Economic and Social Committee,

Having regard to the opinion of the Committee of the Regions,

Acting in accordance with the ordinary legislative procedure,

Whereas:

(1) The protection of natural persons in relation to the processing of personal data is a fundamental right. Article 8(1) of the Charter of Fundamental Rights of the European Union (the 'Charter') and Article 16(1) of the Treaty on the Functioning of the European Union (TFEU) provide that everyone has the right to the protection of personal data concerning him or her.

(2) The principles of, and rules on the protection of natural persons with regard to the processing of their personal data should, whatever their nationality or residence, respect their fundamental rights and freedoms, in particular their right to the protection of personal data. This Regulation is intended to contribute to the accomplishment of an area of freedom, security and justice and of an economic union, to economic and social progress, to the strengthening and the convergence of the economies within the internal market, and to the well-being of natural persons.

(3) Directive 95/46/EC of the European Parliament and of the Council seeks to harmonise the protection of fundamental rights and freedoms of natural persons in respect of processing activities and to ensure the free flow of personal data between Member States.

(4) The processing of personal data should be designed to serve mankind. The right to the protection of personal data is not an absolute right; it must be considered in relation to its function in society and be balanced against other fundamental rights, in accordance with the principle of proportionality. This Regulation respects all fundamental rights and observes the freedoms and principles recognised in the Charter as enshrined in the Treaties, in particular the respect for private and family life, home and communications, the protection of personal data, freedom of thought, conscience and religion, freedom of expression and information, freedom to conduct a business, the right to an effective remedy and to a fair trial, and cultural, religious and linguistic diversity.

(5) The economic and social integration resulting from the functioning of the internal market has led to a substantial increase in cross-border flows of personal data. The exchange of personal data between public and private actors, including natural persons, associations and undertakings across the Union has increased. National authorities in the Member States are being called upon by Union law to cooperate and exchange personal data so as to be able to perform their duties or carry out tasks on behalf of an authority in another Member State.

(6) Rapid technological developments and globalisation have brought new challenges for the protection of personal data. The scale of the collection and sharing of personal data has increased significantly. Technology allows both private companies and public authorities to make use of personal data on an

unprecedented scale in order to pursue their activities. Natural persons increasingly make personal information available publicly and globally. Technology has transformed both the economy and social life, and should further facilitate the free flow of personal data within the Union and the transfer to third countries and international organisations, while ensuring a high level of the protection of personal data.

(7) Those developments require a strong and more coherent data protection framework in the Union, backed by strong enforcement, given the importance of creating the trust that will allow the digital economy to develop across the internal market. Natural persons should have control of their own personal data. Legal and practical certainty for natural persons, economic operators and public authorities should be enhanced. . . .

(10) In order to ensure a consistent and high level of protection of natural persons and to remove the obstacles to flows of personal data within the Union, the level of protection of the rights and freedoms of natural persons with regard to the processing of such data should be equivalent in all Member States. Consistent and homogenous application of the rules for the protection of the fundamental rights and freedoms of natural persons with regard to the processing of personal data should be ensured throughout the Union. Regarding the processing of personal data for compliance with a legal obligation, for the performance of a task carried out in the public interest or in the exercise of official authority vested in the controller, Member States should be allowed to maintain or introduce national provisions to further specify the application of the rules of this Regulation. In conjunction with the general and horizontal law on data protection implementing Directive 95/46/EC, Member States have several sector-specific laws in areas that need more specific provisions. This Regulation also provides a margin of manoeuvre for Member States to specify its rules, including for the processing of special categories of personal data ('sensitive data'). To that extent, this Regulation does not exclude Member State law that sets out the circumstances for specific processing situations, including determining more precisely the conditions under which the processing of personal data is lawful. . . .

(16) This Regulation does not apply to issues of protection of fundamental rights and freedoms or the free flow of personal data related to activities which fall outside the scope of Union law, such as activities concerning national security. This Regulation does not apply to the processing of personal data by the Member States when carrying out activities in relation to the common foreign and security policy of the Union. . . .

(23) In order to ensure that natural persons are not deprived of the protection to which they are entitled under this Regulation, the processing of personal data of data subjects who are in the Union by a controller or a processor not established in the Union should be subject to this Regulation where the processing activities are

related to offering goods or services to such data subjects irrespective of whether connected to a payment. In order to determine whether such a controller or processor is offering goods or services to data subjects who are in the Union, it should be ascertained whether it is apparent that the controller or processor envisages offering services to data subjects in one or more Member States in the Union. Whereas the mere accessibility of the controller's, processor's or an intermediary's website in the Union, of an email address or of other contact details, or the use of a language generally used in the third country where the controller is established, is insufficient to ascertain such intention, factors such as the use of a language or a currency generally used in one or more Member States with the possibility of ordering goods and services in that other language, or the mentioning of customers or users who are in the Union, may make it apparent that the controller envisages offering goods or services to data subjects in the Union.

(24) The processing of personal data of data subjects who are in the Union by a controller or processor not established in the Union should also be subject to this Regulation when it is related to the monitoring of the behaviour of such data subjects in so far as their behaviour takes place within the Union. In order to determine whether a processing activity can be considered to monitor the behaviour of data subjects, it should be ascertained whether natural persons are tracked on the internet including potential subsequent use of personal data processing techniques which consist of profiling a natural person, particularly in order to take decisions concerning her or him or for analysing or predicting her or his personal preferences, behaviours and attitudes. . . .

(26) The principles of data protection should apply to any information concerning an identified or identifiable natural person. Personal data which have undergone pseudonymisation, which could be attributed to a natural person by the use of additional information should be considered to be information on an identifiable natural person. To determine whether a natural person is identifiable, account should be taken of all the means reasonably likely to be used, such as singling out, either by the controller or by another person to identify the natural person directly or indirectly. To ascertain whether means are reasonably likely to be used to identify the natural person, account should be taken of all objective factors, such as the costs of and the amount of time required for identification, taking into consideration the available technology at the time of the processing and technological developments. The principles of data protection should therefore not apply to anonymous information, namely information which does not relate to an identified or identifiable natural person or to personal data rendered anonymous in such a manner that the data subject is not or no longer identifiable. This Regulation does not therefore concern the processing of such anonymous information, including for statistical or research purposes. . . .

(30) Natural persons may be associated with online identifiers provided by their devices, applications, tools and protocols, such as internet protocol addresses,

cookie identifiers or other identifiers such as radio frequency identification tags. This may leave traces which, in particular when combined with unique identifiers and other information received by the servers, may be used to create profiles of the natural persons and identify them. . . .

(32) Consent should be given by a clear affirmative act establishing a freely given, specific, informed and unambiguous indication of the data subject's agreement to the processing of personal data relating to him or her, such as by a written statement, including by electronic means, or an oral statement. This could include ticking a box when visiting an internet website, choosing technical settings for information society services or another statement or conduct which clearly indicates in this context the data subject's acceptance of the proposed processing of his or her personal data. Silence, pre-ticked boxes or inactivity should not therefore constitute consent. Consent should cover all processing activities carried out for the same purpose or purposes. When the processing has multiple purposes, consent should be given for all of them. If the data subject's consent is to be given following a request by electronic means, the request must be clear, concise and not unnecessarily disruptive to the use of the service for which it is provided.

(33) It is often not possible to fully identify the purpose of personal data processing for scientific research purposes at the time of data collection. Therefore, data subjects should be allowed to give their consent to certain areas of scientific research when in keeping with recognised ethical standards for scientific research. Data subjects should have the opportunity to give their consent only to certain areas of research or parts of research projects to the extent allowed by the intended purpose. . . .

(38) Children merit specific protection with regard to their personal data, as they may be less aware of the risks, consequences and safeguards concerned and their rights in relation to the processing of personal data. Such specific protection should, in particular, apply to the use of personal data of children for the purposes of marketing or creating personality or user profiles and the collection of personal data with regard to children when using services offered directly to a child. The consent of the holder of parental responsibility should not be necessary in the context of preventive or counselling services offered directly to a child.

(39) Any processing of personal data should be lawful and fair. It should be transparent to natural persons that personal data concerning them are collected, used, consulted or otherwise processed and to what extent the personal data are or will be processed. The principle of transparency requires that any information and communication relating to the processing of those personal data be easily accessible and easy to understand, and that clear and plain language be used. That principle concerns, in particular, information to the data subjects on the identity of the controller and the purposes of the processing and further information to ensure fair and transparent processing in respect of the natural persons concerned and their

right to obtain confirmation and communication of personal data concerning them which are being processed. Natural persons should be made aware of risks, rules, safeguards and rights in relation to the processing of personal data and how to exercise their rights in relation to such processing. In particular, the specific purposes for which personal data are processed should be explicit and legitimate and determined at the time of the collection of the personal data. The personal data should be adequate, relevant and limited to what is necessary for the purposes for which they are processed. This requires, in particular, ensuring that the period for which the personal data are stored is limited to a strict minimum. Personal data should be processed only if the purpose of the processing could not reasonably be fulfilled by other means. In order to ensure that the personal data are not kept longer than necessary, time limits should be established by the controller for erasure or for a periodic review. Every reasonable step should be taken to ensure that personal data which are inaccurate are rectified or deleted. Personal data should be processed in a manner that ensures appropriate security and confidentiality of the personal data, including for preventing unauthorised access to or use of personal data and the equipment used for the processing. . . .

(43) In order to ensure that consent is freely given, consent should not provide a valid legal ground for the processing of personal data in a specific case where there is a clear imbalance between the data subject and the controller, in particular where the controller is a public authority and it is therefore unlikely that consent was freely given in all the circumstances of that specific situation. Consent is presumed not to be freely given if it does not allow separate consent to be given to different personal data processing operations despite it being appropriate in the individual case, or if the performance of a contract, including the provision of a service, is dependent on the consent despite such consent not being necessary for such performance. . . .

(46) The processing of personal data should also be regarded to be lawful where it is necessary to protect an interest which is essential for the life of the data subject or that of another natural person. Processing of personal data based on the vital interest of another natural person should in principle take place only where the processing cannot be manifestly based on another legal basis. Some types of processing may serve both important grounds of public interest and the vital interests of the data subject as for instance when processing is necessary for humanitarian purposes, including for monitoring epidemics and their spread or in situations of humanitarian emergencies, in particular in situations of natural and man-made disasters.

(47) The legitimate interests of a controller, including those of a controller to which the personal data may be disclosed, or of a third party, may provide a legal basis for processing, provided that the interests or the fundamental rights and freedoms of the data subject are not overriding, taking into consideration the reasonable expectations of data subjects based on their relationship with the controller. Such

legitimate interest could exist for example where there is a relevant and appropriate relationship between the data subject and the controller in situations such as where the data subject is a client or in the service of the controller. At any rate the existence of a legitimate interest would need careful assessment including whether a data subject can reasonably expect at the time and in the context of the collection of the personal data that processing for that purpose may take place. The interests and fundamental rights of the data subject could in particular override the interest of the data controller where personal data are processed in circumstances where data subjects do not reasonably expect further processing. Given that it is for the legislator to provide by law for the legal basis for public authorities to process personal data, that legal basis should not apply to the processing by public authorities in the performance of their tasks. The processing of personal data strictly necessary for the purposes of preventing fraud also constitutes a legitimate interest of the data controller concerned. The processing of personal data for direct marketing purposes may be regarded as carried out for a legitimate interest. . . .

(58) The principle of transparency requires that any information addressed to the public or to the data subject be concise, easily accessible and easy to understand, and that clear and plain language and, additionally, where appropriate, visualisation be used. Such information could be provided in electronic form, for example, when addressed to the public, through a website. This is of particular relevance in situations where the proliferation of actors and the technological complexity of practice make it difficult for the data subject to know and understand whether, by whom and for what purpose personal data relating to him or her are being collected, such as in the case of online advertising. Given that children merit specific protection, any information and communication, where processing is addressed to a child, should be in such a clear and plain language that the child can easily understand.

(59) Modalities should be provided for facilitating the exercise of the data subject's rights under this Regulation, including mechanisms to request and, if applicable, obtain, free of charge, in particular, access to and rectification or erasure of personal data and the exercise of the right to object. The controller should also provide means for requests to be made electronically, especially where personal data are processed by electronic means. The controller should be obliged to respond to requests from the data subject without undue delay and at the latest within one month and to give reasons where the controller does not intend to comply with any such requests. . . .

(65) A data subject should have the right to have personal data concerning him or her rectified and a 'right to be forgotten' where the retention of such data infringes this Regulation or Union or Member State law to which the controller is subject. In particular, a data subject should have the right to have his or her personal data erased and no longer processed where the personal data are no longer necessary in relation to the purposes for which they are collected or otherwise processed, where

a data subject has withdrawn his or her consent or objects to the processing of personal data concerning him or her, or where the processing of his or her personal data does not otherwise comply with this Regulation. That right is relevant in particular where the data subject has given his or her consent as a child and is not fully aware of the risks involved by the processing, and later wants to remove such personal data, especially on the internet. The data subject should be able to exercise that right notwithstanding the fact that he or she is no longer a child. However, the further retention of the personal data should be lawful where it is necessary, for exercising the right of freedom of expression and information, for compliance with a legal obligation, for the performance of a task carried out in the public interest or in the exercise of official authority vested in the controller, on the grounds of public interest in the area of public health, for archiving purposes in the public interest, scientific or historical research purposes or statistical purposes, or for the establishment, exercise or defence of legal claims. . . .

(71) The data subject should have the right not to be subject to a decision, which may include a measure, evaluating personal aspects relating to him or her which is based solely on automated processing and which produces legal effects concerning him or her or similarly significantly affects him or her, such as automatic refusal of an online credit application or e-recruiting practices without any human intervention. Such processing includes 'profiling' that consists of any form of automated processing of personal data evaluating the personal aspects relating to a natural person, in particular to analyse or predict aspects concerning the data subject's performance at work, economic situation, health, personal preferences or interests, reliability or behaviour, location or movements, where it produces legal effects concerning him or her or similarly significantly affects him or her. However, decision-making based on such processing, including profiling, should be allowed where expressly authorised by Union or Member State law to which the controller is subject, including for fraud and tax-evasion monitoring and prevention purposes conducted in accordance with the regulations, standards and recommendations of Union institutions or national oversight bodies and to ensure the security and reliability of a service provided by the controller, or necessary for the entering or performance of a contract between the data subject and a controller, or when the data subject has given his or her explicit consent. In any case, such processing should be subject to suitable safeguards, which should include specific information to the data subject and the right to obtain human intervention, to express his or her point of view, to obtain an explanation of the decision reached after such assessment and to challenge the decision. Such measure should not concern a child. . . .

(78) The protection of the rights and freedoms of natural persons with regard to the processing of personal data require that appropriate technical and organisational measures be taken to ensure that the requirements of this Regulation are met. In order to be able to demonstrate compliance with this Regulation, the controller should adopt internal policies and implement measures which meet in

particular the principles of data protection by design and data protection by default. Such measures could consist, inter alia, of minimising the processing of personal data, pseudonymising personal data as soon as possible, transparency with regard to the functions and processing of personal data, enabling the data subject to monitor the data processing, enabling the controller to create and improve security features. When developing, designing, selecting and using applications, services and products that are based on the processing of personal data or process personal data to fulfil their task, producers of the products, services and applications should be encouraged to take into account the right to data protection when developing and designing such products, services and applications and, with due regard to the state of the art, to make sure that controllers and processors are able to fulfil their data protection obligations. The principles of data protection by design and by default should also be taken into consideration in the context of public tenders. . .

(87) It should be ascertained whether all appropriate technological protection and organisational measures have been implemented to establish immediately whether a personal data breach has taken place and to inform promptly the supervisory authority and the data subject. The fact that the notification was made without undue delay should be established taking into account in particular the nature and gravity of the personal data breach and its consequences and adverse effects for the data subject. Such notification may result in an intervention of the supervisory authority in accordance with its tasks and powers laid down in this Regulation. . .

(101) Flows of personal data to and from countries outside the Union and international organisations are necessary for the expansion of international trade and international cooperation. The increase in such flows has raised new challenges and concerns with regard to the protection of personal data. However, when personal data are transferred from the Union to controllers, processors or other recipients in third countries or to international organisations, the level of protection of natural persons ensured in the Union by this Regulation should not be undermined, including in cases of onward transfers of personal data from the third country or international organisation to controllers, processors in the same or another third country or international organisation. In any event, transfers to third countries and international organisations may only be carried out in full compliance with this Regulation. A transfer could take place only if, subject to the other provisions of this Regulation, the conditions laid down in the provisions of this Regulation relating to the transfer of personal data to third countries or international organisations are complied with by the controller or processor. . . . .

(103) The Commission may decide with effect for the entire Union that a third country, a territory or specified sector within a third country, or an international organisation, offers an adequate level of data protection, thus providing legal certainty and uniformity throughout the Union as regards the third country or international organisation which is considered to provide such level of protection. In such cases, transfers of personal data to that third country or international

organisation may take place without the need to obtain any further authorisation. The Commission may also decide, having given notice and a full statement setting out the reasons to the third country or international organisation, to revoke such a decision. . . .

(117) The establishment of supervisory authorities in Member States, empowered to perform their tasks and exercise their powers with complete independence, is an essential component of the protection of natural persons with regard to the processing of their personal data. Member States should be able to establish more than one supervisory authority, to reflect their constitutional, organisational and administrative structure.

(118) The independence of supervisory authorities should not mean that the supervisory authorities cannot be subject to control or monitoring mechanisms regarding their financial expenditure or to judicial review. . . .

(123) The supervisory authorities should monitor the application of the provisions pursuant to this Regulation and contribute to its consistent application throughout the Union, in order to protect natural persons in relation to the processing of their personal data and to facilitate the free flow of personal data within the internal market. For that purpose, the supervisory authorities should cooperate with each other and with the Commission, without the need for any agreement between Member States on the provision of mutual assistance or on such cooperation. . . .

(146) The controller or processor should compensate any damage which a person may suffer as a result of processing that infringes this Regulation. The controller or processor should be exempt from liability if it proves that it is not in any way responsible for the damage. The concept of damage should be broadly interpreted in the light of the case-law of the Court of Justice in a manner which fully reflects the objectives of this Regulation. This is without prejudice to any claims for damage deriving from the violation of other rules in Union or Member State law. Processing that infringes this Regulation also includes processing that infringes delegated and implementing acts adopted in accordance with this Regulation and Member State law specifying rules of this Regulation. Data subjects should receive full and effective compensation for the damage they have suffered. Where controllers or processors are involved in the same processing, each controller or processor should be held liable for the entire damage. However, where they are joined to the same judicial proceedings, in accordance with Member State law, compensation may be apportioned according to the responsibility of each controller or processor for the damage caused by the processing, provided that full and effective compensation of the data subject who suffered the damage is ensured. Any controller or processor which has paid full compensation may subsequently institute recourse proceedings against other controllers or processors involved in the same processing.

HAVE ADOPTED THIS REGULATION:

CHAPTER I
GENERAL PROVISIONS

Article 1
Subject-matter and objectives

1. This Regulation lays down rules relating to the protection of natural persons with regard to the processing of personal data and rules relating to the free movement of personal data.

2. This Regulation protects fundamental rights and freedoms of natural persons and in particular their right to the protection of personal data.

3. The free movement of personal data within the Union shall be neither restricted nor prohibited for reasons connected with the protection of natural persons with regard to the processing of personal data.

Article 2
Material scope

1. This Regulation applies to the processing of personal data wholly or partly by automated means and to the processing other than by automated means of personal data which form part of a filing system or are intended to form part of a filing system.

2. This Regulation does not apply to the processing of personal data:

   (a) in the course of an activity which falls outside the scope of Union law;

   (b) by the Member States when carrying out activities which fall within the scope of Chapter 2 of Title V of the TEU;

   (c) by a natural person in the course of a purely personal or household activity;

   (d) by competent authorities for the purposes of the prevention, investigation, detection or prosecution of criminal offences or the execution of criminal penalties, including the safeguarding against and the prevention of threats to public security. . . .

Article 3
Territorial scope

1. This Regulation applies to the processing of personal data in the context of the activities of an establishment of a controller or a processor in the Union, regardless of whether the processing takes place in the Union or not.

2. This Regulation applies to the processing of personal data of data subjects who are in the Union by a controller or processor not established in the Union, where the processing activities are related to:

> (a) the offering of goods or services, irrespective of whether a payment of the data subject is required, to such data subjects in the Union; or

> (b) the monitoring of their behaviour as far as their behaviour takes place within the Union.

(3) This Regulation applies to the processing of personal data by a controller not established in the Union, but in a place where Member State law applies by virtue of public international law.

Article 4
Definitions

For the purposes of this Regulation:

(1) 'personal data' means any information relating to an identified or identifiable natural person ('data subject'); an identifiable natural person is one who can be identified, directly or indirectly, in particular by reference to an identifier such as a name, an identification number, location data, an online identifier or to one or more factors specific to the physical, physiological, genetic, mental, economic, cultural or social identity of that natural person;

(2) 'processing' means any operation or set of operations which is performed on personal data or on sets of personal data, whether or not by automated means, such as collection, recording, organisation, structuring, storage, adaptation or alteration, retrieval, consultation, use, disclosure by transmission, dissemination or otherwise making available, alignment or combination, restriction, erasure or destruction; . .
. .

(5) 'pseudonymisation' means the processing of personal data in such a manner that the personal data can no longer be attributed to a specific data subject without the use of additional information, provided that such additional information is kept separately and is subject to technical and organisational measures to ensure that

the personal data are not attributed to an identified or identifiable natural person;

(6) 'filing system' means any structured set of personal data which are accessible according to specific criteria, whether centralised, decentralised or dispersed on a functional or geographical basis;

(7) 'controller' means the natural or legal person, public authority, agency or other body which, alone or jointly with others, determines the purposes and means of the processing of personal data; where the purposes and means of such processing are determined by Union or Member State law, the controller or the specific criteria for its nomination may be provided for by Union or Member State law;

(8) 'processor' means a natural or legal person, public authority, agency or other body which processes personal data on behalf of the controller;

(9) 'recipient' means a natural or legal person, public authority, agency or another body, to which the personal data are disclosed, whether a third party or not. However, public authorities which may receive personal data in the framework of a particular inquiry in accordance with Union or Member State law shall not be regarded as recipients; the processing of those data by those public authorities shall be in compliance with the applicable data protection rules according to the purposes of the processing;

(10) 'third party' means a natural or legal person, public authority, agency or body other than the data subject, controller, processor and persons who, under the direct authority of the controller or processor, are authorised to process personal data;

(11) 'consent' of the data subject means any freely given, specific, informed and unambiguous indication of the data subject's wishes by which he or she, by a statement or by a clear affirmative action, signifies agreement to the processing of personal data relating to him or her;

(12) 'personal data breach' means a breach of security leading to the accidental or unlawful destruction, loss, alteration, unauthorised disclosure of, or access to, personal data transmitted, stored or otherwise processed; . . . .

(20) 'binding corporate rules' means personal data protection policies which are adhered to by a controller or processor established on the territory of a Member State for transfers or a set of transfers of personal data to a controller or processor in one or more third countries within a group of undertakings, or group of enterprises engaged in a joint economic activity;

(21) 'supervisory authority' means an independent public authority which is established by a Member State pursuant to Article 51; . . . .

(23) 'cross-border processing' means either:

(a) processing of personal data which takes place in the context of the activities of establishments in more than one Member State of a controller or processor in the Union where the controller or processor is established in more than one Member State; or

(b) processing of personal data which takes place in the context of the activities of a single establishment of a controller or processor in the Union but which substantially affects or is likely to substantially affect data subjects in more than one Member State. . . .

CHAPTER II
PRINCIPLES

Article 5
Principles relating to processing of personal data

1. Personal data shall be:

(a) processed lawfully, fairly and in a transparent manner in relation to the data subject ('lawfulness, fairness and transparency');

(b) collected for specified, explicit and legitimate purposes and not further processed in a manner that is incompatible with those purposes; further processing for archiving purposes in the public interest, scientific or historical research purposes or statistical purposes shall, in accordance with Article 89(1), not be considered to be incompatible with the initial purposes ('purpose limitation');

(c) adequate, relevant and limited to what is necessary in relation to the purposes for which they are processed ('data minimisation');

(d) accurate and, where necessary, kept up to date; every reasonable step must be taken to ensure that personal data that are inaccurate, having regard to the purposes for which they are processed, are erased or rectified without delay ('accuracy');

(e) kept in a form which permits identification of data subjects for no longer than is necessary for the purposes for which the personal data are processed; personal data may be stored for longer periods insofar as the personal data will be processed solely for archiving purposes in the public interest, scientific or historical research purposes or statistical purposes in accordance with Article 89(1) subject to implementation of the appropriate technical and organisational measures required by this Regulation in order to safeguard the rights and freedoms of the data subject ('storage limitation');

(f) processed in a manner that ensures appropriate security of the personal data, including protection against unauthorised or unlawful processing and against accidental loss, destruction or damage, using appropriate technical or organisational measures ('integrity and confidentiality').

2. The controller shall be responsible for, and be able to demonstrate compliance with, paragraph 1 ('accountability').

Article 6
Lawfulness of processing

1. Processing shall be lawful only if and to the extent that at least one of the following applies:

(a) the data subject has given consent to the processing of his or her personal data for one or more specific purposes;

(b) processing is necessary for the performance of a contract to which the data subject is party or in order to take steps at the request of the data subject prior to entering into a contract;

(c) processing is necessary for compliance with a legal obligation to which the controller is subject;

(d) processing is necessary in order to protect the vital interests of the data subject or of another natural person;

(e) processing is necessary for the performance of a task carried out in the public interest or in the exercise of official authority vested in the controller; .
. . .

3. The basis for the processing referred to in point (c) and (e) of paragraph 1 shall be laid down by:

(a) Union law; or

(b) Member State law to which the controller is subject.

The purpose of the processing shall be determined in that legal basis or, as regards the processing referred to in point (e) of paragraph 1, shall be necessary for the performance of a task carried out in the public interest or in the exercise of official authority vested in the controller. That legal basis may contain specific provisions to adapt the application of rules of this Regulation, inter alia: the general conditions governing the lawfulness of processing by the controller; the types of data which are subject to the processing; the data subjects concerned; the entities to, and the purposes for which, the personal data may be disclosed; the purpose limitation; storage periods; and processing operations and processing procedures, including measures to ensure lawful and fair processing such as those for other specific processing situations as provided for in Chapter IX. The Union or the Member State law shall meet an objective of public interest and be proportionate to the legitimate aim pursued.

4. Where the processing for a purpose other than that for which the personal data have been collected is not based on the data subject's consent or on a Union or Member State law which constitutes a necessary and proportionate measure in a democratic society to safeguard the objectives referred to in Article 23(1), the controller shall, in order to ascertain whether processing for another purpose is compatible with the purpose for which the personal data are initially collected, take into account, inter alia:

(a) any link between the purposes for which the personal data have been collected and the purposes of the intended further processing;

(b) the context in which the personal data have been collected, in particular regarding the relationship between data subjects and the controller;

(c) the nature of the personal data, in particular whether special categories of personal data are processed, pursuant to Article 9, or whether personal data related to criminal convictions and offences are processed, pursuant to Article 10;

(d) the possible consequences of the intended further processing for data subjects;

(e) the existence of appropriate safeguards, which may include encryption or pseudonymisation.

Article 7
Conditions for consent

1. Where processing is based on consent, the controller shall be able to demonstrate that the data subject has consented to processing of his or her personal data.

2. If the data subject's consent is given in the context of a written declaration which also concerns other matters, the request for consent shall be presented in a manner which is clearly distinguishable from the other matters, in an intelligible and easily accessible form, using clear and plain language. Any part of such a declaration which constitutes an infringement of this Regulation shall not be binding.

3. The data subject shall have the right to withdraw his or her consent at any time. The withdrawal of consent shall not affect the lawfulness of processing based on consent before its withdrawal. Prior to giving consent, the data subject shall be informed thereof. It shall be as easy to withdraw as to give consent.

4. When assessing whether consent is freely given, utmost account shall be taken of whether, inter alia, the performance of a contract, including the provision of a service, is conditional on consent to the processing of personal data that is not necessary for the performance of that contract.

Article 8
Conditions applicable to child's consent
in relation to information society services

1. Where point (a) of Article 6(1) applies, in relation to the offer of information society services directly to a child, the processing of the personal data of a child shall be lawful where the child is at least 16 years old. Where the child is below the age of 16 years, such processing shall be lawful only if and to the extent that consent is given or authorised by the holder of parental responsibility over the child.

Member States may provide by law for a lower age for those purposes provided that such lower age is not below 13 years . . .

Article 9
Processing of special categories of personal data

1. Processing of personal data revealing racial or ethnic origin, political opinions, religious or philosophical beliefs, or trade union membership, and the processing of genetic data, biometric data for the purpose of uniquely identifying a natural

person, data concerning health or data concerning a natural person's sex life or sexual orientation shall be prohibited.

2. Paragraph 1 shall not apply if one of the following applies:

(a) the data subject has given explicit consent to the processing of those personal data for one or more specified purposes, except where Union or Member State law provide that the prohibition referred to in paragraph 1 may not be lifted by the data subject;

(b) processing is necessary for the purposes of carrying out the obligations and exercising specific rights of the controller or of the data subject in the field of employment and social security and social protection law in so far as it is authorised by Union or Member State law or a collective agreement pursuant to Member State law providing for appropriate safeguards for the fundamental rights and the interests of the data subject;. . . .

(e) processing relates to personal data which are manifestly made public by the data subject;. . . .

(g) processing is necessary for reasons of substantial public interest, on the basis of Union or Member State law which shall be proportionate to the aim pursued, respect the essence of the right to data protection and provide for suitable and specific measures to safeguard the fundamental rights and the interests of the data subject;. . . .

(j) processing is necessary for archiving purposes in the public interest, scientific or historical research purposes or statistical purposes in accordance with Article 89(1) based on Union or Member State law which shall be proportionate to the aim pursued, respect the essence of the right to data protection and provide for suitable and specific measures to safeguard the fundamental rights and the interests of the data subject.. . . .

CHAPTER III
RIGHTS OF THE DATA SUBJECT

Section 1
Transparency and modalities

Article 12
Transparent information, communication and modalities for the exercise of the rights of the data subject

1. The controller shall take appropriate measures to provide any information referred to in Articles 13 and 14 and any communication under Articles 15 to 22 and 34 relating to processing to the data subject in a concise, transparent, intelligible and easily accessible form, using clear and plain language, in particular for any information addressed specifically to a child. The information shall be provided in writing, or by other means, including, where appropriate, by electronic means. When requested by the data subject, the information may be provided orally, provided that the identity of the data subject is proven by other means.

2. The controller shall facilitate the exercise of data subject rights under Articles 15 to 22. In the cases referred to in Article 11(2), the controller shall not refuse to act on the request of the data subject for exercising his or her rights under Articles 15 to 22, unless the controller demonstrates that it is not in a position to identify the data subject.

3. The controller shall provide information on action taken on a request under Articles 15 to 22 to the data subject without undue delay and in any event within one month of receipt of the request. That period may be extended by two further months where necessary, taking into account the complexity and number of the requests. The controller shall inform the data subject of any such extension within one month of receipt of the request, together with the reasons for the delay. Where the data subject makes the request by electronic form means, the information shall be provided by electronic means where possible, unless otherwise requested by the data subject.

4. If the controller does not take action on the request of the data subject, the controller shall inform the data subject without delay and at the latest within one month of receipt of the request of the reasons for not taking action and on the possibility of lodging a complaint with a supervisory authority and seeking a judicial remedy.

5. Information provided under Articles 13 and 14 and any communication and any actions taken under Articles 15 to 22 and 34 shall be provided free of charge. Where requests from a data subject are manifestly unfounded or excessive, in particular because of their repetitive character, the controller may either:

(a) charge a reasonable fee taking into account the administrative costs of providing the information or communication or taking the action requested; or

(b) refuse to act on the request.

The controller shall bear the burden of demonstrating the manifestly unfounded or excessive character of the request.

6. Without prejudice to Article 11, where the controller has reasonable doubts concerning the identity of the natural person making the request referred to in Articles 15 to 21, the controller may request the provision of additional information necessary to confirm the identity of the data subject.. . . .

Section 2
Information and access to personal data

Article 13
Information to be provided where personal data are collected from the data subject

1. Where personal data relating to a data subject are collected from the data subject, the controller shall, at the time when personal data are obtained, provide the data subject with all of the following information:

(a) the identity and the contact details of the controller and, where applicable, of the controller's representative;

(b) the contact details of the data protection officer, where applicable;

(c) the purposes of the processing for which the personal data are intended as well as the legal basis for the processing;

(d) where the processing is based on point (f) of Article 6(1), the legitimate interests pursued by the controller or by a third party;

(e) the recipients or categories of recipients of the personal data, if any;

(f) where applicable, the fact that the controller intends to transfer personal data to a third country or international organisation and the existence or absence of an adequacy decision by the Commission, or in the case of transfers referred to in Article 46 or 47, or the second subparagraph of Article 49(1), reference to the appropriate or suitable safeguards and the means by which to obtain a copy of them or where they have been made available.

2. In addition to the information referred to in paragraph 1, the controller shall, at the time when personal data are obtained, provide the data subject with the following further information necessary to ensure fair and transparent processing:

(a) the period for which the personal data will be stored, or if that is not possible, the criteria used to determine that period;

(b) the existence of the right to request from the controller access to and rectification or erasure of personal data or restriction of processing concerning the data subject or to object to processing as well as the right to data portability;

(c) where the processing is based on point (a) of Article 6(1) or point (a) of Article 9(2), the existence of the right to withdraw consent at any time, without affecting the lawfulness of processing based on consent before its withdrawal;

(d) the right to lodge a complaint with a supervisory authority;

(e) whether the provision of personal data is a statutory or contractual requirement, or a requirement necessary to enter into a contract, as well as whether the data subject is obliged to provide the personal data and of the possible consequences of failure to provide such data;

(f) the existence of automated decision-making, including profiling, referred to in Article 22(1) and (4) and, at least in those cases, meaningful information about the logic involved, as well as the significance and the envisaged consequences of such processing for the data subject.

3. Where the controller intends to further process the personal data for a purpose other than that for which the personal data were collected, the controller shall provide the data subject prior to that further processing with information on that other purpose and with any relevant further information as referred to in paragraph 2. . . .

Article 15
Right of access by the data subject

1. The data subject shall have the right to obtain from the controller confirmation as to whether or not personal data concerning him or her are being processed, and, where that is the case, access to the personal data and the following information:

(a) the purposes of the processing;

(b) the categories of personal data concerned;

(c) the recipients or categories of recipient to whom the personal data have been or will be disclosed, in particular recipients in third countries or international organisations;

(d) where possible, the envisaged period for which the personal data will be stored, or, if not possible, the criteria used to determine that period;

(e) the existence of the right to request from the controller rectification or erasure of personal data or restriction of processing of personal data concerning the data subject or to object to such processing;

(f) the right to lodge a complaint with a supervisory authority;

(g) where the personal data are not collected from the data subject, any available information as to their source;

(h) the existence of automated decision-making, including profiling, referred to in Article 22(1) and (4) and, at least in those cases, meaningful information about the logic involved, as well as the significance and the envisaged consequences of such processing for the data subject.

2. Where personal data are transferred to a third country or to an international organisation, the data subject shall have the right to be informed of the appropriate safeguards pursuant to Article 46 relating to the transfer.

3. The controller shall provide a copy of the personal data undergoing processing. For any further copies requested by the data subject, the controller may charge a reasonable fee based on administrative costs. Where the data subject makes the request by electronic means, and unless otherwise requested by the data subject, the information shall be provided in a commonly used electronic form.

4. The right to obtain a copy referred to in paragraph 3 shall not adversely affect the rights and freedoms of others.

Section 3
Rectification and erasure

Article 16
Right to rectification

The data subject shall have the right to obtain from the controller without undue delay the rectification of inaccurate personal data concerning him or her. Taking into account the purposes of the processing, the data subject shall have the right to have incomplete personal data completed, including by means of providing a supplementary statement.

Article 17
Right to erasure ('right to be forgotten')

1. The data subject shall have the right to obtain from the controller the erasure of personal data concerning him or her without undue delay and the controller shall have the obligation to erase personal data without undue delay where one of the following grounds applies:

(a) the personal data are no longer necessary in relation to the purposes for which they were collected or otherwise processed;

(b) the data subject withdraws consent on which the processing is based according to point (a) of Article 6(1), or point (a) of Article 9(2), and where there is no other legal ground for the processing;

(c) the data subject objects to the processing pursuant to Article 21(1) and there are no overriding legitimate grounds for the processing, or the data subject objects to the processing pursuant to Article 21(2);

(d) the personal data have been unlawfully processed;

(e) the personal data have to be erased for compliance with a legal obligation in Union or Member State law to which the controller is subject;

(f) the personal data have been collected in relation to the offer of information society services referred to in Article 8(1).

2. Where the controller has made the personal data public and is obliged pursuant to paragraph 1 to erase the personal data, the controller, taking account of available technology and the cost of implementation, shall take reasonable steps, including technical measures, to inform controllers which are processing the personal data that the data subject has requested the erasure by such controllers of any links to, or copy or replication of, those personal data.

3. Paragraphs 1 and 2 shall not apply to the extent that processing is necessary:

(a) for exercising the right of freedom of expression and information;

(b) for compliance with a legal obligation which requires processing by Union or Member State law to which the controller is subject or for the performance of a task carried out in the public interest or in the exercise of official authority vested in the controller;

(c) for reasons of public interest in the area of public health in accordance with points (h) and (i) of Article 9(2) as well as Article 9(3);

(d) for archiving purposes in the public interest, scientific or historical research purposes or statistical purposes in accordance with Article 89(1) in so far as the right referred to in paragraph 1 is likely to render impossible or seriously impair the achievement of the objectives of that processing; or

(e) for the establishment, exercise or defence of legal claims.

Article 18
Right to restriction of processing

1. The data subject shall have the right to obtain from the controller restriction of processing where one of the following applies:

(a) the accuracy of the personal data is contested by the data subject, for a period enabling the controller to verify the accuracy of the personal data;

(b) the processing is unlawful and the data subject opposes the erasure of the personal data and requests the restriction of their use instead;

(c) the controller no longer needs the personal data for the purposes of the processing, but they are required by the data subject for the establishment, exercise or defence of legal claims; . . . .

Article 19
Notification obligation regarding rectification or erasure of personal data or restriction of processing

The controller shall communicate any rectification or erasure of personal data or restriction of processing carried out in accordance with Article 16, Article 17(1) and Article 18 to each recipient to whom the personal data have been disclosed, unless this proves impossible or involves disproportionate effort. The controller shall inform the data subject about those recipients if the data subject requests it.

Article 20
Right to data portability

1. The data subject shall have the right to receive the personal data concerning him or her, which he or she has provided to a controller, in a structured, commonly used and machine-readable format and have the right to transmit those data to another controller without hindrance from the controller to which the personal data have been provided, where:

(a) the processing is based on consent pursuant to point (a) of Article 6(1) or point (a) of Article 9(2) or on a contract pursuant to point (b) of Article 6(1); and

(b) the processing is carried out by automated means. . . .

Section 4
Right to object and automated individual decision-making

Article 21
Right to object

1. The data subject shall have the right to object, on grounds relating to his or her particular situation, at any time to processing of personal data concerning him or her which is based on point (e) or (f) of Article 6(1), including profiling based on those provisions. The controller shall no longer process the personal data unless the controller demonstrates compelling legitimate grounds for the processing which override the interests, rights and freedoms of the data subject or for the establishment, exercise or defence of legal claims. . . .

Article 22
Automated individual decision-making, including profiling

1. The data subject shall have the right not to be subject to a decision based solely on automated processing, including profiling, which produces legal effects concerning him or her or similarly significantly affects him or her.

2. Paragraph 1 shall not apply if the decision:

(a) is necessary for entering into, or performance of, a contract between the data subject and a data controller;

(b) is authorised by Union or Member State law to which the controller is subject and which also lays down suitable measures to safeguard the data subject's rights and freedoms and legitimate interests; or

(c) is based on the data subject's explicit consent.

3. In the cases referred to in points (a) and (c) of paragraph 2, the data controller shall implement suitable measures to safeguard the data subject's rights and freedoms and legitimate interests, at least the right to obtain human intervention on the part of the controller, to express his or her point of view and to contest the decision.

4. Decisions referred to in paragraph 2 shall not be based on special categories of personal data referred to in Article 9(1), unless point (a) or (g) of Article 9(2) applies and suitable measures to safeguard the data subject's rights and freedoms and legitimate interests are in place.

Section 5
Restrictions

Article 23
Restrictions

1. Union or Member State law to which the data controller or processor is subject may restrict by way of a legislative measure the scope of the obligations and rights provided for in Articles 12 to 22 and Article 34, as well as Article 5 in so far as its provisions correspond to the rights and obligations provided for in Articles 12 to 22, when such a restriction respects the essence of the fundamental rights and freedoms and is a necessary and proportionate measure in a democratic society to safeguard:

(a) national security;

(b) defence;

(c) public security;

(d) the prevention, investigation, detection or prosecution of criminal offences or the execution of criminal penalties, including the safeguarding against and the prevention of threats to public security; . . . .

CHAPTER IV
CONTROLLER AND PROCESSOR

Section 1
General obligations

Article 24
Responsibility of the controller

1. Taking into account the nature, scope, context and purposes of processing as well as the risks of varying likelihood and severity for the rights and freedoms of natural persons, the controller shall implement appropriate technical and organisational measures to ensure and to be able to demonstrate that processing is performed in accordance with this Regulation. Those measures shall be reviewed and updated where necessary. . . .

Article 25
Data protection by design and by default

1. Taking into account the state of the art, the cost of implementation and the nature, scope, context and purposes of processing as well as the risks of varying likelihood and severity for rights and freedoms of natural persons posed by the processing, the controller shall, both at the time of the determination of the means for processing and at the time of the processing itself, implement appropriate technical and organisational measures, such as pseudonymisation, which are designed to implement data-protection principles, such as data minimisation, in an effective manner and to integrate the necessary safeguards into the processing in order to meet the requirements of this Regulation and protect the rights of data subjects.

2. The controller shall implement appropriate technical and organisational measures for ensuring that, by default, only personal data which are necessary for each specific purpose of the processing are processed. That obligation applies to the amount of personal data collected, the extent of their processing, the period of their storage and their accessibility. In particular, such measures shall ensure that by default personal data are not made accessible without the individual's intervention to an indefinite number of natural persons. . . .

Article 28
Processor

1. Where processing is to be carried out on behalf of a controller, the controller shall use only processors providing sufficient guarantees to implement appropriate technical and organisational measures in such a manner that processing will meet the requirements of this Regulation and ensure the protection of the rights of the data subject.

2. The processor shall not engage another processor without prior specific or general written authorisation of the controller. In the case of general written authorisation, the processor shall inform the controller of any intended changes concerning the addition or replacement of other processors, thereby giving the controller the opportunity to object to such changes.

3. Processing by a processor shall be governed by a contract or other legal act under Union or Member State law, that is binding on the processor with regard to the controller and that sets out the subject-matter and duration of the processing, the nature and purpose of the processing, the type of personal data and categories of data subjects and the obligations and rights of the controller. That contract or other legal act shall stipulate, in particular, that the processor:

> (a) processes the personal data only on documented instructions from the controller, including with regard to transfers of personal data to a third country or an international organisation, unless required to do so by Union or Member State law to which the processor is subject; in such a case, the processor shall inform the controller of that legal requirement before processing, unless that law prohibits such information on important grounds of public interest;

> (b) ensures that persons authorised to process the personal data have committed themselves to confidentiality or are under an appropriate statutory obligation of confidentiality; . . . .

9. The contract or the other legal act referred to in paragraphs 3 and 4 shall be in writing, including in electronic form.

10. Without prejudice to Articles 82, 83 and 84, if a processor infringes this Regulation by determining the purposes and means of processing, the processor shall be considered to be a controller in respect of that processing.

Article 29
Processing under the authority of the controller or processor

The processor and any person acting under the authority of the controller or of the processor, who has access to personal data, shall not process those data except on instructions from the controller, unless required to do so by Union or Member State law.

Article 30
Records of processing activities

1. Each controller and, where applicable, the controller's representative, shall maintain a record of processing activities under its responsibility. That record shall contain all of the following information:

(a) the name and contact details of the controller and, where applicable, the joint controller, the controller's representative and the data protection officer;

(b) the purposes of the processing;

(c) a description of the categories of data subjects and of the categories of personal data;. . . .

3. The records referred to in paragraphs 1 and 2 shall be in writing, including in electronic form.

4. The controller or the processor and, where applicable, the controller's or the processor's representative, shall make the record available to the supervisory authority on request. . . . .

Article 31
Cooperation with the supervisory authority

The controller and the processor and, where applicable, their representatives, shall cooperate, on request, with the supervisory authority in the performance of its tasks.

Section 2
Security of personal data

Article 32
Security of processing

1. Taking into account the state of the art, the costs of implementation and the nature, scope, context and purposes of processing as well as the risk of varying likelihood and severity for the rights and freedoms of natural persons, the controller and the processor shall implement appropriate technical and organisational measures to ensure a level of security appropriate to the risk, including inter alia as appropriate:

   (a) the pseudonymisation and encryption of personal data;

   (b) the ability to ensure the ongoing confidentiality, integrity, availability and resilience of processing systems and services;

   (c) the ability to restore the availability and access to personal data in a timely manner in the event of a physical or technical incident;

   (d) a process for regularly testing, assessing and evaluating the effectiveness of technical and organisational measures for ensuring the security of the processing.

2. In assessing the appropriate level of security account shall be taken in particular of the risks that are presented by processing, in particular from accidental or unlawful destruction, loss, alteration, unauthorised disclosure of, or access to personal data transmitted, stored or otherwise processed.. . . .

Article 33
Notification of a personal data breach to the supervisory authority

1. In the case of a personal data breach, the controller shall without undue delay and, where feasible, not later than 72 hours after having become aware of it, notify the personal data breach to the supervisory authority competent in accordance with Article 55, unless the personal data breach is unlikely to result in a risk to the rights and freedoms of natural persons. Where the notification to the supervisory authority is not made within 72 hours, it shall be accompanied by reasons for the delay.

2. The processor shall notify the controller without undue delay after becoming aware of a personal data breach.

3. The notification referred to in paragraph 1 shall at least:

(a) describe the nature of the personal data breach including where possible, the categories and approximate number of data subjects concerned and the categories and approximate number of personal data records concerned;

(b) communicate the name and contact details of the data protection officer or other contact point where more information can be obtained;

(c) describe the likely consequences of the personal data breach;

(d) describe the measures taken or proposed to be taken by the controller to address the personal data breach, including, where appropriate, measures to mitigate its possible adverse effects.

4. Where, and in so far as, it is not possible to provide the information at the same time, the information may be provided in phases without undue further delay.

5. The controller shall document any personal data breaches, comprising the facts relating to the personal data breach, its effects and the remedial action taken. That documentation shall enable the supervisory authority to verify compliance with this Article.

Article 34
Communication of a personal data breach to the data subject

1. When the personal data breach is likely to result in a high risk to the rights and freedoms of natural persons, the controller shall communicate the personal data breach to the data subject without undue delay.

2. The communication to the data subject referred to in paragraph 1 of this Article shall describe in clear and plain language the nature of the personal data breach and contain at least the information and measures referred to in points (b), (c) and (d) of Article 33(3).

3. The communication to the data subject referred to in paragraph 1 shall not be required if any of the following conditions are met:

(a) the controller has implemented appropriate technical and organisational protection measures, and those measures were applied to the personal data affected by the personal data breach, in particular those that render the personal data unintelligible to any person who is not authorised to access it, such as encryption;

(b) the controller has taken subsequent measures which ensure that the high risk to the rights and freedoms of data subjects referred to in paragraph 1 is no longer likely to materialise;

(c) it would involve disproportionate effort. In such a case, there shall instead be a public communication or similar measure whereby the data subjects are informed in an equally effective manner. . . .

Section 3
Data protection impact assessment and prior consultation

Article 35
Data protection impact assessment

1. Where a type of processing in particular using new technologies, and taking into account the nature, scope, context and purposes of the processing, is likely to result in a high risk to the rights and freedoms of natural persons, the controller shall, prior to the processing, carry out an assessment of the impact of the envisaged processing operations on the protection of personal data. A single assessment may address a set of similar processing operations that present similar high risks. . . .

4. The supervisory authority shall establish and make public a list of the kind of processing operations which are subject to the requirement for a data protection impact assessment pursuant to paragraph 1. The supervisory authority shall communicate those lists to the Board referred to in Article 68. . . .

Article 36
Prior consultation

1. The controller shall consult the supervisory authority prior to processing where a data protection impact assessment under Article 35 indicates that the processing would result in a high risk in the absence of measures taken by the controller to mitigate the risk.

2. Where the supervisory authority is of the opinion that the intended processing referred to in paragraph 1 would infringe this Regulation, in particular where the controller has insufficiently identified or mitigated the risk, the supervisory authority shall, within period of up to eight weeks of receipt of the request for consultation, provide written advice to the controller and, where applicable to the processor, and may use any of its powers referred to in Article 58. That period may be extended by six weeks, taking into account the complexity of the intended processing. The supervisory authority shall inform the controller and, where

applicable, the processor, of any such extension within one month of receipt of the request for consultation together with the reasons for the delay. Those periods may be suspended until the supervisory authority has obtained information it has requested for the purposes of the consultation . . .

Section 4
Data protection officer

Article 37
Designation of the data protection officer

1. The controller and the processor shall designate a data protection officer in any case where:

(a) the processing is carried out by a public authority or body, except for courts acting in their judicial capacity;

(b) the core activities of the controller or the processor consist of processing operations which, by virtue of their nature, their scope and/or their purposes, require regular and systematic monitoring of data subjects on a large scale; or

(c) the core activities of the controller or the processor consist of processing on a large scale of special categories of data pursuant to Article 9 and personal data relating to criminal convictions and offences referred to in Article 10. . . .

7. The controller or the processor shall publish the contact details of the data protection officer and communicate them to the supervisory authority.

Article 38
Position of the data protection officer

1. The controller and the processor shall ensure that the data protection officer is involved, properly and in a timely manner, in all issues which relate to the protection of personal data. . . .

3. The controller and processor shall ensure that the data protection officer does not receive any instructions regarding the exercise of those tasks. He or she shall not be dismissed or penalised by the controller or the processor for performing his tasks. The data protection officer shall directly report to the highest management level of the controller or the processor.

4. Data subjects may contact the data protection officer with regard to all issues related to processing of their personal data and to the exercise of their rights under this Regulation.

5. The data protection officer shall be bound by secrecy or confidentiality concerning the performance of his or her tasks, in accordance with Union or Member State law.

6. The data protection officer may fulfil other tasks and duties. The controller or processor shall ensure that any such tasks and duties do not result in a conflict of interests.

Article 39
Tasks of the data protection officer

1. The data protection officer shall have at least the following tasks:

(a) to inform and advise the controller or the processor and the employees who carry out processing of their obligations pursuant to this Regulation and to other Union or Member State data protection provisions;. . . .

(d) to cooperate with the supervisory authority; . . . .

Section 5
Codes of conduct and certification. . . .

Article 42
Certification

1. The Member States, the supervisory authorities, the Board and the Commission shall encourage, in particular at Union level, the establishment of data protection certification mechanisms and of data protection seals and marks, for the purpose of demonstrating compliance with this Regulation of processing operations by controllers and processors. The specific needs of micro, small and medium-sized enterprises shall be taken into account. . . .

CHAPTER V
TRANSFERS OF PERSONAL DATA TO THIRD COUNTRIES OR INTERNATIONAL ORGANISATIONS

Article 44
General principle for transfers

Any transfer of personal data which are undergoing processing or are intended for processing after transfer to a third country or to an international organisation shall take place only if, subject to the other provisions of this Regulation, the conditions laid down in this Chapter are complied with by the controller and processor, including for onward transfers of personal data from the third country or an international organisation to another third country or to another international organisation. All provisions in this Chapter shall be applied in order to ensure that the level of protection of natural persons guaranteed by this Regulation is not undermined.

Article 45
Transfers on the basis of an adequacy decision

1. A transfer of personal data to a third country or an international organisation may take place where the Commission has decided that the third country, a territory or one or more specified sectors within that third country, or the international organisation in question ensures an adequate level of protection. Such a transfer shall not require any specific authorisation.

2. When assessing the adequacy of the level of protection, the Commission shall, in particular, take account of the following elements:

(a) the rule of law, respect for human rights and fundamental freedoms, relevant legislation, both general and sectoral, including concerning public security, defence, national security and criminal law and the access of public authorities to personal data, as well as the implementation of such legislation, data protection rules, professional rules and security measures, including rules for the onward transfer of personal data to another third country or international organisation which are complied with in that country or international organisation, case-law, as well as effective and enforceable data subject rights and effective administrative and judicial redress for the data subjects whose personal data are being transferred;

(b) the existence and effective functioning of one or more independent supervisory authorities in the third country or to which an international organisation is subject, with responsibility for ensuring and enforcing compliance with the data protection rules, including adequate enforcement powers, for assisting and advising the data subjects in exercising their rights and for cooperation with the supervisory authorities of the Member States; and

(c) the international commitments the third country or international organisation concerned has entered into, or other obligations arising from legally binding conventions or instruments as well as from its participation in multilateral or regional systems, in particular in relation to the protection of personal data. . . .

8. The Commission shall publish in the Official Journal of the European Union and on its website a list of the third countries, territories and specified sectors within a third country and international organisations for which it has decided that an adequate level of protection is or is no longer ensured. . . .

Article 46
Transfers subject to appropriate safeguards

1. In the absence of a decision pursuant to Article 45(3), a controller or processor may transfer personal data to a third country or an international organisation only if the controller or processor has provided appropriate safeguards, and on condition that enforceable data subject rights and effective legal remedies for data subjects are available.

2. The appropriate safeguards referred to in paragraph 1 may be provided for, without requiring any specific authorisation from a supervisory authority, by:

(a) a legally binding and enforceable instrument between public authorities or bodies;

(b) binding corporate rules in accordance with Article 47; . . . .

Article 47
Binding corporate rules

1. The competent supervisory authority shall approve binding corporate rules in accordance with the consistency mechanism set out in Article 63, provided that they:

(a) are legally binding and apply to and are enforced by every member concerned of the group of undertakings, or group of enterprises engaged in a joint economic activity, including their employees;

(b) expressly confer enforceable rights on data subjects with regard to the processing of their personal data; and

(c) fulfil the requirements laid down in paragraph 2.. . . .

Article 49
Derogations for specific situations

1. In the absence of an adequacy decision pursuant to Article 45(3), or of appropriate safeguards pursuant to Article 46, including binding corporate rules, a transfer or a set of transfers of personal data to a third country or an international organisation shall take place only on one of the following conditions:

(a) the data subject has explicitly consented to the proposed transfer, after having been informed of the possible risks of such transfers for the data subject due to the absence of an adequacy decision and appropriate safeguards;

(b) the transfer is necessary for the performance of a contract between the data subject and the controller or the implementation of pre-contractual measures taken at the data subject's request;

(c) the transfer is necessary for the conclusion or performance of a contract concluded in the interest of the data subject between the controller and another natural or legal person;

(d) the transfer is necessary for important reasons of public interest; . . . .

CHAPTER VI
INDEPENDENT SUPERVISORY AUTHORITIES

Section 1
Independent status

Article 51
Supervisory authority

1. Each Member State shall provide for one or more independent public authorities to be responsible for monitoring the application of this Regulation, in order to protect the fundamental rights and freedoms of natural persons in relation to processing and to facilitate the free flow of personal data within the Union ('supervisory authority'). . . .

Article 52
Independence

1. Each supervisory authority shall act with complete independence in performing its tasks and exercising its powers in accordance with this Regulation.

2. The member or members of each supervisory authority shall, in the performance of their tasks and exercise of their powers in accordance with this Regulation, remain free from external influence, whether direct or indirect, and shall neither seek nor take instructions from anybody.

3. Member or members of each supervisory authority shall refrain from any action incompatible with their duties and shall not, during their term of office, engage in any incompatible occupation, whether gainful or not.

4. Each Member State shall ensure that each supervisory authority is provided with the human, technical and financial resources, premises and infrastructure necessary for the effective performance of its tasks and exercise of its powers, including those to be carried out in the context of mutual assistance, cooperation and participation in the Board. . . .

Section 2
Competence, tasks and powers

Article 55
Competence

1. Each supervisory authority shall be competent for the performance of the tasks assigned to and the exercise of the powers conferred on it in accordance with this Regulation on the territory of its own Member State. . . .

Article 57
Tasks

1. Without prejudice to other tasks set out under this Regulation, each supervisory authority shall on its territory:

(a) monitor and enforce the application of this Regulation;

(b) promote public awareness and understanding of the risks, rules, safeguards and rights in relation to processing. Activities addressed specifically to children shall receive specific attention; . . . .

(v) fulfil any other tasks related to the protection of personal data. . . .

Article 58
Powers

1. Each supervisory authority shall have all of the following investigative powers:

(a) to order the controller and the processor, and, where applicable, the controller's or the processor's representative to provide any information it requires for the performance of its tasks;

(b) to carry out investigations in the form of data protection audits; . . . .

2. Each supervisory authority shall have all of the following corrective powers:

(a) to issue warnings to a controller or processor that intended processing operations are likely to infringe provisions of this Regulation; . . . .

3. Each supervisory authority shall have all of the following authorisation and advisory powers:

(a) to advise the controller in accordance with the prior consultation procedure referred to in Article 36; . . . .

4. The exercise of the powers conferred on the supervisory authority pursuant to this Article shall be subject to appropriate safeguards, including effective judicial remedy and due process, set out in Union and Member State law in accordance with the Charter.

5. Each Member State shall provide by law that its supervisory authority shall have the power to bring infringements of this Regulation to the attention of the judicial authorities and where appropriate, to commence or engage otherwise in legal proceedings, in order to enforce the provisions of this Regulation. . . .

Article 59
Activity reports

Each supervisory authority shall draw up an annual report on its activities, which may include a list of types of infringement notified and types of measures taken in accordance with Article 58(2). Those reports shall be transmitted to the national parliament, the government and other authorities as designated by Member State law. They shall be made available to the public, to the Commission and to the Board.

CHAPTER VII
COOPERATION AND CONSISTENCY

Section 3
European data protection board

Article 68
European Data Protection Board

1. The European Data Protection Board (the 'Board') is hereby established as a body of the Union and shall have legal personality. . . .

Article 69
Independence

1. The Board shall act independently when performing its tasks or exercising its powers pursuant to Articles 70 and 71. . . .

Article 70
Tasks of the Board

1. The Board shall ensure the consistent application of this Regulation. To that end, the Board shall, on its own initiative or, where relevant, at the request of the Commission, in particular:

(a) monitor and ensure the correct application of this Regulation in the cases provided for in Articles 64 and 65 without prejudice to the tasks of national supervisory authorities; . . . .

Article 71
Reports

1. The Board shall draw up an annual report regarding the protection of natural persons with regard to processing in the Union and, where relevant, in third countries and international organisations. The report shall be made public and be transmitted to the European Parliament, to the Council and to the Commission.

2. The annual report shall include a review of the practical application of the guidelines, recommendations and best practices referred to in point (l) of Article 70(1) as well as of the binding decisions referred to in Article 65. . . .

CHAPTER VIII
REMEDIES, LIABILITY AND PENALTIES

Article 77
Right to lodge a complaint with a supervisory authority

1. Without prejudice to any other administrative or judicial remedy, every data subject shall have the right to lodge a complaint with a supervisory authority, in particular in the Member State of his or her habitual residence, place of work or place of the alleged infringement if the data subject considers that the processing of personal data relating to him or her infringes this Regulation.

2. The supervisory authority with which the complaint has been lodged shall inform the complainant on the progress and the outcome of the complaint including the possibility of a judicial remedy pursuant to Article 78.

Article 78
Right to an effective judicial remedy against a supervisory authority

1. Without prejudice to any other administrative or non-judicial remedy, each natural or legal person shall have the right to an effective judicial remedy against a legally binding decision of a supervisory authority concerning them.

2. Without prejudice to any other administrative or non-judicial remedy, each data subject shall have the right to a an effective judicial remedy where the supervisory authority which is competent pursuant to Articles 55 and 56 does not handle a complaint or does not inform the data subject within three months on the progress or outcome of the complaint lodged pursuant to Article 77.

3. Proceedings against a supervisory authority shall be brought before the courts of the Member State where the supervisory authority is established.

4. Where proceedings are brought against a decision of a supervisory authority which was preceded by an opinion or a decision of the Board in the consistency mechanism, the supervisory authority shall forward that opinion or decision to the court.

Article 79
Right to an effective judicial remedy against a controller or processor

1. Without prejudice to any available administrative or non-judicial remedy, including the right to lodge a complaint with a supervisory authority pursuant to Article 77, each data subject shall have the right to an effective judicial remedy where he or she considers that his or her rights under this Regulation have been infringed as a result of the processing of his or her personal data in non-compliance with this Regulation.

2. Proceedings against a controller or a processor shall be brought before the courts of the Member State where the controller or processor has an establishment. Alternatively, such proceedings may be brought before the courts of the Member State where the data subject has his or her habitual residence, unless the controller or processor is a public authority of a Member State acting in the exercise of its public powers. . . .

Article 82
Right to compensation and liability

1. Any person who has suffered material or non-material damage as a result of an infringement of this Regulation shall have the right to receive compensation from the controller or processor for the damage suffered.

2. Any controller involved in processing shall be liable for the damage caused by processing which infringes this Regulation. A processor shall be liable for the damage caused by processing only where it has not complied with obligations of this Regulation specifically directed to processors or where it has acted outside or contrary to lawful instructions of the controller.

3. A controller or processor shall be exempt from liability under paragraph 2 if it proves that it is not in any way responsible for the event giving rise to the damage.
. . .

Article 83
General conditions for imposing administrative fines

1. Each supervisory authority shall ensure that the imposition of administrative fines pursuant to this Article in respect of infringements of this Regulation referred to in paragraphs 4, 5 and 6 shall in each individual case be effective, proportionate and dissuasive.

2. Administrative fines shall, depending on the circumstances of each individual case, be imposed in addition to, or instead of, measures referred to in points (a) to (h) and (j) of Article 58(2). When deciding whether to impose an administrative fine and deciding on the amount of the administrative fine in each individual case due regard shall be given to the following:

(a) the nature, gravity and duration of the infringement taking into account the nature scope or purpose of the processing concerned as well as the number of data subjects affected and the level of damage suffered by them;

(b) the intentional or negligent character of the infringement;

(c) any action taken by the controller or processor to mitigate the damage suffered by data subjects; . . . .

3. If a controller or processor intentionally or negligently, for the same or linked processing operations, infringes several provisions of this Regulation, the total

amount of the administrative fine shall not exceed the amount specified for the gravest infringement.

4. Infringements of the following provisions shall, in accordance with paragraph 2, be subject to administrative fines up to 10 000 000 EUR, or in the case of an undertaking, up to 2 % of the total worldwide annual turnover of the preceding financial year, whichever is higher:

(a) the obligations of the controller and the processor pursuant to Articles 8, 11, 25 to 39 and 42 and 43;

(b) the obligations of the certification body pursuant to Articles 42 and 43;

(c) the obligations of the monitoring body pursuant to Article 41(4).

5. Infringements of the following provisions shall, in accordance with paragraph 2, be subject to administrative fines up to 20 000 000 EUR, or in the case of an undertaking, up to 4 % of the total worldwide annual turnover of the preceding financial year, whichever is higher:

(a) the basic principles for processing, including conditions for consent, pursuant to Articles 5, 6, 7 and 9;

(b) the data subjects' rights pursuant to Articles 12 to 22;

(c) the transfers of personal data to a recipient in a third country or an international organisation pursuant to Articles 44 to 49;

(d) any obligations pursuant to Member State law adopted under Chapter IX;

(e) non-compliance with an order or a temporary or definitive limitation on processing or the suspension of data flows by the supervisory authority pursuant to Article 58(2) or failure to provide access in violation of Article 58(1).

6. Non-compliance with an order by the supervisory authority as referred to in Article 58(2) shall, in accordance with paragraph 2 of this Article, be subject to administrative fines up to 20 000 000 EUR, or in the case of an undertaking, up to 4 % of the total worldwide annual turnover of the preceding financial year, whichever is higher. . . .

Article 84
Penalties

1. Member States shall lay down the rules on other penalties applicable to infringements of this Regulation in particular for infringements which are not subject to administrative fines pursuant to Article 83, and shall take all measures necessary to ensure that they are implemented. Such penalties shall be effective, proportionate and dissuasive. . . .

CHAPTER IX
PROVISIONS RELATING TO SPECIFIC
PROCESSING SITUATIONS

Article 85
Processing and freedom of expression and information

1. Member States shall by law reconcile the right to the protection of personal data pursuant to this Regulation with the right to freedom of expression and information, including processing for journalistic purposes and the purposes of academic, artistic or literary expression.

2. For processing carried out for journalistic purposes or the purpose of academic artistic or literary expression, Member States shall provide for exemptions or derogations from Chapter II (principles), Chapter III (rights of the data subject), Chapter IV (controller and processor), Chapter V (transfer of personal data to third countries or international organisations), Chapter VI (independent supervisory authorities), Chapter VII (cooperation and consistency) and Chapter IX (specific data processing situations) if they are necessary to reconcile the right to the protection of personal data with the freedom of expression and information.

3. Each Member State shall notify to the Commission the provisions of its law which it has adopted pursuant to paragraph 2 and, without delay, any subsequent amendment law or amendment affecting them.

Article 86
Processing and public access to official documents

Personal data in official documents held by a public authority or a public body or a private body for the performance of a task carried out in the public interest may be disclosed by the authority or body in accordance with Union or Member State law to which the public authority or body is subject in order to reconcile public access to official documents with the right to the protection of personal data pursuant to this Regulation. . . .

Article 89
Safeguards and derogations relating to processing for archiving purposes in the public interest, scientific or historical research purposes or statistical purposes

1. Processing for archiving purposes in the public interest, scientific or historical research purposes or statistical purposes, shall be subject to appropriate safeguards, in accordance with this Regulation, for the rights and freedoms of the data subject. Those safeguards shall ensure that technical and organisational measures are in place in particular in order to ensure respect for the principle of data minimisation. Those measures may include pseudonymisation provided that those purposes can be fulfilled in that manner. Where those purposes can be fulfilled by further processing which does not permit or no longer permits the identification of data subjects, those purposes shall be fulfilled in that manner.

2. Where personal data are processed for scientific or historical research purposes or statistical purposes, Union or Member State law may provide for derogations from the rights referred to in Articles 15, 16, 18 and 21 subject to the conditions and safeguards referred to in paragraph 1 of this Article in so far as such rights are likely to render impossible or seriously impair the achievement of the specific purposes, and such derogations are necessary for the fulfilment of those purposes. . . .

CHAPTER XI
FINAL PROVISIONS

Article 94
Repeal of Directive 95/46/EC

1. Directive 95/46/EC is repealed with effect from 25 May 2018. . . .

Article 99
Entry into force and application

1. This Regulation shall enter into force on the twentieth day following that of its publication in the Official Journal of the European Union.

2. It shall apply from 25 May 2018.

This Regulation shall be binding in its entirety and directly applicable in all Member States.

Done at Brussels, 27 April 2016.

For the European Parliament   *For the Council*

The President   *The President*

M. SCHULZ   *J.A. HENNIS-PLASSCHAERT*

INDEX